Socialism in Yiddish

Socialism in Yiddish

The Jewish Labor Bund in Sweden

Håkan Blomqvist

Södertörns högskola

Original title: *Socialism på jiddisch: Judiska Arbeter Bund i Sverige*
First published in Swedish by Carlsson bokförlag, 2020

Translated in to English by Håkan Blomqvist and Paul (Hershl) Glasser

Södertörn University
Library
SE-141 89 Huddinge
www.sh.se/publications

Cover layout: Jonathan Robson
Cover image: The Stockholm Bund marching in the social democratic first of May demonstration (1946), YIVO photo archive
Graphic form: Per Lindblom & Jonathan Robson
Stockholm 2022

Södertörn Academic Studies 87
ISSN 1650-433X

ISBN 978-91-89109-90-2 (print)
ISBN 978-91-89109-91-9 (digital)

Acknowledgments

Many have helped to make this book possible. The Publications Committee at Södertörn University in Sweden has made an English publication of the Swedish original a reality. David Payne copy edited the translation creating the final version that was then laid out by Jonathan Robson and Per Lindblom. Many warm thanks for that. The Foundation for Baltic and East European Studies in Stockholm, which funded four years of part-time research, paid not only for travel expenses for the undertaking of archival studies but also financed large translation work from Yiddish. Paul (Hershl) Glasser, of course, heroically interpreted and translated from the seemingly never-ending piles of documents in Yiddish and corrected the English. Leo Greenbaum, Gunnar Berg, Vital Zwajka and everyone else's helpful hands – heads and eyes – at YIVO in New York, which over the years rooted out textual treasures and images. Dear Eda and Richard, thank you for all the dinners and care – and friendship – during my often lonely filings in New York! And to Arieh Lebowiz of the Jewish Labor Committee, along with Gail Malmgreen, not only for Ben's Kosher Delicatessen but for all your knowledge of JLC and your joint efforts against right-wing extremism and anti-Semitism. The 2018 Memorial Meetings in Sweden for the victims of the November 1938 pogrom not only took place owing to JLC's appeal following the terrorist attack on Tree of life's synagogue in Pittsburg, but it was probably the first time that *Die Shvue* had sounded at Sergels torg, the central square in Stockholm.

Silke Neunsinger at the Workers' Movement's Archive in Stockholm, thank you for ensuring that the research conference on the Bund at Södertörn University and the Workers' Movement's Archive in 2017 became such a magnificent introduction to transnational labor history. Constance Paris de la Bollardière, Martyna Rusiniak-Karwat and Jack Jacobs with Malin Thor Tureby, Pontus Rudberg and Jan Schwarz, together with Svante Hansson and Per Enerud made it an intellectually inspirational journey, widening our views in the process. And thank you Göran Ericsson at the labor adult education association ABF in Stockholm for arranging a public meeting where interested Stockholmers could for the first time hear about research on the Bund. I would also like to thank Christel Winberg at the Workers' Movement's Archive in Trelleborg who dug into the archives of the local Social Democracy and its youth organization.

The research network Bundism.net, all *tuers*, *khaveyrim* and *leyeners* (active, peers and interested), was a constant source of support. The Institute of Contemporary History at the Södertörn University, where I have been intellectually active, has been of great help; many inspiring colleagues, seminar discussions and a stimulating book project, *The Sea of Identities, history around and across the Baltic Sea.* The JIS network, "The Jews in Sweden – the history of a minority", has contributed with research contacts and invaluable reading material. Moreover, all those friendly invitations to lectures at the Swedish Yiddish Association, Limmud, the Jewish Museum and to Paideia, the Jewish folkshul in Stockholm where I give classes on Jewish socialism, have forced me to learn more – and finally to get this work done.

Thank you also to everyone else who has contributed and inspired in so many ways – most recently Irena Klepfish, the siblings Kshensky in New York, Sara Ferdman Tauben and Irwin in Montreal, and Hanna Cohen in New York with daughter Stacey is warmly thanked here. Most sincerely of course I would like to thank my wife Gudrun. Together we have traveled through places, history, and meetings of socialist Yiddish culture. It is you and all the children who give life itself meaning; the word "we" accompanies this work.

Stockholm August 14, 2021

Contents

Socialism in Yiddish – The Jewish Labor Bund in Sweden

Di Shvue[1]

Brider un shvester fun arbet un noyt,
Ale vos zaynen tsezeyt un tseshpreyt
Tsuzamen, tsuzamen, di fon iz greyt
Zi flatert fun tsorn, fun blut iz zi royt!
A shvue, a shvue, oyf lebn un toyt

Himl un erd veln undz oyshern
Eydes veln zayn di likhtike shtern
A shvue fun blut, a shvue fun trern,
Mir shvern, mir shvern, mir shvern!

Mir shvern a trayhayt on grenetsn tsum Bund
Nor er ken di shklafn bafrayen atsind.
Di fon, di royte, iz hoykh un breyt.
Mir shvern a trayhayt oyf lebn un toyt!
A shvue, a shvue, oyf lebn un toyt.

[1] Bund's anthem, composed by Sh. An-Ski (Shloime Rapaport), 1902, is available in different versions. The following recorded version was performed by a Workmen's Circle choir as a tribute to Bundist Marek Edelman (1919–2009): https://www.youtube.com/watch?v=KZg-5RBFjbA (20190316).

Preface

"Bund was the answer." This is what the filmmaker Eran Torbiner proclaimed when we met him one day in Tel Aviv several years ago. His loving documentary Bunda'im, about the aging Bundists in Israel, portrayed a forgotten Jewish labor movement that turned against both Zionism, Communism and the capitalist system.[2] A party of "naysayers," as they were called by the historian David Slucki in an article.[3] And it is easy to get that impression of the once-powerful Jewish mass movement in the Russian Empire and interwar Poland. Both capitalism and Stalinist communism were among the movement's sworn enemies, but also the rabbis' religious teachings as well as Zionism's quest for a Jewish nation-state. Opposition became the Bund's condition of existence, but not opposition for its own sake. The Bund was founded on the conviction that the "Jewish question" could only be resolved through the liberation of the international working class from all oppression on its way to a world of equality, welfare and democracy without borders – a socialist social order. There, the broad strata of the population would rule, not capitalist elites or communist party despots. The role of "naysayer" became the position of a shrinking space when the Holocaust, or *khurbn* in Yiddish, wiped out the movement's mass base in Poland and Eastern Europe, and the world was divided into the Western and Eastern blocs of the Cold War – and the Zionists established the Jewish state of Israel. The Bund was one of the losers of history. The once deeply-rooted movement was crushed during terror and genocide, dispersed into exile, driven into its shell by overpowering political forces and undermined by assimilation as time wore on and the world changed. The following story is about that process at the micro-level, in a place on the edge of the world.

I do not remember, but it may have started with Noach Zelazo. He was mentioned in Salomon Schulman's fine book *Jiddischland* as an anti-Stalinist socialist and Yiddish journalist who collaborated with the legendary Isaac Deutscher and took part in the Warsaw Ghetto Uprising of 1943.[4] I met Zelazo in Stockholm, where he told me how he had become involved in

[2] The film can be streamed from youtube: https://www.youtube.com/watch?v=3bE6uhKxmYU (20190316)

[3] David Slucki, "A Party of Naysayers: The Jewish Labor Bund after the Holocaust," *AJS Perspectives*. The Magazine of the Association for Jewish Studies, No. 42–43, 2013, https://www.marxists.org/subject/jewish/bund-post-war.pdf

[4] Salomon Shulman, *Jiddischland. Bland rabbiner och revolutionärer* [Yiddishland. Among rabbis and revolutionairies], Nya Doxa, Nora 1996, pp. 161–163

rebuilding Jewish society in Warsaw after the war, but came to be monitored by the communist security service and to be imprisoned for three years in post-war Poland. In Sweden, he devoted all his time to writing about the Holocaust and condemning what he saw as the criminality of the Western world, while nothing was done to prevent the genocide. He was almost as condemnatory of Zionist leaders, whom he considered to have diminished Jewish resistance to the Hitler regime and, after the war, made up for damages to Israel from a Germany he considered not to have been de-nazified. According to his own account, he was excluded from Jewish gatherings and some other Jewish contexts. Perhaps it was so; he hardly seemed to be a man of peace. I helped him publish a brochure about the Holocaust under the heading *Who were exterminated in the depths of loneliness*? He had written it in Yiddish and had it translated into English, apparently not very well.[5] I later handed over the Yiddish original to YIVO in New York (below). Gradually, I came to realize that his unusual combination of stances – and enemy images – could be related to the Bund; perhaps he was even a Bundist. His political example was a call to try to understand what the once-significant movement represented and stood for.

[5] Noach Zelazo, *Who were exterminated in the depths of loneliness by the German caused Jewish Holocaust*, Stockholm, 2001.

Introduction

Internationally, there is an extensive literature on the Bund, and exciting studies of it have been produced in different countries.[6] The movement's women's activism, sports clubs, children's activities, migration, and ideology have been examined from different perspectives. Although research has been conducted on Jewish refugee communities in Sweden during and after World War II, the Bund in Sweden was a largely unknown chapter in both the historiography of the Swedish labor movement and in Swedish–Jewish history.[7] Martin Grass, former archivist at the Workers' Movement's Archives and Library in Stockholm, ARAB, extracted some information about Bundists in Sweden before World War I in his study "Reading room of Russian emigres in Stockholm 1907–1910." A Jewish Social Democratic group rooted in the Russian exile community was formed in Stockholm in 1902 under the name *Zukunft*.[8] The group is also referred to in archival fragments as a department of the Bund, and active behind the Russian Refugee Committee which, after the defeat of the 1905 Russian revolution, fought for the cause of Russian refugees. In the literature on the Russian exile environment in Stockholm during that period, there are also a smattering of references to Bundists.[9] Morten Thing mentions, in his magnificent *De russiske jöder i Köbenhavn 1882–1943*, that the leader of the Bundists in Copenhagen in the 1910s, Anna Mironovna, came from the Bund group in Stockholm (where her name was Anna Brumberg).[10] For the period after 1910, however, Grass could not find anything about the Bund in the Swedish social democratic archives during and after World War I. In 1917, the labor Zionists in *Poalei Zion* moved their international representation to Stockholm, and they seem to have been the

[6] www.bundism.net (20190316).

[7] There is much written about Jewish refugees, legislation, reception, etc., in Sweden. But, when it comes to political projects on Jewish refugee exile, I think primarily of Malin Thor Tureby, *Hechaluz – en rörelse i tid och rum. Tysk-judiska ungdomars exil i Sverige 1933–1943* [Hechaluz – a movement in time and space. Exile of German–Jewish youth in Sweden], Växjö, 2005.

[8] Martin Grass, "Ryska emigranternas läsesal i Stockholm 1907–1910" [Russian emigrants' reading room in Stockholm 1907–1910], ARAB, 2006, http://www.arbark.se/2006/07/ryska-emigranternas-lasesal-i-stockholm-1907-1910/

[9] For example, Hans Björkegren, *Ryska posten: de ryska revolutionärerna i Norden 1906–1917* [The Russian Post: the Russian revolutionaries in the Nordic countries], Stockholm, 1985.

[10] Morten Thing, *De russiske jöder i Köbenhavn 1882–1943* [The Russian Jews in Copenhagen 1882–1943], Gyldendal, Copenhagen, 2008, p. 298.

Jewish party that Swedish Social Democracy mainly had contact with at home.[11] On the other hand, Martin Grass found a few membership cards from the "Stockholm branch of the Jewish Social Democratic Union Bund in Sweden" from the years 1949–50, i.e., forty years after Zukunft in Stockholm. The cards were found in Sara Mehr's and Paul Olberg's archives.[12] Sara Mehr, the mother of the well-known Stockholm politician Hjalmar Mehr and an active Social Democrat, came to play a central role in the building of the Bund in Sweden after the war, along with the Social Democratic writer Paul Olberg. Olberg was usually described in Swedish labour historiography as a "Menshevik" from Russia, without any mention of the Bund. Not that, of course, his affiliation with the Mensheviks contradicted his commitment to the Bund, which was part of the organizational world of Russian social democracy. After the split between the Bolsheviks and the Mensheviks in 1903, the Bund in the Russian Empire generally joined the Menshevik side.

That the Bund would have existed in Sweden for some years after World War II was thus for me, and Swedish labor movement research in general, unknown, at least for those who had not read the books of the sculptor and author Zenia Larsson – Szaina Marcinowski. In particular, her letters to her close friend Chava Rosenfarb in *Brev från en ny verklighet* depict her years as a newly arrived refugee in Sweden, documenting that period from when she belonged to the Bund's political and cultural Yiddish environment to the dissolution of this environment and her own assimilation into Swedish society.[13]

For my own part, it was a newspaper notice about the funeral of Paul Olberg in 1960, which said that he was followed to his eternal rest by "his Bundists,"

[11] Håkan Blomqvist, *Nation, ras och civilisation i svensk arbetarrörelse före nazismen* [Nation, race and civilization in the Swedish labor movement before Nazism], Carlsson bokförlag, Stockholm, 2006, p. 351. However, Poalei Zion was not recognized as a section of the Social Democratic International until it was reestablished in 1924.

[12] Sara Mehr's personal archive, No. 400, ARAB, contains ten volumes, most of them with newspaper clippings. Paul Olberg's personal archive, PO 435, ARAB, contains 38 volumes.

[13] Zenia Larsson, *Brev från en ny verklighet* [Letters from a new reality], Rabén & Sjögren, Stockholm, 1972. An article by Goldie Morgentaler in the online magazine *Tablet*, "Chava and Zenia," depicts the friendship and correspondence between her mother, the author Chava Rosenfarb and Zenia Larsson, the childhood friends from Bund's world in Łódź who lived through Bergen-Belsen together. The two young women separated at the end of the war, Zenia came to Sweden alone as a refugee, Chava, with the help of the Bund, moved to a Jewish communitee in Canada. While Zenia became a well-known author and sculptress in Sweden, with Swedish as her new language, Chava became an acclaimed Yiddish writer – a life-long friendship that would be corrupted by Zenia Larsson's book *Brev från en ny verklighet* [Letters from a new reality] (author's translation), where Chava was given the non-Jewish name "Linn." Why?, was a question that, according to Morgentaler, came to torment Chava, and which she herself discusses in her article: https://www.tabletmag.com/jewish-arts-and-culture/253817/chava-and-zenia (20190321).

which made me wonder: were there Bundists in Sweden in 1960? During a visit to the YIVO Institute for Jewish Research – *Yidisher Visnshaftlekher Institut* – in New York[14] for other research purposes, I could not help but ask Bund archivist Leo Greenbaum about the Bund in Sweden. It turned out that there was an extensive archive under the heading "Bund in Sweden" from 1945. It was about a dozen volumes – or boxes – with an estimated thousand documents in the form of correspondence, letters, reports, and minutes (see source list). The material was partly arranged, or rather roughly sorted, under several English-language main headings, but beyond that, they were only partially sorted by type and date. Coherent protocol booklets and binders appeared in some cases, otherwise letters and notes were mixed. Printed or typed material was available only to a small extent, with most of the documents handwritten – with different handwriting and on different surfaces. Most of these are in Yiddish, some in German and Russian, with only a handful in Swedish.

With the help of studies on the Bund's history from various aspects, exchanges with international researchers and "Bundist children" – with now-departed parents who were once part of the Bund's Swedish environment – and inspiration from my lectures on the Bund in Swedish–Jewish contexts, I have tried to do justice to this impressive empirical material within a reasonably delimited historical context. For the sake of readability, much of the material has been omitted; perhaps it can be a basis for articles in another context. This then also applies to personal data. The source material contains many personal names, of which I only state a small number. These are people who had a certain prominent and, at least in the Yiddish environment, public place during the Bund's operations in Sweden. However, I have as far as possible tried to compile membership lists for the Swedish organization, which I am happy to share with relatives or other interested parties. (The story has really come to life when "Bundist children" from different parts of the world have contacted me with questions about parents and relatives who appear in the archive material.)

[14] https://yivo.org/. The history of YIVO was introduced to the Swedish public in the book by Samuel D. Kassow, *Vem ska skriva vår historia? Det dolda arkivet i Warszawagettot* [Who will write our history? The hidden archive of the Warsaw getto], Bonniers, Stockholm, 2010. For the dramatic history of the archives of the Bund, see: *A Great Collection: The Archives of the Jewish Labor Movement,* New York, 1965 and Marek Web, "Between New York and Moscow: the Fate of the Bund Archives", in Jack Jacobs (ed.), *Jewish Politics in Eastern Europe: The Bund at 100,* Palgrave, Houndmills, 2001.

Translation

From the outset, it should be noted that I write this from the outside. I have no Jewish affiliation, no roots in Jewish culture and speak neither Yiddish nor Hebrew. I came to this topic from research on the Swedish – and to some extent the international – labor movement, as well as on nationalism, racist ideas and anti-Semitism. I received, after several attempts, a four-year part-time research grant from the Swedish Foundation for Baltic and East European Studies for a project located at Södertörn University, near Stockholm. In addition, I have been received, I must say, with open arms by Yiddish associations and other Jewish milieus in Sweden, as well as by children and grandchildren of Bundists both internationally and in Sweden. A special problem here is about translation, both linguistically and culturally. German and Russian, at least typed, I can manage to understand, but Yiddish – in the Hebrew alphabet? "It's upside down," said Paul, or Hershl, Glasser, the translator, as I handed him a document. The Foundation granted funding for the translation of archival material, and Dr Glasser, a specialist in Yiddish, who had just then completed an assignment as dean of the Max Weinreich Center for Advanced Jewish Studies at YIVO, accepted the challenge. So, box after box, the material went from my hands to Glasser's, who read aloud from Yiddish to English, while I took notes and sometimes photographed documents that Glasser later translated in depth in peace and quiet. In this way, we created an archive of printed English translations of the original Yiddish material, together with my notebooks from the oral interviews. My studies of documents – letters, reports, telegrams, lists of names and more – from the Jewish Labor Committee of America, JLC, which concerned Sweden, were conducted in a similar way. But in that case, I scanned the documents directly into my archive and sent them to Glasser for translation. JLC's vast archive is located at the Robert F. Wagner Labor Archives at New York University, in the list of sources here abbreviated WLA, and includes too many documents concerning Sweden to be studied in its entirety within the framework of this project. All the same, it became interesting material for Dr Glasser to handle, alongside a number of documents in Yiddish from Paul Olberg's and Sara Mehr's personal archives in Stockholm (at YIVO there is one further volume with documents from Olberg I have studied).

Without Dr Glasser's great efforts, including correcting the English text, this study would not have been possible at all. He also generously spent a lot of time trying to orient me in Yiddish cultural and linguistic mysteries. Nevertheless, it should be clear that here, of course, there are sources of error, not primarily significant – a large part of the material was translated twice, both orally and in writing with only minor changes. But in the translations, ambiguities may have escaped me, as well as cultural allusions, symbols, and sub-meanings. Not infrequently, laughter and amusing discussions erupted – in Yiddish – when Glasser read aloud from the material in the small archive hall where we mingled with archivists and volunteers from the older generation. "Olbergs shammes!," Ha, ha. "Upfal! Poor man... heh, heh." It was not always easy to keep up. Yiddish is a rich language with many nuances and possibilities for interpretation. The transcription of Jewish names here offers a great deal of variation, both in naming and spelling. The origins of the names in various linguistic and cultural contexts, such as Yiddish with German, Slavic and Latin roots, create a large variety – quite confusing for a Swede, where the state since long homogenized forms and spellings. Ashkenazi forms of, for example, the biblical names – read in Swedish as Moses, Isak and Jakob – are often Moyshe, Itskhok and Yankev in the material, while Sara and Rachel are transformed from Sore and Rokhl. What in the Swedish version can correspond to Samuel is the Jewish Shmul or Shmil (in Polish spelling: Szmul/Szmil); the "Swedish" Boris, taken from Slavic, corresponds to Hebrew Baruch or Yiddish Beynesh.[15] This is not the place for a study of the subject, just a note that the transcription of names from the archival material offers variations when it comes to one and the same person. In addition, there is spelling that of course differs in the target languages. English *y* usually corresponds to Swedish *j* or possibly *i*. Where the Polish sje-sound is written with sz or cz, the English transcription can be ch or tch, while z can be s. The German word for silver can be written zylber and stein spelled shtein, depending on the origin. In my archival material, all these names and spellings are mixed, not least depending on who wrote the letters, kept the minutes or had drawn up lists of names – or depending on Paul Glasser's translation, which generally followed YIVO's standard for transcription (where, for example, Sara Mehr became Sore Mer). Those who held the pencils probably often started from their individual phonetic impressions, with resulting variations: the Bundist Sziah Szechatow, who appears frequently in the material, has also been spelled Shaye Shikhatov[16]; Chaim is sometimes spelled Khayem; Szmul Perl alternates with Shmul Perel; Finkelstajn is Finkelstein; Abraham is Avrom, Avram or Abram; Raphael is Rafal or Rafol,

[15] For an introduction to naming conventions in Yiddish, see: http://www.yivoencyclopedia.org/article.aspx/Names_and_Naming (20190315).

[16] Sara Ferdman Tauben, Szechatow's granddaughter in Montreal, emphasizes that the family has used the spelling Sziah Szechatow throughout the years, which will be used here as well. See e-mail from Sara Ferdman Tauben to Håkan Blomqvist (20190309).

not to mention the Bund leader in New York Emanuel Novogrodski, also spelled Nowogrodsky, Nowogrodzki, Novogrudski, Novogrotski, etc. I have not been able to perform any name analysis in the flow of names, but have chosen to use the forms that most often occur without attempts at consistency, but with a note of other spellings and forms that may occur.

Ethical considerations

But which names should be reproduced at all in a contemporary historical work like this? The Swedish Research Council's research ethics principles in humanities and social science research include instructions and requirements not to disclose privacy-infringing information about persons who have not had the opportunity to give their consent themselves or through relatives. In this very context – where such consent cannot be given – I have generally assumed that politically organized people with some degree of active participation may be named without anonymization. In cases involving conditions that may be perceived as derogatory – for example, accusations in party trials – and in the case of non-prominent persons, I have chosen not to name them. Perhaps more complicated still are the many letters from refugee camps and sanatoriums with personal stories of difficult lives during the war. The letters were not written for any historian's publication seventy-five years after the fact, and they can reproduce close experiences, feelings, and reactions. For us in the future, these testimonies are a kind of human puzzle in understanding what happened and the traces it left in the lives of individuals – in this case, of those who would also try to rebuild a political movement. Should letter writers be named? "But should they be hidden now as well? Was not the Holocaust enough!," exclaimed a colleague who thought it important that the survivors not be kept anonymous, but revealed as subjects in their full identity. There is also a need for information for any survivors and relatives. The source material contains many names of people in and around the Bundist environment, in letters, protocols and not least lists of names for refugee notification. During the project, I have been repeatedly contacted by survivors and relatives from different parts of the world who have wondered about a relative's time in Sweden. My way of dealing with this is to make an assessment from case to case and letter to letter. Where people have expressed themselves in the direction of: "Let the world know!," I have seen it as important to name. In other respects, I have tried to arrange lists of names in my research archive so that those who want to look for relatives can find them.

Background

The Bund, or *Der algemeyner yidisher arbeter-bund in Lite, Poyln un Rusland*, was formed in October 1897 and developed into an unparalleled Jewish labor movement in the Jewish Pale of Settlement of the Russian Empire, from Vilnius in the northwest down through Polish, Belarusian, and Ukrainian communities to the Black OSea.[17] At that time, over five million Jews lived there in poor conditions while incipient industrialization disrupted older lifestyles and trades. A Jewish working class in small workshops and industrialized handicrafts emerged. The Bund would eventually organize it into a proletarian Jewish cosmos around a secular and socialist Yiddish culture in the form of political clubs and unions, children's and youth organizations, schools and orphanages, theater and cultural activities, sports organizations, and self-defense groups, doing so in its own language, Yiddish. The Bund was the initiator of Russian Social Democracy, which was formed the following year, but early on came to clash with both Bolsheviks and Mensheviks, who did not see the point of a special Jewish organization. The Socialist Second International, founded in 1889, was initially reluctant to speak out against anti-Semitic pogroms in the Empire for fear of "splitting" the working class. But the Bund grew, and at the beginning of the 20th century it became a mass organization of Jewish workers which during the first Russian revolution in 1905 played a prominent role. This was not only because of its trade union efforts and political organization, but also through its defensive militias against pogroms and its socialist Yiddish culture. The Jewish working class, the Bund believed, would develop its own secular socialist culture in its own language and in its

[17] For the history of the Bund, Daniel Blatman, *For our freedom and yours: The Jewish Labour Bund in Poland 1939–1949*, Vallentine Mitchell, London, Portland, 2003, Alain Brossat & Sylvia Klingberg, *Revolutionary Yiddishland: A History Of Jewish Radicalism*, Verso, London, New York, 2016 (Balland 1983), Jack Jacobs (ed.), *Jewish Politics in Eastern Europe: The Bund at 100*, Palgrave, Houndmills, 2001, Henri Minczeles, *Histoire générale du BUND: un mouvement révolutionnaire juif*, Denoël, Paris, 1999, David Slucki, *The International Jewish Labor Bund after 1945: Toward a Global History*, Rutger University Press, New Brunswick, New Jersey, and London, 2012. Enzo Traverso, *Les marxistes et la question juive*, Paris, 1997, Nathan Weinstock, *Le pain de misère: Histoire du mouvement ouvrier juif en Europe Tome 1: L'Empire russe jusqu'en 1914*, and *Tome II: L'Europe centrale et occidental jusqu'en 1945*, La Découverte, Paris, 2002. Martyna Rusiniak-Karwat, *Nowe zycie na zgliszczach: Bund w Polsce w latach 1944–1949* [New life in the ruins: Bund in Poland during the years 1944–1949], Instytut Studiów Politycznych Polskiej Akademii Nauk, Warsaw, 2016. In addition, the large number of Bunds and their relatives' have histories which, of course, express the movement's self-perception but contain a lot of knowledge, such as the latest publication for the 120th anniversary, Irena Klepfisz & Daniel Soyer (eds), *The Stars Bear Witness: The Jewish Labor Bund, 1897–2017*, YIVO, New York, 2017.

own cultural forms through Yiddish. And around the Bund, a world of Yiddish culture grew with poetry, literature, theater, and art.

In the same year that the Bund was formed, though a few months earlier, the first Zionist World Congress had taken place under pomp and circumstance in Basel, Switzerland. For the handful of Jewish socialists gathered in Vilnius, however, the congress in Basel was a purely bourgeois event. In contrast to what they saw as Zionism's unrealistic utopianism and bourgeois nationalism, the Bund advocated *doikayt*, a Yiddish neologism meaning "hereness." The Jewish working masses would fight for their rights on the ground where they lived, "here and now." Through Jewish cultural autonomy within democratic nation-states, the way would be paved for the socialist liberation of the people without oppression and subordination. Ideologically, the Bund also differed from the Marxists, both Bolsheviks and Mensheviks, who advocated Jewish assimilation under the sign of universalism. Through its theorists, led by Vladimir Medem, the Bund developed a view of national rights that was close to the theories of so-called Austro-Marxism, formulated primarily by Karl Renner and Otto Bauer.[18] In a similar vein, the Bund operated in a multiethnic empire and did not imagine that the liberation of the proletariat would be achieved through national separation into new nation-states. Here there was a certain ideological kinship between the Bund and the radical, more cosmopolitan Marxism which, embodied by Rosa Luxemburg and others, distanced itself from all nation-state solutions.[19] But unlike Luxemburg, who in the name of internationalism also rejected Jewish identity building, the Bund worked to affirm, strengthen, and develop such an identity intertwined with socialist ideals. Yiddish as a linguistic and cultural, secular, and socialist identity, became the Bund's hallmark. The Russian revolution of 1905 coincided with the Bund's first heyday. The second could have been the Russian February Revolution of 1917, but the movement was already weakened by repression, expulsion, and the collapse of the Russian Empire. With the Bolshevik takeover, the Bund, like Mensheviks and other socialist movements, was gradually faced with an ultimatum to either be suppressed or join the victorious Bolshevik party. During the Russian Civil War, parts of the movement and the Jewish population in general had supported the Red Army and Soviet power in

[18] Karl Renner (1870–1950) and Otto Bauer (1881–1938) were leading Austrian Social Democrats and Marxists. In 1907, Bauer presented his strategy in *Die Nationalitätenfrage und die Sozialdemokratie*.
[19] For the internationalist perspective of Rosa Luxemburg see: Peter Hudis & Kevin B. Anderson (eds), *The Rosa Luxemburg Reader*, New York, London, 2004.

self-defense against the anti-Jewish mass pogroms of the "whites."[20] Under the name *Kombund*, parts of the Russian Bund were included in the Jewish sections of the ruling Communist Party, *yevsektsii*, while non-Bolshevik parties were banned.[21]

It was outside Soviet Russia, in independent Poland, which in 1918 broke away from the former Russian Empire, that the Bund not only lived on in the 1920s, but gained increasing influence in a growing Jewish working class. With trade union organizations for Jewish workers, the youth movement *Tsukunft*, the defensive militia *Tsukunft shturem* and the sports movement *Morgnshtern*, together with the children's organization SKIF – *Sotsyalistishe kinder-farband* and the women's organization YAF – *Yidisher arbeter-froy*, the Bund united a world of Jewish socialist mass organizations. In addition, there was the construction of the secular Jewish school system *Tsysho* (*Tsentrale yidishe shul-organizatsye*), *Kultur-lige's* Yiddish theaters, artists and writers, and a network of social events such as camps, kindergartens and the famous *Medem* sanatorium for the treatment of tuberculosis in Jewish children and young people. In the Polish municipal elections of 1938, the Bund was the largest Jewish party in Warsaw, with over 60 percent of the Jewish electorate. Through the daily *Folkstsaytung*, the youth magazine *Yugnt-veker*, book publishers and educational activities, the Bund's ideological orientation came to characterize large parts of the Jewish working class in Poland until the war and the Holocaust. With the German invasion of Poland in 1939 and the World War, most of the Bund in Europe perished. Through the Soviet occupation of eastern Poland in 1939–41, parts of the organization's leadership, of which Henryk Erlich and Viktor Alter were the best-known representatives, were liquidated. During the Holocaust, the movement's mass base was annihilated. The last big battle of the Polish Bund was the uprising in the Warsaw Ghetto in the spring of 1943, when young Bundists led by, among others, Marek Edelman together with left-wing Zionists, Communists and others challenged the deportations to the death camps. After the war, only remnants of the once powerful Jewish socialist movement remained.

Attempts were made after 1945, however, to gather surviving Bundists from camps and exile to rebuild the movement in Poland. New pogroms in Kielce and elsewhere, along with the establishment of the Stalinist party state, presented the Polish Bund with the choice to join the ruling Communist Party

[20] Oleg Budnitskii, *Russian Jews between the Reds and the Whites 1917–1920*, University of Pennsylvania Press, Philadelphia, 2012 .

[21] Zvi Y. Gitelman, *Jewish Nationality and Soviet Politics. The Jewish sections of the CPSU, 1917–1930*, Princeton New Yersey, 1972.

or to cease, and its survivors to disperse throughout the world. In the labor movement's conflicts between social democracy and communism, the Polish Bund had long chosen to stand outside both the Communist International and the Socialist International, recreated after World War I. In 1930, however, the Bund joined the Socialist International and formed a radical component that turned against both non-revolutionary "ministerial socialism" and "bourgeois nationalism," which was believed to be represented also by Labor Zionism.

Outside Poland, the Bund did not exist as a party, but only as a network and as support groups in various countries where Jewish socialists, primarily with a Russian background, migrated. The individual Bundists were usually part of the social democratic parties, especially after joining the Socialist International. To be, for example, a German or French Social Democrat at the same time as a Bundist did not have to be a contradiction. Bundists in the United States were for a long time the leading force in the textile workers' unions and in the American umbrella organization Jewish Labor Committee of America, JLC, which at the end of World War II numbered a half a million members. After the war and the Polish Bund joining the Communist Party, the support groups were transformed into branches of a world party. The Polish Bund's exile representation in New York became the International Coordinating Committee of the Yiddish Workers' Bund or "Jewish Labor Bund." While the Bund's world organization survived into the 1990s with a major centenary in New York in 1997, the Coordinating Committee was finally dissolved on the eve of the 2000s. Organized Bundists are still, as of this writing, active in some parts of the world, including London, Paris, and Melbourne.[22]

Who were they?

A few had already reached Sweden during the war years, but from the Swedish refugee reception in the spring of 1945, the lists of Jewish men, women, and children from concentration camps and so-called DP (Displaced Persons) camps in Germany, Poland and Austria began to grow, as well as lists of Jewish migrants from Soviet territories. Many of them were Bundists. Through the Jewish Labor Committee of America and the Bund Representation in New York, they sought contact with each other and with relatives around the world.[23] Letters from *khaveyrim* – comrades – in Polish and German camps

[22] For London: https://www.jewishsocialist.org.uk/ Paris: https://www.yiddishweb.com/histoire/ and https://www.centre-medem.org/ Melbourne: https://www.bundist.org/ (20190623).

[23] The archives of the JLC at The Tamiment Library & Robert F. Wagner Labor Archives in New York (TAMWAG) contain extensive material on this activity with correspondence, lists of names and

who were to be evacuated to Sweden arrived in New York. Even Bundists who arrived in Sweden without the help of JLC wrote to New York from refugee camps and sanatoriums in the hope of regaining contact with comrades in the new, unfamiliar country. The letters testified to the catastrophe behind them, to abandonment and despair, but also to the hope that someone would hear their cries of distress, that the world would listen. "Dear, dear comrades, when I write these words I am blinded by tears," begins a letter from a woman somewhere in Sweden in the spring of 1946.[24] "I have lost everything, I am abandoned in the world, I am alone in Sweden, twice alone without family or friends." She appeals for help finding the remains of her relatives somewhere in the world, in America, or in her hometown of Starachowice, Poland, but concludes: "Dear comrades, I cannot now tell you about my experiences. I had a child in Poland, she had Catholic papers, so she survived the war, thanks to our friends who saved her. When the war was over, she went from Warsaw to Starachowice, where Polish hooligans murdered her."

Another woman writes several letters from the industrial city of Norrköping in the autumn and winter of 1945–46. "Dear Bund Comrades, I write to you and can hardly believe that I am Rosa Rosen, one of the thousands who survived. My tears flow, my hands tremble."[25] She was twenty-four years old, from Łódź, and all her relatives had been Bundists. "My father was a well-known Bundist who was missing a foot he lost before the war." She had graduated from a Medem school and been active in the youth organization Tsukunft. When the war broke out, she and most of her Tsukunft comrades remained in the ghetto. "You cannot imagine what it was like, but even in the worst moments we helped each other." Still, "thousands of our comrades died of starvation and tuberculosis." Nevertheless, she continued, they held their meetings at night, and many were shot. After five years in the ghetto, they were transported to Auschwitz, just before the Russians arrived. With the Swedish Red Cross, she had been taken to Sweden at the end of the war. "Now I am completely alone in a new country, I have no friends and know no one." Her father's best friend had once said that in the United States, they had many

accounts of financial items and other support. Name lists, correspondence and telegrams in Box 36, reel 102–105, Box 37, reel 106–109, Box 38 reel 110–111, serie III, JLC, TAMWAG. How JLC organized its support work for the Bund is studied by Constance Pâris de Bollardière, "The Jewish Labor Committee's Bundist Relief Network in France 1945–1948," i *Jewish History Quarterly*, no 2 (246), June 2013. The work of the JLC during the war has been studied by Catherine Collomp, "'Relief is a political gesture:' The Jewish Labor Committee's interventions in war-torn Poland, 1939–1945," *Transatlantica*, No. 1/2014.

[24] Letter from a woman, March 14 1946, Vol. 207, ME18, 1400BA, YIVO.

[25] Letter from Rosa Rosen, Norrköping, November 15, 1945. Vol. 207, ME18, 1400BA, YIVO.

friends who were willing to help. "Therefore, I pray you in my loneliness, you are my only hope," and signed "Your Lonely Comrade from Łódź."[26]

A month later, she is happy to have found her sister in Sweden who lost a finger in a machine in Berlin.[27] The sister had previously been admitted to the Medem Sanatorium in Warsaw. Now she wrote about life in the ghetto, about deportations and about starvation. "For just a little water and soup, we gave up resisting." She had worked in various factories and finally in a hospital. One morning in 1943, when she had just returned to work, an alarm sounded in the street. The entire hospital had been surrounded by Nazi soldiers, a terrible panic ensued: patients ran in all directions, the sickest prayed for their lives. In a post-natal ward, a mother with a three-day-old baby pleaded, "Please, nurse, I am strong, I can go with you, I want to find my husband." Together they had run across the yard and through the kitchen to a basement, where the mother and child were left. The woman, though, ran back, and was met with a heinous sight. The German soldiers threw women and babies out of the windows on the second floor, the blood flowing over the cobblestones. "I will never forget the screams." She herself survived another year in the ghetto until the last deportation in August 1944, when she and her family were "forced to give ourselves to the killers." In closed railway carriages, they were transported to Auschwitz; one of her cousins traveled together with her eight-year-old daughter, who comforted her mother: "Look at me, Mom, I'm big and strong now, we will not be separated." But the mother's appeals on arrival were in vain: "At the selection, the German officer did not see how big her daughter was."

The letter writer was also separated from her sister and parents. She was sent to an ammunition factory in Berlin, where she was forced to work until the end of the war. "We were bombed every day." With the Swedish Red Cross, she was taken to Sweden, "thanks to that, I can become human again." But what hope did she have for the future? "I miss our party, I miss our comrades, I miss our Yiddish literature and our language." She wanted to be active in the party again, but it was impossible in Sweden. "My only hope that keeps me alive is that I have devoted friends in you," she wrote to her comrades in New York, hoping they could help her find surviving relatives.[28]

From the Koppardal camp outside the small town of Nyköping, two women wrote to Bund general secretary, Emanuel Novogrodski, in April 1946.[29] They

[26] Ibid.

[27] Letter from Rosa Rosen, Norrköping, December 15, 1945. Vol. 207, ME18, 1400BA, YIVO.

[28] Also letter from Rosa (Rochel) Rosenblaum, February 9, 1946, "My last hope is with you, that you may find my uncles in New York.," Vol. 207, ME18, 1400BA, YIVO.

[29] Letter from Lea Finkelman and Maria Fajnmesser to Emanuel Novogrodski, April 21, 1946. Box 36, folder 25, reel 105, ser. III, JLC, TAMWAG.

promised to resume their activities in the Bund as soon as they regained their strength. About their experiences, they wrote that "every day was a tragedy," especially when they were deported from Łódź to Kielce in 1942. One thousand two hundred Jews were driven into the city's ghetto, "we came with our children and husbands." May 29, 1943 was the most heartbreaking day of their lives: "My only child was killed by the Nazis," writes one of the women. By three in the morning, the "Ukrainian killers" had arrived, followed by the Gestapo. They drove the Jews out of their houses and lined them up in the square. A few hundred here, a few hundred there. "There, the murderers tore the children out of our hands, it is impossible to describe, you who were not there can never imagine it." Forty "innocent children" were murdered. Mass shootings began, people had to dig their own graves … "I was the only one in the family that survived. Why?" The two women thanked their comrades in New York for the help they received in Sweden. "Please do not forget us; perhaps working for the Bund can make us feel better."

From a small place called Fagersjö outside Stockholm, a male comrade, in ten handwritten pages, talks about his war experiences in Kraków.[30] "We understood when the war came that something terrible was going to happen, but we had no idea it was going to be so horrible." The leading and well-known comrades had to flee, those who could went to the Soviet Union, some to "Lembrik," Yiddish for L'viv. He himself remained in Kraków together with several of the comrades who later came to Sweden. In June 1943, a terrible deportation took place in Kraków, "half of the deported died." Many had thought that with the war against the Soviet Union, the situation for Jews would ease, but the opposite was in fact the case. Kraków was liberated by the Russians on January 17, 1945, "but by then, there were no Jews left." The last transport had left at midnight the day before. "When we heard the shots, we thought we would make it, but we were transported to the Grossrosen camp, where it all took a terrible turn, but I cannot write about that." Now he was in "free Sweden," but in a camp with only Poles: "Life is empty, impossible!" And he hoped to contact the movement again.

From Halmstad, a woman writes long handwritten letters about her personal fate and her experiences during the war years, about becoming acquainted with Sweden and her ideological convictions.[31] What impression had she and the Jewish camp prisoners made on the Swedish population? "We were all sick, we had to go to bed, but who followed that good advice? We stood

[30] Letter from Jakob Kshienski to Emanuel Novogrodski, Fagersjö, November 15, 1945. Box 36, folder 19, reel 102, ser. III, JLC, TAMWAG.
[31] Letter from Hella Rudnitska, Halmstad, February 22, 1946, Vol. 207, ME18, 1400BA, YIVO.

by the window, slipped out into the yard and ran like wild dogs from captivity." The yard was surrounded by barbed wire, and the gate was guarded by two armed men, Swedish soldiers, "two soldiers of the same race as our murderers, but still so different, so good. They calmed us down with their cheerful blue eyes." The women had to do as the doctors said in order not to spread diseases. But people came with packages to the other side of the fence, "we cried, and they cried, we laughed, and they laughed"; a soldier tried to keep them apart, but the women talked to him, held his weapon and cried: "Although he did not understand what we said, he knew what we meant." "Dear comrades," she continued, "the first weeks, we were not normal. No matter how much food they gave us, we could not get enough. We lied when we said we had not received seconds, so we got a third portion. We hid food under the pillows …, milk and bread under the beds." And clothes! "For five years I had not had any real leather shoes." Silk underwear and silk socks, nice clothes, the women got what they asked for, and lied to get more. "We must have another pair of shoes, another dress, which we immediately hid in the bed." For the sick, the clothes were hung above the beds, "and the eyes of the half-dead came back to life as they looked at the new clothes and fantasized about how nice they would look on them." To her, it was as if the clothes were embarrassed by just hanging there to make the owners' death easier. But soon, the hunger for food and clothing was sated. "Take back the clothes! Give us back our families, our mothers, fathers, spouses, children … Swedes, why do you save us, we do not want to live! Why are they all dead! And why are we alive?"[32]

After nine months in Sweden, she had regained her physical and mental health and was working in a textile factory. "I am convinced that I am now able to work and live my life." Finally, she had been reached by a letter from the Bund in New York and was overwhelmed by emotions: "Dear comrades, I was so happy to have the first letter from you. You, just you, woke me from my sleep and revived in me what fascism had poisoned. You [illegible] surviving teachers gave me a life injection and brought me back to socialism." And she quoted the Bund anthem *Di Shvue* about the oath in blood and tears they once swore to socialism. The war experience stood as a confirmation of those words. "Oh, people," she urged, "ask us what the difference is between one people and another. Come to Auschwitz, come to Buchenwald, [illegible] Berlin's arms factories. Get burned, be tortured by hunger, cold and heat [illegible], lying on planks with lice, stone [illegible] with Russian women, with German women, with Jewish women, French women, Yugoslav women, Greek women," then

[32] Ibid.

people would see what humanity is, and the difference between fascism and socialism. When the bombs fell on a concentration camp in Berlin with five hundred Jewish women from Łódź, they were all in the same inferno.[33]

Reunification

The letters written by Bund's representation in New York and JLC appealed for help with, among other things, the Swedish authorities, practical issues, financial support and contacting other comrades. The addressee in Stockholm was Paul Olberg, who during the 1930s was a leader in the construction of the Swedish Labor Movement's refugee aid.

Paul Olberg

Paul Olberg, or Pavel Karlovitch, whose Jewish birth name was Hirsch Schuschkowitz, was not young. He was born in 1878 into a Jewish family in the Latvian city of Jakobstadt (now Jekabpils) within the then-Russian Empire.[34] At the age of seventeen, he joined the emerging Jewish labor movement, which merged into the Bund in 1897. Olberg himself had already had a few years of illegal activity behind him as a participant in underground *kruzhiki* – workers' circles – and as a distributor of Marxist literature. For that, he was arrested and imprisoned, but as for so many other radicals, the year he spent in prison became, in Olberg's own words, his "literary faculty."[35] With Marx, Engels, Lassalle and Plekhanov in his intellectual arsenal, he resumed his post-liberation activity, took part in the first Russian revolution in 1905, moved between different places in the Russian Empire, and worked as a journalist for the socialist press. With the split of Russian Social Democracy in 1903, Olberg sided with the Mensheviks.[36] In the wake of the Russian February Revolution

[33] Ibid.
[34] For Olberg see: the biography by Per Enerud, *Den farligaste av flyktingar. Paul Olberg – antinazist, antikommunist och dissident i folkhemmet* [The most dangerous of refugees. Paul Olberg – anti-Nazi, anti-communist and dissident in the folk home], Carlsson bokförlag, Stockholm, 2017. See also: Håkan Blomqvist "Lost Worlds of Labour: Paul Olberg, the Jewish Labour Bund, and Menshevik Socialism" in Norbert Götz (ed.), *The Sea of Identities: A Century of Baltic and East European Experiences with Nationality, Class and Gender*, Södertörn Academic Studies, Huddinge, 2014.
[35] "75-årige Paul Olberg är glad att aldrig ha varit bolsjevik" [75-year-old Paul Olberg is happy to have never been a Bolshevik], *Morgon-Tidningen* [The Morning-paper], November 21, 1953.
[36] For the history of Menshevism see: Abraham Ascher, *Pavel Axelrod and the Development of Menshevism*, Harvard University Press, Cambridge, Massachusetts, 1972, Vladimir N. Brovkin, *The Mensheviks after October: Socialist Opposition and the Rise of the Bolshevik Dictatorship*, Cornell University Press, Ithaca and London, 1987, Leopold H. Haimson (ed.), *The Mensheviks: from the revolution of 1917 to the second world war*, The University of Chicago Press, Chicago and London, 1974, and André Liebich, *From*

of 1917, Olberg participated in the transit of Russian exile socialists who went back to Russia from various parts of Europe via Sweden.[37] Together with leading Mensheviks, he set up an information agency in Stockholm for the Russian Petrograd Soviet, which at that time was dominated by Mensheviks.[38] For a time Stockholm became the meeting place of international socialism, the city to which revolutionaries and reformists, internationalists and social patriots, pacifists and Leninists would flock. Here, Olberg was not only part of the Menshevik circle, but also met prominent figures of the Swedish Social Democrats, such as the founder Hjalmar Branting and leaders Gustav Möller and Arthur Engberg, as well as the left-wing socialists and future communists Fredrik Ström, Zeth Höglund and Ture Nerman. Here, he got to know the Zimmerwald movement's Angelica Balabanoff, who a few years later would join the Communist International, and many other notable figures from the revolutionary years. Already during the year of the revolution in 1917 and the first post-war years, Paul Olberg became a contributor to the Swedish Social Democratic press, writing articles increasingly critical of the Bolshevik reign of terror, of its corruption, misrule, and its handling of the famine.[39]

He went to Berlin and reported from the German November Revolution of 1918 and the Spartacus uprising in January 1919, and was already experienced as a political writer. At the age of forty, he had experienced the birth and emergence of the Russian labor movement with its ideological and political struggles, the Russian revolutions of 1905 and 1917, the Bolsheviks' takeover, and the initial civil war. He had broad contacts in the Russian, Swedish and European social democratic movements and experience as a socialist writer in several countries. As a writer in the German Social Democratic press, Olberg got to know many of the German Social Democrats' prominent figures such as Eduard Bernstein and Karl Kautsky. When Hitler took power in 1933, Olberg and his wife Frida Markovna went to Sweden. It was the year after the Swedish Social Democrats' great election victory, with the launch of the crisis program and with the popular movements' growing influence in the development of

the Other Shore: Russian Social Democracy after 1921, Harvard University Press, Cambridge, Massachusetts, and London, England, 1997.

[37] Enerud, pp. 50–53 and Björkegren, p. 251.

[38] Aleksander Kan, *Hemmabolsjevikerna: Den svenska socialdemokratin, ryska bolsjeviker och mensjeviker under världskriget och revolutionsåren 1914–1920* [The Home Bolsheviks: The Swedish Social Democrats, Russian Bolsheviks and Mensheviks during the World War and the Revolutionary Years 1914–1920], Carlsson bokförlag, Stockholm, 2005, p. 128.

[39] "Sovjet-Ryssland i verkligheten. Brev till *Social-Demokraten* från P. Olberg" [Soviet Russia in reality. Letter to the Social Democrat from P. Olberg], part 1–3, *Social-Demokraten* [The Social Democrat], August 25, October 28 and October 29, 1919.

society. 1932 marked the beginning of 44 years of uninterrupted Social Democratic governments in Sweden and the birth of the so-called "people's home," the welfare state.

He immediately joined the Swedish Social Democrats and was involved in building up the labor movement's refugee assistance. After only having temporary addresses during their early years in Sweden, the Olbergs moved into a simple one-room apartment on Luxgatan in the heavy industrialized Stockholm island of Lilla Essingen's working class quarters.[40] It was here that Paul Olberg's reception center for emergency calls from Bundists in refugee camps and care facilities around Sweden took shape.

It was through the labor movement's refugee aid (*Arbetarrörelsens flyktinghjälp*) and its international network of contacts that Olberg became the important link for JLC and the Bund in its relief work for comrades, or "like-minded people," as Olberg usually put it.[41] Even before the war, he had sought to assist individual persecuted comrades of Jewish background. The Kautsky family had fled Austria after the Anschluss in 1938, and 84-year-old Karl Kautsky died on arrival in the Netherlands. When Kautsky's elderly Jewish wife Luise appealed to Olberg in 1942 for help in going to Sweden, he contacted the Social Democratic leadership, but apparently without result. Luise Kautsky was deported to Auschwitz, where she died on arrival.[42] During the war years, he continued to play a role as a contact between and support for Bundists, Mensheviks and Social Democrats on the run. Olberg's archive in Stockholm contains correspondence with a large number of socialists in different parts of the world.[43] YIVO's archives also contain a volume with accounts of aid packages, books, travel, mail, telegrams and telephones, and more concerning

[40] The first lease on Lilla Essingen is from 1942. Vol. 30, PO 435, ARAB.

[41] For example, the report from Olberg in German to JLC in New York, August 29, 1945, which only in exceptional cases uses the word "comrades" (*genossen*), otherwise the term *freunde* is used even for leading Bundists. A reply letter from JLC Secretary General Jacob Pat, September 18, 1945, also emphasizes that JLC is one *unparteilische Organisation*. Box 36, reel 102, ser. III, JLC, TAMWAG.

[42] Postcard to Paul Olberg from Luise Kautsky, Amsterdam, July 16, 1942. Copy of a letter from Zeth Höglund to Swedish foreign minister Christian Günther in 1942, concerning Luise Kautsky. About the death of Luise Kautsky in Auschwitz Birkenau, see: the letter to Paul Olberg from the prisoner Lucie Adelsberger who stayed with Mrs Kautsky until the end of the war, October 13, 1945. All the documents are in Vol. 23, PO 435, ARAB.

[43] The correspondence is spread over the volumes, but Vol. 20, 22–25 contain an exceptionally large number of letters linked to both international and Swedish Social Democracy, including correspondence with the prominent Menshevik leader Rafael Abromovich and the Ukrainian–Jewish socialist Angelica Balabanoff. PO 435, ARAB.

Olberg's activities from January 1943 on.[44] It otherwise seems to have been Axel Granath, secretary of the labor movement's refugee aid, with whom JLC collaborated at the beginning of the war to mediate contacts, to offer financial means and to help with transit visas for Bundists on the run from occupied Europe. These efforts intensified after the Soviet annexation of the Baltic states in 1940, where Jewish Vilnius, or Vilna, previously had become a refuge for many socialists fleeing Nazism, but was now also threatened by Soviet security forces.[45]

With the transports to Sweden from the concentration camps in Germany and Poland taking place during the summer of 1945, contacts with the Bund's representation in New York and JLC reached another level. From Jacob (Yankev) Pat, JLC secretary general, the telegrams and letters arrived in an ever-increasing stream from comrades in need of help. Lists of people on the road, telegrams with arrival times and places were sent to Olberg, as well as money to provide for their initial time, both necessities and accommodation.[46]

JLC in Sweden

Pat was a fifty-five-year-old veteran of the Bund, born into a working-class family in Białystok, in present-day Poland. After a background as a workers' Zionist, he had joined the Bund in Poland, become a prominent Yiddish writer, and in the 1920s built up the secular Jewish school system Tsysho, becoming its general secretary. He also represented the Bund in the Jewish parliamentary delegation in Warsaw.[47] At the outbreak of the war, he was traveling in the

[44] Vol. 205, ME18, 1400BA, YIVO. Some documents in the archive of the JLC concern Olberg's refugee aid during the war, Box 36, folder 14–16 reel 102, ser. III, JLC, TAMWAG and Box 39, folder 46, reel 115, ser. IV, JLC, TAMWAG.

[45] Axel Granath has otherwise probably been unjustly described as one of those who hand-picked Social Democratic refugees from occupied Czechoslovakia in 1938 and "opted out of Communists and Jews." Klas Åmark, *Att bo granne med ondskan: Sveriges förhållande till nazismen, Nazityskland och Förintelsen* [Living next door to evil: Sweden's relationship to Nazism, Nazi Germany and the Holocaust], Albert Bonniers förlag, Stockholm, 2011, pp. 478–479. However, JLC's archive footage shows that Granath was important in helping the transit of Jewish Bundists to safety in the United States, among others, the Bundist leader Emanuel Sherer during his flight from Vilnius. See: telegram January 17, 1940, to Axel Granath from the chairman of the JLC, Adolph Held, who sends him one-thousand dollars to guarantee Sherer a visa. Sherer managed to reach Stockholm where in 1940, together with the Bundist leader Shloime Mendelsohn and Axel Granath, he worked to put more Bundists to safety. In a number of letters and telegrams from the summer of 1940, their efforts flash past, as does Sherer's despair over the American consul's inaction in Kaunas and the dismantling of the Jewish aid organization JOINT's relief work in Vilnius. Box 36, folder 14, reel 102, ser. III, JLC, TAMWAG.

[46] Box 36, folder 16–20, reel 102 and 103, ser. III, JLC, TAMWAG, for 1945.

[47] "Yankev [Jacob] Pat (1890–1966) http://yleksikon.blogspot.com/2018/06/yankev-jacob-pat.html (20190623).

United States to raise funds for the movement; he remained there and became part of the Bund's exile representation in New York, as well as of JLC's management. Together with Benjamin Tabachynski from the same region, he came to be responsible for the Bund's and JLC's fundraising and support activities for Jewish and other non-communist labor movements in occupied Europe. In his intensive correspondence, Olberg described in detail Swedish regulations on refugee transit and visa rules, accommodation and daily allowances, postal and parcel postage, as well as Swedish and Polish customs regulations, all to facilitate JLC's relief shipments, contact connections and assist comrades to reach relatives and friends, especially in the United States.[48]

To facilitate contacts with the Swedish authorities, Olberg proposed in September 1945 that he be appointed JLC's Swedish representative, which was immediately welcomed in New York.[49] The Bundists in JLC already knew Olberg, not least the Menshevik veteran Lazar Epstein, whose niece Beba was found by Olberg in a Swedish refugee camp, enabling them to resume contact.[50] Olberg was also not modest in emphasizing his good contacts with representatives from Swedish authorities and Social Democratic politicians up to the top level, such as the Minister of Social Affairs Gustav Möller and the Prime Minister himself, Per Albin Hansson. On JLC's hopes that Olberg would present himself to the American Legation for visa applications, Olberg empha-

[48] Letter from Olberg in German to JLC in New York, October 4, 1945, about package prices, customs fees, contact persons etc. Letter from Olberg to JLC in New York, October 13, 1945, on Swedish rules for refugees' living conditions, work permits, transit visas, etc. Box 36, folder 18, reel 102, ser. III, JLC, TAMWAG. For the Swedish rules regarding refugee reception, permits, support, etc. Mikael Byström, *Utmaningen: Den svenska välfärdsstatens möte med flyktingar i andra världskrigets tid* [The challenge: The Swedish welfare state's meeting with refugees during the Second World War], Nordic Academic Press, Lund, 2012.

[49] Letter from Jacob Pat, Secretary General and Adolph Held, Chairman to Paul Olberg, October 2, 1945: "We hereby, authorize you to represent the Jewish Labor Committee in all your activities to ease the plight of these victims of fascism…". Box 36, folder 18, reel 102, ser. III, JLC, TAMWAG.

[50] Several letters in German show that Beba Epstein made direct contact with Olberg from a camp, or a sanatorium, from the seaside resort of Mölle in August 1945, where she was transported via Helsingborg. Olberg apparently managed to arrange temporary housing for her with friends in Stockholm so that "she would not feel alone." He announced that he met her almost daily as she seems to have helped him with refugee work. Lazar Epstein sent funds to Olberg to finance her upkeep. Letter from Beba Epstein to Olberg from Mölle, August 29, 1945. Box 51, folder 40, reel 152, ser IV, JLC, TAMWAG. Letter from Jacob Pat, JLC to Olberg, September 18, 1945, about "Fräulein Beba Epstein." Letter from Olberg to JLC, October 4, 1945, about contact with the niece who is going to write to her uncle. Letter from Jacob Pat to Olberg in Russian, September 26, 1945, containing information about sending 600 dollars in support of bundists, of which 100 dollars were from "our" Lazar Epstein to his *plemjanitsy*. Box 36, folder 17, 18, reel 102, ser. III, JLC, TAMWAG.

sized that his personal friendship with Gunnar Myrdal, well known for his social science research on the United States, would surely open the door.[51]

Before the visit of an American trade union delegation in October 1945, JLC had acquired full knowledge of Olberg's skills and his network of contacts. It was Irving Brown from the central trade union AFL and Charles Zimmermann from the JLC who traveled around Europe for several months to form an opinion on the situation and establish contacts with non-communist trade union and labor movement representatives.[52] Olberg planned the Swedish visit in detail, asking JLC to send congratulatory telegrams on the sixtieth birthdays of both prime minister Per Albin Hansson and the chairman of the blue-collar trade union central, LO, August Lindberg. JLC also sent an appeal to the Minister of Social Affairs Gustav Möller and Foreign Minister Östen Undén not to repatriate the labor movement activists who had lost all human contact with their countries of origin, as well as their relatives, having also lost their homes and belongings. The Committee thanked "democratic Sweden" for its "outstanding humanitarian efforts" during the war years, especially the rescue operation for Danish Jews, and hoped that those who were now worried about being sent back would stay in Sweden for a while and receive work or education "which did not infringe on the interests of the country." It was a time-limited period because most of "this group" sought to reunite with relatives in America. Editor Paul Olberg at the social democratic morning paper in Stockholm, the JLC informed, had the names of those concerned, and JLC took responsibility for seeing that the people in question "not be a burden for Sweden."[53]

Olberg was later able to report the whole thing as a success. The two Americans had been received in Bromma Stockholm airport by government representatives, and the American minister in Stockholm, Hershel Johnson, had arranged a lunch for the guests where Prime Minister Hansson, the Minister of Social Affairs, Möller, LO chairman Lindberg, JLC's Swedish

[51] Letters from Olberg to JLC, October 4, 1945. Box 36, folder 18, reel 102, ser. III, JLC, TAMWAG.

[52] Irving Brown (1911–1989) was the emissary of the American Trade Union Confederation (AFL) for building up pro-Western trade union movements in post-war Europe, later known for his CIA contacts. See: Anthony Carew, *American Labour's Cold War Abroad: From Deep Freeze to Détente, 1945–1970*, AU Press, Edmonton, 2018. See also: Harry Kelber, "AFL-CIO's Dark Past (3)," 2004, http://www.laboreducator.org/darkpast3.htm (20190604). Charles Zimmerman from the American textile union ILGWU represented JLC.

[53] Telegram, September 22, 1945, from Adolph Held, President of the JLC, and Jacob Pat, Secretary General, to the Minister of Social Affairs Gustav Moeller [Möller] and Foreign Minister Oesten [Östen] Unden. Box 36, folder 17, reel 102, ser. III, JLC, TAMWAG.

representative Olberg, and some other well-known figures participated.[54] Zimmermann had further conferred with Möller and Undén, thanked them for Sweden's humanitarian aid to the Jews and discussed the problems of the detention of Jews from different countries.[55] Olberg was able to report that the Swedish government had granted a visa quota for the transit of refugees through the JLC. The American visit was widely reported in the press, not least JLC's contribution of $10,000 to Swedish aid for Denmark's Jews.[56]

It all opened the way for the formation of a Swedish branch of JLC in December of 1945 under the prominent leadership of LO's vice-chairman Gunnar Andersson.[57] The chief accountant of Stockholm municipality and Social Democrat Hjalmar Mehr, the son of Sara Mehr, was involved early in the relief work, and became a member of the board, appointed as its vice chairman.

Sara Mehr

Sara Mehr, or Sara Mobschebna Matles before her marriage, was born in 1887 in Grodno in present-day Belarus, then within the Russian Empire. As a 17-year-old tobacco worker, she had in 1904 participated in a long-running strike that was suppressed by force, and fled to Sweden.[58] This is how, many decades later, she described it in a short memoir:

> I had to leave my homeland after a long strike, where 2,500 workers demanded a small wage increase and slightly better conditions. After three months of famine, the employers hired the Cossacks of the Russian authorities, who cracked down on the strikers, and the workers lost the strike, and

[54] Telegram from Olberg to JEWLABCOM New York, November 9, 1945, Box 36, folder 19, reel 102, ser. III, JLC, TAMWAG.

[55] Ibid.

[56] *Dagens Nyheter* [The Daily News], October 26, 1945, *Expressen* [The Express], November 2, 1945.

[57] Minutes taken at a constituent meeting with the founders of the Jewish Labor Committee in Stockholm, December 17, 1945.Box 36, folder 20, reel 103, ser. III, JLC, TAMWAG.

[58] According to the Swedish journalist Björn Elmbrant, *Stockholmskärlek. En bok om Hjalmar Mehr* [Stockholm love. A book about Hjalmar Mehr], Atlas, Stockholm, 2010, pp. 21–23 and 374–375, Sara Mehr did not arrive in Sweden until 1905. Based on various statements from family stories, Elmbrant discusses information about her arrival and age. According to her own information above and "Ansökan om uppehållsbok 1918–1924" [Application for a residence book 1918–1924], she was born in 1887 and arrived in Sweden in 1904, *Stadsarkivet* [The Stockholm City Archive] http://digitalastadsarkivet.stockholm.se/Databas/ansokan-om-uppehallsbok-1918-1924/Visa/sara-mehr-fodd-matles/731?sid index=73 (20181123).

> when the workers staged a demonstration in protest and at that time pulled out a single red cloth, the result was beatings and arrests.[59]

It was the famous strike at the Shereshevsky factory from December 1903, when the tobacco workers fought a long battle in which growing hunger and distress, strikebreakers and Cossacks gradually tore apart and crushed the strike. Behind the union struggle were the Bund and other Jewish socialists in a region where a growing Jewish working class had been organizing since the 1890s. The Bund's secret factory newspaper, *Grodner fabriks bletel*, had been distributed in the tobacco factories since the turn of the century and described the working conditions of the mainly female workers at Shereshevski. Without fans and ventilation, the tobacco dust made the workers sick; many suffered from kidney disease or tuberculosis and were described as "pale and yellow."[60] According to her own information, Sara Matles arrived in Sweden on the last day of April in 1904. In Stockholm the next day, she saw the great First of May demonstration, a transformative experience for her.

> Already on Vasagatan, I saw the hundreds of red flags and the standards, thousands of people all the way up to Odengatan. Most of the protesters were well-dressed and seemed enthusiastic, but at the same time solemn. I was in seventh heaven! To imagine such a splendor of red flags! A demonstration! Freedom! And this the working class had fought for.[61]

When the Tobacco Industry Workers' Union's column came marching, she ran enthusiastically into line, marching to the vast field of Gärdet, where the chairwoman Anna Sterky spoke: "of her speech, I understood only the word 'golden calf.'" Thus began her lifelong involvement in the Swedish labor movement. She could almost have been the girl in the little pamphlet *Erinerungen fun a papirosen makherke* – Memoirs of a woman cigarette maker – distributed by the Bund in Grodno, where the young tobacco worker, after participating in a strike, became a committed socialist.[62] Among those who welcomed Sara Matles in Stockholm the night before the First of May demon-

[59] "Mina första intryck av Stockholm" [My first impressions of Stockholm], undated typewritten manuscript, probably late 1950s, early 1960s. Vol. 1, SM400, ARAB.
[60] History of the Jewish Community of Grodno: https://www.jewishgen.org/Yizkor/grodno/gro137.html (20181123).
[61] Vol. 1, SM400, ARAB.
[62] History of the Jewish Community of Grodno: https://www.jewishgen.org/Yizkor/grodno/gro137.html (20181123).

stration was, according to the memoir, her future husband, the twenty-seven-year-old journalist Bejnes Meyerowitch. He was to change his name to the more Swedish Bernhard Mehr.[63] Born in Dvinsk, now Daugavpils in Latvia, he was a socialist and Bundist who managed to reach Sweden after escaping from a political prison sentence.[64] Bernhard and Sara Mehr became a hub in the relief work for Russian political migrants during the stormy periods of revolution around both 1905 and 1917. At their home in Stockholm, Bundists, Mensheviks and Bolsheviks met on the run from tsarist repression or on their way back from exile to participate in the revolution.

Another of those who in 1917 worked in the Mensheviks' exile environment in Stockholm was Paul Olberg. Much later, in a quite different historical period, Olberg and Mehr would meet again, around a new relief effort for socialist refugees. By then, Bernhard had been dead for several years, while world history had experienced revolutions, stock market crashes and depression, fascism, and Stalinist terror as well as two devastating world wars. Sara Mehr, who, like her husband, became involved in Swedish social democracy, was still active at the age of 58, and her thirty-five-year-old son Hjalmar was about to take a leading role in Stockholm's social democracy. Her address in these contexts was the sewing studio Chic in Riksby, a then-modern suburb of Stockholm. Her personal archive at the labor movement's archive and library in Stockholm contains fragments of lectures and activities in Jewish and Social Democratic women's clubs as well as for TOZ, the aid organization for Jewish children's health in Poland.[65] A speech at the Jewish Women's Club in Stockholm in 1936 shows that her commitment to the health of Jewish children was directed at her hometown, Grodno.[66] In personal notebooks, Yiddish is mixed with a bit of broken Swedish, as well as letters in Russian, information about fiction she read, developments in the Soviet Union, and questions about anti-Semitism and Jewish identity. And of course, there are bundles of newspaper clippings about her son Hjalmar Mehr's exploits plus excerpts from the French Bund's daily newspaper in Yiddish, *Unzer Shtime*. At the same time, acting in Jewish amateur theater in Yiddish seems to have been one of her great joys.

[63] According to Elmbrant, p. 15, they met a year later.

[64] Elmbrant, p. 18.

[65] TOZ, *Towarzystwo Ochrony Zdrowia Ludności Żydowskiej* [The Society for the Protection of the Health of the Jewish Population] was founded in Warsaw, 1921: http://www.yivoencyclopedia.org/article.aspx/TOZ (20181227).

[66] From a lecture, held at the Jewish Women's Club in Stockholm, January 28, 1936, on TOZ's activities in the Grodno district, Poland. Manuscript in SM400, ARAB.

Contact channels

Rina Branting, the daughter-in-law of social democratic founder Hjalmar Branting, was first curator at the Immigration Commission and thus strategically well positioned to support Olberg's efforts. She was also on the board of the JLC's Swedish department. At the age of fifty-five, she had extensive experience of international support work within the Nordic Association, Central Finland Aid and Save the Children. She oversaw the counseling department, *Sociala Byrån* (Social Agency), which had recently been established at the Immigration Commission to help refugees in personal matters and with entertainment and work in the camps.[67] The board of the Swedish JLC department also included others from the Social Democratic trade union central, the Labor Adult Education Association, and Social Democratic aid organizations. It was a closely-knit social democratic circle, but with influence in several areas. However, the Swedish JLC branch was mostly regarded as a paper organization to give its "executive member," Paul Olberg, increased legitimacy. It was Olberg and Sara Mehr who came to run the business themselves, sometimes with the help of a social democratic ombudsman who was formally the chairman, and Rina Branting.

That the American JLC was characterized by the Bundist tradition and with prominent Bundists in its leadership was not highlighted in the Swedish context. In Olberg's articles on the JLC for the Social Democratic daily *Morgon-Tidningen* and in public speeches, JLC was portrayed solely as an anti-fascist umbrella organization for half a million Jewish workers in the United States who during the war supported persecuted Jews and democratic labor movements in Europe – and now, after the war, supported reconstruction and refugee aid.[68] Of course, this was not an incorrect picture. However, what it did omit was the fact that care was targeted to members of the Bundist movement and, to some extent, the left wing of workers' Zionism, *Linke poalei tsion*.

Although the correspondence with Jacob Pat at JLC seldom explicitly concerned the Bund, but rather "like-minded people" and "our friends," the correspondence with Emanuel Novogrodski at the Bund's representation in New York was explicitly about the Bund and its dispersed members. The fifty-five-year-old Novogrodski was a veteran of the movement. Born in Warsaw within the Russian Empire, he had joined the Bund at the outbreak of World War I, and in independent Poland he worked for the party's daily *Folkstsaytung*; shortly before World War II he was elected general secretary of

[67] *Dagens Nyheter*, September 20, 1945.

[68] For example, Olberg's manuscript about JLC in Vol. 210, ME18, 1400 BA, YIVO.

the organization. On the run from Poland, he built up the Polish Bund's representation in New York and later became secretary general of the International Coordinating Committee of the Bund there, contributing to the magazine *Unzer Tsayt*, which had started publication during the war in 1941.[69] He wrote letters which, together with Yiddish literature and magazines such as *Forverts* and *Unzer Tsayt*, were sent to Sweden with the message: "Please contact Paul Olberg in Stockholm for material support."[70]

An important contact channel for the Bundists in Sweden was the Swedish biweekly newspaper *Via Suecia*. It was published during the year 1945–46 by *Samarbetskommittén för demokratiskt uppbyggnadsarbete* [the Cooperation Committee for Democratic Building Work], an umbrella organization for various Swedish peace and aid associations formed in the final stages of the war.[71] With the social democratic leader Alva Myrdal as one of the publishers, and with an introductory article by Prime minister Per Albin Hansson, the magazine was explicitly aimed at refugees in Sweden in different languages: German; Polish; Romanian; Czech and Hungarian. Among the writers contributing to the broad material covered in the newspaper were well-known names such as the Swedish feminist Elin Wägner, Soviet ambassador and famous Bolshevik Aleksandra Kollontaj, and the American first lady Eleanor Roosevelt. With news, culture, and social information – as well as "hygienic advice, women's talk, entertainment and jokes," as the Swedish evening paper *Expressen* put it[72] – the newspaper was an important link, or "lifeline," for thousands of people in Swedish refugee camps where it was distributed.[73] The columns listed people who sought contact with relatives and friends and with political comrades. Here, several Bundists found each other.

Camps and sanatoriums

Many of the emergency calls initially came from sanatoriums and hospitals in various parts of Sweden, including the war hospital in Lärbro on the island of Gotland, Sweden's largest and most modern hospital of its kind at the time. It had been built during the war and from 1944 received many Baltic refugees,

[69] About Emanuel Novogrodski (1891–1967) YIVO http://www.yivoarchives.org/index.php?p=collections/controlcard&id=34168 (20181227).

[70] Examples of Novogrodski's standard letters from the *American Representation of the General Jewish Workers' Union of Poland* in February, 1946, Box 36, folder 23, reel 104, ser. III, JLC, TAMWAG.

[71] Christin Mays, "For the Sake of Democracy – Samarbetskommittén för demokratiskt uppbyggnadsarbete and the the Cultural Reconstruction of Post-World War II Europe," master thesis, Uppsala University 2011.

[72] *Expressen*, August 3, 1945.

[73] Mays, p. 53.

and later also fleeing and wounded German soldiers. Beginning in the summer of 1945, five hundred concentration camp prisoners arrived, many of them Jews. The conditions were difficult due to the patients' ill health, with tuberculosis, typhus, and other diseases, but also due to the inmates' varied backgrounds and accompanying conflicts. Local anecdotes even talk about anxious staff who hid knives and other things. Several of the prisoners' lives could not be saved; of the forty-five war graves at Lärbro cemetery, nine are listed as "mosaic confessors," most of whom died of tuberculosis.[74]

"We are the only survivors of our families that we lost in fascist Germany," five *khaveyrim* write from a tuberculosis ward on the 4 November 1945, in order in their time of distress to ask Olberg for help, using the words of the legendary Bundist leader: "As Comrade Erlich said, to save a comrade is to save oneself." Another patient with lung disease from ward 10 writes in hope for help: "I am in a difficult situation, seriously ill and alone. Of my brothers and sisters, wife and two children, I am the only one left. I am very weak and depressed after what I have been through the last six years." He had heard a lot from friends at the hospital about Olberg's helpfulness, had hoped for letters and that "the sun will one day shine on me too, and I will be able to leave this sad island of Gotland."[75]

From the war hospital in Lärbro and sanatoriums elsewhere, patients who had begun to recover were evacuated to refugee camps around the country. The letters Olberg received were sent from an ever-growing number of camp addresses: Bettna, Doverstorp, Fagersjö, Grangärde, Kjesäter, Skärplinge, Overyd… From the "Polish camp" in Mora in the forest region of Dalarna, a comrade says that he was to leave Lärbro and is now convalescing, "not completely healthy yet, but much better," and relieved to have left the hospital. "You get sicker just by lying there and watching other sick people." For a while, he would try to regain his personal health, but he feared what awaited him. "Dear comrade, after all we have been through and survived the barbarism of Hitlerism, the real tragedy of our lives has only just begun." Most of the

[74] https://www.hembygd.se/larbro/krigssjukhusmuseet (20180721), also Läkartidningen [the Medical journal]: http://www.lakartidningen.se/Aktuellt/Kultur/Kultur/2014/10/Krigssjukhuset-pa-Gotland-en-tillflykt-for-krigets-offer-/ (20181227). The hospital is today a hostel after serving for many years as a prison. About the war hospital: https://www.hembygd.se/larbro/krigssjukhusmuseet, http://www.tjelvar.se/sjalavard/7-1.htm (20180623).

[75] The letters below to Paul Olberg from Zabludowicz etc., Lärbro, November 19, 1945, Box 36, folder 19, reel 102, ser. III, JLC, TAMWAG. Dawid Mermelstein and Yankev Shifer, Lärbro, November 22, 1945, Box 36, folder 19, reel 102, ser. III, JLC, TAMWAG. Shamo Milshteyn, Lärbro, November 28, 1945, Box 36, folder 19, reel 102, ser. III, JLC, TAMWAG. Rafael Goldberg, Mora, November 24, 1945, Box 36, folder 19, reel 102, ser. III, JLC, TAMWAG. Herman Grinberg, Mora, November 22, 1945. Box 36, folder 19, reel 102, ser. III, JLC, TAMWAG.

survivors of the concentration camps were, he said, physically and mentally broken. It was only "nature that forces us to live on" after losing so much. He himself had reported to the employment service, but the doctor had not allowed him to work yet. "It's hard to walk around idle here, you think too much about your memories and everything that has been lost."

Another Bundist who, after a German concentration camp and sanatorium in Sweden, was placed in Mora says that he had learned that there was a member of the movement in Sweden. After writing to the Bund in New York and quickly receiving a warm response, he now hoped for contact with Olberg. "Since we are cut off from our movement, we would very much like to dedicate our free time – of which we have a lot – to Yiddish books, newspapers and other reading that we do not have here." He also invited Olberg to visit his comrades in the camp.

In fact, Olberg visited more and more camps from the autumn of 1945 and received proposals for travel plans from the Immigration Commission. That the authority did not always have a clear idea of the purpose of Olberg's visits is evident from the proposed destinations. Among the "alien camps for ex-prisoners from the German labor and concentration camps," there were equally camps for Baltic refugees, "female Romanian Orthodox repatriandi," "mixed nationality" and more.[76]

Communicating greetings and contacts and visiting Bundists in camps and sanatoriums became a huge effort for Olberg, then sixty-seven and in recurrent failing health. Sara Mehr assisted in traveling around and performing small pieces with her Jewish amateur theater group. From Rosöga sanatorium outside the idyllic town of Strängnäs not far from Stockholm, Olberg received a warm thank-you from a young woman for a letter with ten kronor (the equivalence of about $20 in today's currency value[77]) and for Sara Mehrs performance. "We were all so happy with the show. I hope they can visit us again soon. Comrade Mehr made the greatest impression on us. She is so

[76] Letter to Paul Olberg from bureau director M Perslow, Social Bureau, *Statens Utlänningskommission* [Immigration Commission], Stockholm, November 3, 1945, including "Proposed itinerary for visits to certain alien camps…". Box 36, folder 19, reel 102, ser. III, JLC, TAMWAG. See also: "Permit certificate" from the Immigration Commission "for editor Paul Olberg to visit the Commission's camp for repatriation in Kopparberg County on November 17–20, 1945," November 16, 1945, on behalf of J.A.C.K. Bonde, amanuensis. The permit was valid on the condition that the medical doctor in charge had no objection and that Olberg himself paid for food and accommodation. Box 36, folder 19, reel 102, ser. III, JLC, TAMWAG.

[77] The value of the Swedish krona fluctuated a great deal during the first post-war years. A conversion factor of 20 seems to get rather close to today's value in US dollars. In the following I have however adjusted some sums to the more exact current value depending on the level of inflation in the early 1950s.

beautiful and such a natural talent."[78] But Mehr also seems to have conveyed something else, concerns about Olberg's workload and health. "How is your health, dear comrade Paul? I fully understand that you have too much to do to write to me."

The same concern was expressed by another young woman at the tuberculosis ward at Rosöga, the seventeen-year-old Fela or Fajgele Falz, who also received a letter from Olberg. Arriving at the Sigtuna sanatorium in September, the destination for many ill female refugees from the concentration camps, she had been greeted in *Via Suecia* by an ad from the Bund Coordinating Committee in the US, and she replied: "If any of us can once again have a few happy moments in life, I had it when I received the happy greeting," she wrote with the hope of regaining contact with "my party, my ideals."[79]

She wrote that she was born in Łódź in 1928, graduated from the Medem School, and from the age of ten was active in the Łódź department of the Bund's children's organization SKIF. By August 1944, their underground work had collapsed, she recalled, and the ghetto had been emptied through deportations to concentration camps. But in 1942, she had already lost her home and her parents. Her mother, "sick with hunger and cold," had been sent away with her little brother, "you know where…". Two months later, her father died of starvation. She then survived after arriving in Bergen-Belsen with an aunt. "Sadly, even this person who was so kind and motherly to me died on the great day of liberation and salvation." So now she was "completely alone" with pneumonia, but through the greeting from her comrades in the Bund, she could again feel that she was "part of a large family that I can live and fight for."[80]

In a long letter to Olberg after Sara Mehr's performance at Rosöga's sanatorium, where she had been moved, the seventeen-year-old shook Olberg's hand "in Bundist *khavershaft*" – comradeship – and urged him not to overwork; she would have been able to help if she were not imprisoned at the sanatorium. "I wait impatiently for the moment when I can regain my freedom and do what my heart, my soul and my ideals need."[81] And she continued in a slightly precocious tone: "You are the leader of our party here in Sweden. You complete our work as our predecessors would have liked. You do everything,

[78] Letter to Paul Olberg from Ruta Taflowicz, Rosöga, avd. 4, Strängnäs, December 3, 1945. Box 36, folder 20, reel 103, ser. III, JLC, TAMWAG.

[79] Letter from Fela (Feygele) Falz to *American Representation of the General Jewish Workers' Union of Poland*, September 20, 1945. Box 36, folder 17, reel 102, ser. III, JLC, TAMWAG.

[80] Ibid.

[81] Letter to Paul Olberg from Fela Falz, Rosöga, avd. 4, Strängnäs, December 11, 1945. Box 36, folder 20, reel 103, ser. III, JLC, TAMWAG.

day, and night, far beyond what is required by duty. But Comrade Olberg, you must live, you must! You, the right person in the right place, you must not risk your health by overworking. You must think about yourself too. I know and understand that, as Comrade Mehr said, you feel guilty and helpless when it comes to us, survivors of the war. I know you want to [unreadable] and free us from the worries of our past. Comrade Paul, you cannot take on that responsibility. You do everything. You do too much, too much. You should not have the slightest sense of guilt." Among her thanks for letters, newspapers and contacts, along with her assurances that she felt good, she urged her fifty-year-older *khaver*: "Dear comrade, I am seventeen years old, and it may seem funny that I am writing this to you. But no, my childhood and naivety have long since disappeared. I am no longer a child. I understand everything and look at everything realistically. I already understand life. And repeat, take care of yourself, you must continue to live."[82] It was clear that the young Fajgele Falz would have a special place in Olberg's heart. Her postal address is mentioned at one point in a list of refugees, such as Olberg's home address at Lilla Essingen.[83] She also later wrote to Olberg from the Bund home, established in the guest house Mälarbaden (see below), between X-ray examinations at the sanatorium in Sigtuna, where she was to return. "I am very happy to be in Mälardalen, it is difficult to leave a place where everyone cares about each other comradely and fraternally." There had on her bed been a big surprise waiting for her: a bag of sweets, some underwear, and a small handbag of cosmetics. "I do not need it, but the handbag had my monogram," plus photos of her father, perhaps from an uncle in the United States. "Dear comrade, thank you for all your help." And she writes to Olberg's wife Frida and thanks her for a pair of shoes, "but unfortunately not my size, a pity because I really liked them."[84]

[82] Ibid.

[83] In a list of people in various Swedish camps/sanatoriums, is attributed by hand: "Feige Falz from Łódź, born January 18, 1928, with the address: c/o Paul Olberg on Luxgatan." Box 36, folder 19, reel 102, ser. III, JLC, TAMWAG.

[84] Letter from Faige Fals to Paul Olberg, March 6, 1946. Box 36, folder 24, reel 105, ser. III, JLC, TAMWAG and to Olbergs wife Frida Olberg, February 6, 1947. Box 231, Doss 22, Paul Olberg, corr 1919–1950s, RG1400, ME17, YIVO.

The Bund *mishpokhe* – the family

The Bund homes

The scattered Bundists in sanatoriums and camps could gradually gather in shared housing, at least if they were received in the Stockholm area. While these collective housing units were regarded as refugee settlements and were under the supervision of the Swedish Immigration Service's social agency, JLC was responsible for a large, perhaps the larger, share of the funding.

Neglinge

One of these collective housings was the guest house Wermé in Neglinge, Saltsjöbaden, an affluent suburb outside Stockholm, not far from the archipelago. From January 1946, it rented out two villas in the area and made another available to the "Polish delegates." The wording possibly suggests some initial uncertainty about the nature of the lease to JLC's Swedish representative, Olberg. The agreed price per day and person was rather high if the number of guests was under forty. For more guests, the price was reduced. Olberg, who stated that the number of residents would eventually amount to 60–65 people, would also pay an extra amount before the tenants began to arrive. They were two "fully modern" villas, one with five rooms, the other with seven. The accommodation period was of indefinite duration, but first and foremost it would begin in the spring, with a one-month notice period.[85] Soon the villas began to be filled with Bundists from sanatoriums and arrival camps. The invoice from March 20 – accounts were settled every fortnight – refers to five families with a total of seventeen people, including five children with a lower fee. Two weeks later, the invoice mentions twenty-six people with eight families or couples, as well as five individuals. By mid-April, the number of residents passed forty, with a resultant reduction in the daily price.

The lists now contain the names of several of those who would be important for the attempt to gather the Bundists in Sweden or elsewhere in the world. There is Chaim Elenbogen, or "Bolek," 26 years old with his sister Perla; Roza Klepfisz, 31-year-old widow of the Bundist leader in the Warsaw ghetto uprising Michal Klepfisz, with her six-year-old daughter Irena. Also, the name Channa, "Hanka," Fryszdorf is recorded, a widow of one of the Bundists,

[85] Accommodation agreement, Saltsjöbaden on January 17, 1946, and letter from editor Paul Olberg, JLC representative in Sweden, to Mrs. H. G. Wermé, Stockholm, January 16, 1946. Box 36, folder 22, reel 104, ser. III, JLC, TAMWAG.

Gavrish Fryszdorf, who took part in the ghetto uprising and in the Jewish Defense Committee, ZOB's, continued armed struggle. He died during battles in the Wyszków Forest when Channa was pregnant with their son, who was born after his father's death under difficult conditions. According to the ghetto fighter, Simha Rotem (Kazik), a decision had been made that Channa would have an abortion, because "under the conditions in the forest in 1943, without any peace in sight, female combatants could not afford to have children."[86] One of the members of the ZOB group was a doctor and performed the abortion one night in a shooting range out in the woods, by candlelight. But something went wrong, and the pregnancy progressed, Channa was taken to Warsaw where in the seventh month, in the middle of the catastrophic Polish uprising in late summer 1944, she gave birth to a healthy boy named after his father, in the lists of Guest house Wermé in Neglinge, spelled Gabriel.

Long, long afterwards, in 2013, Eda Rak, a psychologist from New York, visited the places around Stockholm where she spent some childhood years in Bundist refugee groups. Her father, Mayer Rak, and mother Guta were among the first to be housed in Neglinge in the spring of 1946 with their daughter "Ida." Mayer and Guta had fled east from Warsaw during the German invasion in 1939 and survived the war in Soviet labor camps on the Arctic Ocean. With peace, they returned to a Poland where nothing was left for them, but their daughter Eda was born in Łódź before the family went to Sweden, perhaps in the hope of traveling on to America.[87] Together with her husband Richard, Eda, more than sixty years later, searched for the houses in Neglinge with the help of sender addresses from old envelopes and faded photographs. In a travel story to childhood friends whose families also lived for a time in the collective, she describes her impressions and memories:

> So this past Monday we set out in a hired car (...). Though I can't possibly remember our lives in Neglinge I was especially eager to visit there, as it was their first respite after the horrors of the war, the camps in Archangelsk and the depressing aftermath in Poland. I figured it was a possibility that the house was recognizable from the photo (it's quite distinctive) and I also had a wonderful description of the location from Jerry Glickson* who has, astonishingly, seemingly total recall of just about everything. He said the house was on a hill that sloped down to the train station, somewhere on the left. Arriving at Neglinge train station (which is as quaint as a Lionel train

[86] Kazik (Simha Rotem), *Memoirs of a Warsaw Ghetto Fighter*, Yale University Press, New Haven and London, 1994, pp. 94–95.

[87] Conversation with Eda Rak, (20131010), New York, YIVO.

* Jerry Glikson, the son of Josef Glikson and Tsipojre (Cipora) Fajnsilber Glikson.

> model and feels almost as miniature), we saw that it is in a dip and all roads leading to it are hilly. Additionally, left on Stockholm side or left on Saltsjöbaden? So, we drove about admiring this lovely town of trees and water, incredibly lush and green. It is so tranquil and so cozy, how like paradise it must have seemed to them![88]

Aided with a photograph, they searched for the whereabouts of that somewhat peculiar house. Passing through the idyllic and picturesque surroundings, they finally found a woman who recognized it as the place where her children went to kindergarten. "Most houses had traditional Sateeritak [manor house roofs] that look like hats with ear flaps, but this was flat with ornate patterns on the porch." It was hidden from the road by trees, "but there it was, dear fellow travelers!" The house was empty for renovation, but Eda recognized the place well from fading family photographs, the large kitchen, and the dining room "where all those quarrels over food could take place." In personal conversations, Eda Rak has talked about disputes among the women in the collective over potatoes and household chores, while the men generally worked at factories elsewhere.[89] One of her memories is of widows from the Warsaw ghetto uprising being considered exempt from some of the everyday tasks, receiving extra support from the JLC. "The companion was also a little taken aback when she told me that her grandmother also lived in the house for a while in the 1940s, as a refugee from Estonia." Exactly how long the villas in Neglinge were rented to the Bundists is difficult to ascertain. The last invoice in the archive is valid for fourteen residents on November 25, 1946, all from the first list in the spring and winter of the same year. In mid-April 1946, Olberg was informed by the owner Mrs Wermé that she intended to evict the residents from mid-May, "since I will hand over the business, and those taking it over will not want any refugees at all."[90] In addition, there was apparently a growing irritation over the development of the accommodation. "I cannot cope with the demands placed on me," Mrs. Wermé explained in a letter to Olberg, complaining that she was forced to make her large rooms, which the Immigrant Commission had calculated for 6–8 people, available for "2 pers. with a baby." Then there could

[88] E-mail from Eda Rak, "Greetings from Stockholm", July 31, 2013. "Dear childhood friends."
[89] Conversation with Eda Rak (20131010), New York, YIVO.
[90] Letter from Alma-Gret Wermé to editor Olberg, Saltsjöbaden, April 14, 1946. Box 36, folder 25, reel 105, ser. III, JLC, TAMWAG.

no longer be talk of the lower rent, and she would be grateful if Olberg could get these people placed elsewhere by April 30.[91]

Kumla Herrgård

Apparently, during the year Olberg managed to rent a new house for those Bundists who could not stay in Neglinge, as well as for newcomers. It was Kumla Herrgård, a mansion in Trollbäcken, south of Stockholm. The manor, which dates from the 17th century or even further back, and which is now owned by the Tyresö municipality, had during the interwar period been periodically used as a guest house and at the beginning of the war even as a detergent factory. However, the building eventually housed Norwegian refugees and then, for two years, some of the Jewish "transmigrants and repatriandi" for whom Olberg sought housing. Without access to the lists of those housed at Kumla, however, it appears from the Swedish Bund's membership lists that several of the Bundists in the Stockholm area lived on the manor.[92] Zenia Larsson's letter also describes the Bund home at Kumla as, "for a short period of glory, the center of Eastern Jewish culture."[93] Living here were the "ghetto widows" along with of the leading Bundists. From here, the artists from the Young Theater in Warsaw, Josef Glikson and Tsipojre Fajnzilber Glikson, traveled around to refugee camps and cities with Jewish refugees desperate for Yiddish culture. The Rak family also came here, an experience that Eda Rak describes in her travel story:

> Kumla Herrgård was easily locatable, since it is now a fancy restaurant and conference center. We had to drive back towards Stockholm, as it is due South, and 15km away (Neglinge is 15km East), but it was just as Jerry described and as I dimly remember. A long tree-lined avenue ending in a cul-de-sac, with a large well-proportioned house in its center. To the right is the neighbors' house, with whom we engaged in sandbox wars, and behind a large lawn, now very manicured with a gazebo, but still with a squint you could recreate the more wild and untended yard. My most ecstatic moment was when I found the dirt path between the trees in the back which led to a larger road which crested at a view of the beautiful lake where Ludvig Svedosh, the only athlete among us, would swim and canoe. How amazing it must have

[91] Letter from A. Wermé to editor Olberg, April 18, 1946. Box 36, folder 25, reel 105, ser. III, JLC, TAMWAG.
[92] Membership lists are scattered throughout the material, here in Vol. 211, ME18, 1400 BA, YIVO.
[93] Zenia Larsson, p. 128.

> been for them to find themselves among these large and friendly people, so welcoming and tolerant![94]

That here, too, economic questions came to arouse irritation is evident from a registered letter to the "Jewish Labor Committee of America" in Stockholm from the owner of Kumla Manor.[95] The letter writer explains that "the extension of the rent at Kumla Herrgård requested by you and by the municipal rent board will not under any circumstances be voluntarily extended by me after 1/4 1949." And the continuation of the rental agreement is characterized by barely restrained anger towards both Olberg and the authorities: "Should you now neglect to provide other accommodation, you will be responsible for the consequences."[96]

Mälarbaden

From late autumn 1945 until May 1946, the largest Bund home outside Stockholm was located at Mälarbaden's *Herrgårdspensiona*t – the mansion guest house – in Torshälla outside the industrial town of Eskilstuna. Here again, the archives do not contain invoices or lists of those living there, except for occasional documents about transfers of persons from other camps inland, like Mora, Rättvik and Furudal.[97] A letter to Olberg in early May 1946 states that the residents have been discharged from the guest house and transferred to the rural village of Kjesäter outside the small town of Vingåker. This is the place to which, in the autumn of 1945, Zenia Larsson came, after the first weeks of isolation in quarantine. About this period, she wrote:

> Soon, these weeks of quarantine would appear to be pure heaven compared to what followed. We were sent to a distant and gloomy little village, which seems to be completely deserted. It is just a single house you see, and for several kilometers, you may only meet a single person. It will never be more than that. Instead, cows and birds, snakes and wasps seem to have taken possession of this village. And as far as the eye can see, it is just forest and trees and meadows... Beautiful? Believe me, my love of nature has taken a real hit,

[94] E-mail from Eda Rak, Greetings from Stockholm (20130731). "Dear childhood friends."
[95] Recommended letter from Afr. A [unreadable] Katarina Bangata 38, to "Hrr Mendel Leff... [unreadable], Jewish Labor Committe av Amerika", July 18, 1948. Box 45, Vol. 206, ME18, 1400 BA, YIVO.
[96] Ibid.
[97] Letter from Paul Olberg, February 11, 1946, with a request for transfers of persons to Mälardalens *Herrgårdspensionat* [the mansion guest house], Torshälla, Box 36, folder 23, reel 104, ser. III, JLC, TAMWAG.

> my whole romantic attitude to what grows and germinates has disappeared like a burst balloon.[98]

She describes the housing conditions as unbearable: "From the beginning, we were three hundred women here – only women! – Polish together with Jewish women, several dozen crowded into each barrack, with bunks in two or three floors sleeping on straw mattresses." Hopefully, the experience was different for the Bundists who moved to Kjesäter from Torshälla six months later. Through Mälarbaden's owner Margit Larsson's many letters to Paul Olberg, a personal overview of the business, large and small, is provided. After Olberg visited the somewhat chilly guest house in January 1946, Mrs. Larsson wonders if there will be more guests than the thirty or so who have already been housed. She has an even larger room available for six people and a smaller one for three to four, but it takes her almost two weeks to transport sheets and blankets from her brother-in-law's and sister's camp in northern Rättvik. Her concern, however, is with the level of uncertainty about how long the boarding house will be rented out to the refugees. Summer guests have already contacted her about making a reservation, and therefore she risks losing loyal guests if she is unable to respond.[99] And no one at the Immigration Commission, who helped to set up the arrangement, seems able to give information.

Unlike in Neglinge and at Kumla, however, Margit Larsson does not want to get rid of the refugees, on the contrary: "For my part, I must say that I mourn the day when everyone is traveling. They are all such cute, nice and fine people in the true sense of the word. Always polite and friendly, young, and happy songbirds. I mourned deeply when my 'girls' left – they also all came at the same time, and we had for over five months camped together and shared sorrow and joy. When happy letters came, we were all delighted; when the message was sadder, we all shared it. I never thought I could live without all the friends I made during that time." Contact with the women was maintained even after they left the guest house and for Olberg's new group, things started to improve considerably. "I just wish with all my heart that they will be able to thrive and have a little sense of home in Mälarbaden – that their poor wounded lives will have strength and courage, after all the ordeal and unjustified torment they have been through." Yes, she could house "refugees for any length of time, for years if need be. It's fun and interesting, 'heart-warming' work". She understood, however, that it was for a limited time; if Olberg did not need rooms for

[98] Kjesäter, December 26, 1945 and Larsson, 1972, p. 24.

[99] Letter from Margit Larsson to editor Olberg, February 5, 1946. Box 36, folder 23, reel 104, ser. III, JLC, TAMWAG.

a convalescing center, then perhaps they could be used for studies, practicing handicrafts or something else. Alas, her health was not up to all the nice things she had planned for her guests, though they also seemed to entertain themselves. The letter was written at half past ten in the evening, laughter and singing could be heard, and a boy dressed as a girl "was a great success."

One of the residents at Mälarbaden was Markus or Motl Kshienski, sometimes written as Ksieski, K'ieski, Chensky or similar in the source material. He was a leading Bundist from Kraków who survived the war in Bergen-Belsen and was taken by one of the white buses to Sweden.[100] As early as August 1945, Olberg had reported to JLC that he had been in personal contact with "Comrade Ksieski," whom he had known before the war and who was also trying to reach Stockholm.[101] It was Kshienski who, according to Olberg, wrote a greeting from JLC to all its "friends" in Swedish camps, which was published in *Via Suecia* with the response "Bund", reaching out to lonely Bundists in camps and sanatoriums around Sweden.[102] In mid-January 1946, Kshienski was able to inform Novogrodski in New York: "We have received a house via Olberg and the Swedish Ministry of Foreign Affairs, so that we Bundists can be together."[103] He said he led the group that planned courses in Swedish, English and science at the guest house in Mälarbaden. On January 19, it was time for the opening, including a song that he had himself composed, "To socialism and the Bund." After the inauguration, he was able to happily report to New York on the "opening of our Bund home" just two and a half hours from Stockholm.[104] Olberg had himself given the inaugural speech, speaking for the Jewish Labor Committee, and thanking the Swedish Social Democrats for their

[100] Information from *Unzer tsait*, undated, by Leo Greenbaum, YIVO.

[101] Letter from Olberg to JLC, August 29, 1945. Box 36, folder 16, reel 102, ser. III, JLC, TAMWAG.

[102] Ibid. In the various letters from Kshienski to JLC and Olberg, there is a certain risk of confusion. A couple of letters from the refugee camp in Fagersjö, in the autumn of 1945, to Olberg and Novogrodski, respectively, are signed by Jakob Kshienski. To Novogrodski, Kshienski wrote on November 15, 1945, from the refugee camp that life "in free Sweden" as the only Jew among Poles was "empty and impossible" and he hoped for help in moving from there. Vol. 207, ME18, 1400 BA, YIVO. Even the letter to Olberg, September 5, 1945, had been about how difficult it was to live in the camp as a lone Jew, not knowing the language and not knowing anyone and he asked for advice as to how to move on to France. Box 51, folder 40, reel 152, ser. IV, JLC, TAMWAG. According to Markus [Motl] Kshienski's children in the USA, Marcel Kshensky and Liliane Kshensky Baxter, Markus was one of four brothers, at least one of whom, Jakob, also came to Sweden. However, according to them, he was not active in the Bund and after a short time managed to get to Paris. E-mail to Håkan Blomqvist from Liliane Kshensky Baxter and Marcel Kshensky (20190319) and (20180321).

[103] Letter from M Kshienski to Novogrodski, Mälarbaden, January 15, 1946. Vol. 207, ME18, 1400 BA, YIVO.

[104] Letter from M Kshienski to Novogrodski, Torshälla, January 22, 1946. Vol. 206, ME18, 1400 BA, YIVO.

help for the Bundists. Representatives of the Swedish Social Democrats had themselves participated, and members of the children's organization SKIF were symbolically hailed "with tears in their eyes," since so few children had survived. "No matter what miserable state we are in, we will be loyal to the Bund and socialism," Kshienski wrote, adding: "While the Zionists are doing everything to confuse the survivors with the illusion of Palestine, socialism is closer than ever." Whereupon the evening ended with the singing in unison of Di Shvue, "after having not been able to sing it for six years."[105]

This event received much attention from the local Social Democratic newspaper *Folket* [the People] under the front-page headline "Festive evening with Jewish socialists in Mälarbaden," with an account of the Bund's role in Poland before the war and attempts to assemble the Bundists among refugees in Sweden.[106] The paper called the thirty Bundists assembled a "youth club"; most were in the 20–25 age group and some even younger, while the oldest "would be around 40." According to police constable Nils Jansson, who was responsible for the place, they were "alert and intelligent young people." They also had a "qualified leader," called by the newspaper an "elder" (spelled Kusieski by *Folket*), "during the war one of the foremost members of the Polish underground movement." The program had, according to the newspaper, been a "classy" affair with recitals, choir singing and classical music, which even impressed "poor Swedes who were not so at home in Yiddish": "The talented artists and the strong socialist mood among the young Jews came together to give the Swedish guests a strong impression of what this movement must have meant socially and culturally and can still mean in international socialism and its struggle for "a freer, more beautiful, younger and wiser world."[107] How important the Bund home in Torshälla was for Bundists who would later be accommodated there is shown in letters to both Olberg and the Coordinating Committee in New York. A resident writes how he is finally among "comrades in the Bund home"; he now finds help to live a normal life. He plans to get married and to start a family in the hope of living his life, as he had been able to do before the war.[108]

Soon, however, the owner of the house, Margit Larsson, began to raise some reservations, such as the late night life, cautiously addressing it to Olberg as "an

[105] Ibid.

[106] *Folket*, January 21, 1946.

[107] Ibid.

[108] Letter from Boruch Weinkranz to Novogrodski, Mälarbadens Herrgårdspensionat, February 17, 1946. Box 45, Vol. 206, ME18, 1400 BA, YIVO.

insignificant matter."[109] Could the editor possibly persuade the guests to change their circadian rhythms somewhat, which made her "simply helpless." "It is the case that breakfast would be served at 9:00 as in all camps, but so that everyone could come on time, we have set the time to 9:30. Nothing helps, although I ask politely and say firmly. A few arrive on time, but most are not in order. Many come undressed, and others remain in bed, and their comrades fetch the food for them." Larsson surmised that it all had to do with the residents turning time around by going to bed very late: "You often hear singing and talking at midnight." Being slovenly in the mornings – and not being ready for breakfast at half past nine – was, she considered, improper behavior. She hoped for support from Olberg, adding that "tomorrow, we will have a choir here for a visit and a coffee table in the salon." In a later letter, Margit Larsson asks for help with compensation for broken crockery, a mirror, a couple of chairs and windows for which the Immigration Commission did not want to pay, as "the cancellation price is so incredibly low." The costs for damages amounted to 150 kronor (around $343 today). Though she added, it was not at all her intention to complain, and that there was a particularly good atmosphere at the guest house, it was nonetheless the fact "that the men were more careless with the equipment than the ladies we had before. It can also be understood that young boys cannot move as calmly. They slam the doors, and it startles you; chairs and other furniture are damaged."

After the group moved out, Margit Larsson warmly thanked Olberg for "all the personal kindness during the time the 'Bundists' had shared their home with me, and for the understanding Olberg also showed me, as I came with my worries about one thing or another." She was now preparing for the arrival of a new group appointed by the Immigration Commission and hoped "by God" to have the strength and ability to solve the big tasks that awaited again: "I must try to succeed in everything, and to create as much as possible from home in this small refugee camp, where so many are trying to gather strength to start living again after difficult years and illness." She was not alone in her hopes; from an earlier letter, she writes: "It was a long and difficult winter this year. We are starting to long for spring out here. Then you must come out and see how beautiful it will be. Yes, spring break is

[109] The following letters from Margit Larsson to editor Olberg are from February 5 1946. Box 36, folder 23, reel 104, ser. III, JLC, TAMWAG. Bill for broken things, Mälarbaden, 1946, Box 36, folder 1, reel 106, ser. III, JLC, TAMWAG. To editor Olberg, April 28, 1946. Box 36, folder 25, reel 105, ser. III, JLC, TAMWAG. Undated, Box 36, folder 2, reel 106, ser. III, JLC, TAMWAG and from Larsson to Olberg, March 7, 1946. Box 36, folder 24, reel 105, ser. III, JLC, TAMWAG.

needed all over the world, with new life, new greenery and new hope after the severe winter that humanity has endured."

The barracks

It was not only Margit Larsson in Torshälla who made every effort to solve urgent tasks in receiving refugees. Olberg hunted around for solutions when either the Immigration Commission or a landlord needed the housing for some other reason. In order to keep Bundists from Mälarbaden together in nearby Eskilstuna, an almost drastic measure was to rent four labor barracks from the State Labor Market Commission in April 1946. Kshienski had alerted Olberg in March that they risked being forced to leave Mälarbaden to travel to other camps, "which we'll never get away from."[110] It was all related to the work requirement to obtain housing. The Bundists at Mälarbaden were no longer perceived to need rehabilitation and thus were to be relocated. Olberg had previously been told by Rina Branting at the Immigration Commission that "all repatriandi" would begin to be regarded as ordinary refugees with compulsory labor once their six-month special status as "guests" had been expired. "This will, of course, also affect the group in Mälarbaden. As the refusal to take assigned work can lead to relocation to special camps, this may mean that those with a clean bill of health cannot be guaranteed to remain in this boarding house."[111]

Olberg found a solution at a reasonable cost. The contract meticulously reports the equipment: 13 wardrobes; 11 iron beds; 3 tables; 14 foot stools; 3 wooden drawers; 1 washbasin; 1 drying rack; 1 step pump with hose; 2 fire buckets in three of the barracks, as well as 3 stoves with flues. The fourth barrack was intended as a kitchen, with 2 heating stoves, 1 oven and "complete kitchen furnishings."[112] The barracks were intended as "housing for 35 Polish Jewish refugees" who could find work in Eskilstuna.[113] That the solution was not completely successful is evident from letters to Olberg from residents in the

[110] Letter from Kshienski to Olberg, Mälarbaden, March 7, 1946. Box 36, folder 24, reel 105, ser. III, JLC, TAMWAG.

[111] Letter from Rina Branting, *Statens Utlänningskommission* [Immigration Commission], to Olberg, January 24, 1946, Box 36, folder 22, reel 104, ser. III, JLC, TAMWAG.

[112] Contract, Stockholm, April 18, for the State Labor Market Commission Hans Hollander, for the Committee for Repatriation and Transemigration, Paul Olberg. Box 36, folder 25, reel 105, ser. III, JLC, TAMWAG.

[113] Confirmation from the Swedish Labor Market Commission, F. Hedlund, to the Committee for Repatriation and Transemigration, Secretary Paul Olberg, Stockholm, April 24, 1946. Box 36, folder 25, reel 105, ser. III, JLC, TAMWAG.

barracks.[114] Already in July, a letter writer appeals that a sick friend is getting worse by the day in the barracks, and must be moved to a sanatorium in order not to risk his life. On October 1, Kshienski, who had lived at Mälarbaden for the longest time, writes that winter has already come to Eskilstuna, and that it was very cold in the barracks, which were now impossible to live in.[115] His wife, who finally managed to reunite with her husband, had caught a cold and, he said, they now risked becoming extremely ill if they did not leave there. It was impossible to find accommodation in Eskilstuna, so he hoped that the couple could instead be moved to the Stockholm area. "Please, help me with a room in Neglinge, there should be room there [...]. We could freeze even before the real winter comes."[116] After Olberg had apparently replied that it was equally difficult for everyone, Kshienski was upset by the fact that not only should Olberg, who visited the barracks, already know that they are uninhabitable during the winter ("We thought we would only live here in the summer"), Kshienski took particular offense that Olberg "compares us with others in the barracks." [117] "You know who lives here in the barracks, if you think I should trust them, I have nothing to tell you." The bitterness had already emerged during the summer, when Kshienski described what he found to be an intolerable cultural and social climate in the cramped barracks: "Here in the barracks, the atmosphere is such that it is difficult to breathe."[118] He had, according to his own statement, tried to take the initiative for arranging social activities and a library, but nothing came of his efforts. "When something is to be done, they either quarrel or beat each other up."

It is not clear from the material when the barracks in Eskilstuna were closed. But there, as elsewhere, the housing issue came to be handled gradually, either by families and individuals being given the opportunity of proper housing or by their taking leave of Sweden. With his wife and a daughter born in Sweden Markus Kshienski left for Paris, where his brother Jakob had previously gone

[114] Letter from Ozholek to Olberg, July 15, 1946, Vol. 206, ME18, 1400BA, YIVO.

[115] Letter from Kshienski to Olberg, Eskilstuna, October 1, 1946. Vol. 206, ME18, 1400BA, YIVO. As for Kshienski's accommodation at Mälarbaden, see the letter from Margit Larsson to editor Olberg, May 18, 1946, which states that "Mr. Ksienski must unconditionally stay until the barracks have been completed, which will happen any day." Box 36, folder 1, reel 106, ser. III, JLC, TAMWAG.

[116] Ibid.

[117] Letter from Kshienski to Olberg, Eskilstuna, October 9, 1946. Vol. 206, ME18, 1400BA, YIVO.

[118] Ibid.

and had become a shoemaker. A few years later, the family moved on to the United States.[119]

[119] In the Holocaust Survivors and Victims Database, a Markus Kshienski, along with his wife Berta, is found in the register of the Australian Jewish Welfare and Relief Society. But, according to the daughter Liliane Kshensky Baxter, born in Stockholm, 1949, the family never traveled there but first left for Paris where his brother Jacob had already gone and later, in 1955, to the USA. E-mail from Liliane Kshensky Baxter to Håkan Blomqvist (19.03.2019).

The party

Rebuilding the Bund

The Bundists in refugee homes around Stockholm and Eskilstuna were gradually joined by groups elsewhere. In Uppsala, several *khaverim* were gathered on the initiative of twenty-five-year-old Tobias Amster, who in the spring of 1945 arrived from Auschwitz at the refugee camp in Fagersjö. He had been active in Tsukunft since his teens and was listed as a "weaver" in a member inventory.[120] He was joined by thirty-five-year-old Anshel Rotenberg, who had been a Bund member since 1926 and who, during the war, lived in exile in Soviet Russia.[121] The group was joined by a forty-year-old tailor, Ber Perelmutter, from a camp in Vagnhärad. He had been a Bundist since the early 1930s and arrived in Sweden via Finland.[122] Among a few hundred Jewish refugees in Uppsala, the Bundists were able to start activities primarily around Jewish culture. They formed the association *Jiddisher Kultur-Vinkl*, which also welcomed non-party members around a small Yiddish library with literature that Olberg requested from JLC. In Malmö, a Bundist group was formed in 1945 under the leadership of Khayem Borenstein, a thirty-six-year-old painter from Pabianice, outside Łódź.[123] He had survived the war in the Soviet Union, was said to have belonged to the Bund's regional board in Łódź, and was the director of the library named after Beinish Michalewicz, one of the Bund's early leaders and theorists, who represented the party in Warsaw's Jewish Council.[124] There was also the typographer Henryk Levkovich, 33 years old, who during the war was "in a ghetto and labor camp."[125] As a sixteen-year-old, he had in 1928 joined the youth organization Tsukunft, and belonged to its national council as well as being the leadership of the youth militia Tsukunft Shturem. The group in Malmö also started a cultural association, *Jiddisher Kulturfarband Arbeter-Ring*, with Yiddish literature, readings, and music on the program. *Arbeter-Ring*, or in the English-speaking world Workmen's [now Workers] Circle, belonged to the Bund's cultural sphere, but was open to non-members as well.

[120] Questionnaire to delegates, appendix to the Minutes of the 1948 National Assembly in Stockholm. He is written there as Tevje Amster. Vol. 206, ME18, 1400 BA, YIVO.
[121] Ibid.
[122] Ibid. sometimes spelled Perlmutter.
[123] Ibid. sometimes spelled Chaim and Bornstein.
[124] For Beinish Michalewicz (1876–1928) see: *The Jewish Labor Bund Bulletin* (Henceforth *Bund Bulletin*), no. 14, 1949. https://www.marxists.org/subject/jewish/bund-bulletin/two-14.pdf (20181126).
[125] Questionnaire to delegates, appendix to the Minutes of the 1948 National Assembly in Stockholm. Vol. 206, ME18, 1400 BA, YIVO.

For the year 1946, little archival material exists from local groups. There seems to have been no other national coordination beyond Olberg's and Mehr's letters and travels, nor does there seem to have been any clear distinction between JLC and the Bund in Sweden, a dilemma that would constantly accompany their work. Olberg was able to deal with party issues using JLC's letterheading; the address in Stockholm for the two branches was the same. Olberg was in fact paid by JLC, which also financed housing and emergency aid.[126] Yiddish literature was sent from JLC and was distributed within the country together with Bund's monthly magazine *Unzer Tsayt* and the Bund newspaper in Paris, *Unzer Shtime*, where Olberg was a correspondent. Correspondence from individual Bundists and groups went to Olberg and Mehr or directly to Novogrodski in New York.

Poland

In their attempts to keep in touch and resolve housing issues, developments in Poland soon overshadowed their efforts. Despite liberation from German occupation, anti-Semitic violence did not cease. Of Poland's more than three million Jews, only a quarter of a million survived the Holocaust. Returning Jews from camps and the Soviet Union were once more targeted. Hundreds were thrown out of trains, individuals were murdered, and pogroms took place, as early as July 1945 in Kraków. In Kielce in the first days of July 1946, some forty Jews were massacred, and many were injured by police and locals after false accusations of kidnapping a Christian child.[127] The pogrom in Kielce convinced many survivors that they no longer had a future in Poland, and they left the country in the tens of thousands. For Olberg and JLC in Sweden, it meant a new wave of Jewish comrades to shelter – and a difficult political dilemma to negotiate. From the Polish Bund, reports reached Olberg that Jews in Kielce organized self-defense instead of leaving, and the Bund's strategy was not to let anti-Semites drive away the Jewish population, which had begun to rebuild itself.[128] The Polish Bund was on its way to reorganize local branches and

[126] For example, letter from Olberg on JLC's letterhead to Chezes, chairman of the Bundgroup in Eskilstuna, November 21, 1950, regarding the national conference of the Bund in Sweden. Vol. 213, ME18, 1400BA, YIVO. The address of the Jewish Labor Committee of America, the Committee for Aid to Repatriandi and Transmigrants and the Bund, was for a long time Wallingatan 21 in Stockholm (i.e. the Social Democrats' People's House).

[127] For an analysis of anti-Semitic violence in Poland after the war, see: Jan T. Gross, *Fear: Anti-Semitism in Poland after Auschwitz*, New York, Random House, 2006.

[128] Letter from 'Abraham' in Poland to Olberg, July 21, 1946 with information about Kielce and self-defense and that the leaders of the Polish Bund, Fishgrund and Schuldenfrei, met Polish leaders. Vol. 206, ME18, 1400BA, YIVO.

operations in the rubble of the mass movement they once constituted. Contacts were forged between survivors, meetings were held in ruined landscapes, labor cooperatives were formed, Yiddish culture began to sprout cautiously, and the Bundist press was revived. With *Naye folkstsaytung*, the movement's legendary flagship resurfaced. Encouraging emigration was foreign to the Bund, instead of "emigrationism" was, as before, "here-ism" – to fight on the spot, in the here and now. Bundists in Sweden participated in a campaign to finance the reorganization at the same time as JLC in Stockholm was reached by emergency calls for help with visas and travel.[129] In January 1947, the board of the Bund group in Stockholm was visited by Israel Falk from the Polish Bund's central committee. The minutes summarize Falk's report:

> The issue of emigration is tragic for the Jewish people. The existence of the Jewish people in Poland is at stake. Most people want to leave. Cause: Kielce, anti-Semitism, and safety. It is safer now, but there are no guarantees. Central Committee: we cannot force any Bundists to stay in Poland, but we must not make it easier to leave either. If the Jewish community in Poland is wiped out, it will be a precedent for the whole of Central Europe. The Bund must fight! Ordinary members can do as they please, but cadres and activists must request permission. Even the Zionists are trying to keep their members from leaving. Illegal emigration has been stopped, but the legal continues.[130]

From the discussion, an opinion is noted that the Swedish Bund should not help Jews to leave Poland. Falk emphasized that emigration was no solution, though there was uncertainty about its development and about Sovietization's relation to socialism. At a later meeting, Falk wanted to address the pressure from the Soviet Union, the decline of Jewish culture in Poland, and the decline of the Bund as an independent Jewish party.[131] In an undated letter, a frustrated Bundist writes, possibly from New York, that JLC has received 1,300 visas to France, Sweden, Norway and perhaps later to Belgium and that lists must be made up for Polish comrades. The Bund's central committee in Poland, the letter writer continues, believes that "this is a crime and threatens the Bund's future" and refuses to help. "Then it will instead be the left-wing Zionists" who take care of emigration. Therefore, Bundists in Poland must themselves try to

[129] Letter from the Central Committee of the Bund in Poland with a collection list for 1 million zlotys. "Sthlm, National", Vol. 206, ME18, 1400BA, YIVO.
[130] Minutes, January 2, 1947, Board meeting, Stockholm, attendees: Olberg, Mehr, Vinegrad, Elenbogen, Papier and Falk, CK member from the Polish Bund. "Stockholm". Vol. 211, ME18, 1400BA, YIVO.
[131] Ibid.

obtain a visa. "There is a possibility that hundreds of our comrades can travel west freely and legally. Our own party prevents that. I know that I read in SKIF and *Tsukunft*, that there will come a time when you must break the discipline. I'm the black sheep," the letter writer concludes.[132]

The Bund in Poland and the Bundists in the West still belonged to the same political community, but during that year, they would be torn apart under the pressure of the intensification of the Cold War. It was also in 1947 that, together with new migrants from Poland and camps in Germany and Austria, the Bund in Sweden began to organize a firmer structure at both local and national level.

Age, gender, and occupations

In the years immediately after the Second World War, the Bundists arrived in Sweden one by one or in groups and at different times. While the first organized Bund groups were formed in 1945, the last one was added in the textile town of Borås in the southwest only in 1950. Olberg officially stated before the Swedish Social Democratic Party that the Bund in Sweden numbered five hundred members, but they can hardly have included more than three hundred at the same time, even if their sympathizers were larger. Refugees arrived only to pass through; local groups came and went. In total, there were groups in the capital, Stockholm, the university town of Uppsala with its nearby industries, Eskilstuna, Vetlanda, Huskvarna, and for a noticeably short time in both Nässjö (spelled Netje in Bund documents) and Norrköping; there were groups also in industrial towns (specializing in engineering, timber, and textiles) in central Sweden. A group was organized in 1945 in the large southern industrial town of Malmö – with the harbor at which many of the refugees first arrived – and later in Landskrona and Trelleborg (from the spring of 1949) also farthest south, plus the last added group in Borås in 1950.[133]

In the First of May greetings to the Bund's ideological magazine *Unzer Tsayt* in New York, the individual names from Sweden were never more than 95. Though, admittedly, this was in 1950, once the high watermark of both Bund membership and activities had already passed. In previous years, greetings

[132] Letter from "Monja" undated and without specified addressee. Vol. 214, ME18, 1400BA, YIVO.
[133] The Borås group was formed in September, 1950. Vol. 206, ME18, 1400 BA, YIVO. On 22 December 1948 a Bund group in Norrköping reported a list of seven members, five men and two women, to the secretariat in Stockholm. Vol. 206, ME18, 1400 BA, YIVO.

were not individual, but represented local groups.[134] Individual greetings also required a fee that not everyone could pay. At the first and only National Assembly in 1948 (see below), local groups appointed one representative per ten members; the conference included 25 delegates. There were furthermore several scattered members without group affiliation.[135]

At the National Assembly, a survey was conducted among the representatives, addressing name, age, occupation, domicile, year of joining the Bund and any previous positions held within the organization. Fifteen responses to the survey are preserved.[136] All were filled out by men, most of whom were between 32 and 44 years old, four in their late 20s, several from Łódź. Most had been members of the Bund since the 1920s, four since the 1930s; several had held positions of trust, such as secretaries in local branches of *Tsukunft*, chairman and board members of local and regional Bund organizations. One had been part of the leadership of the youth militia *Tsukunft Shturem*, one in the Polish Bund's press commission and one in charge of a library. Among their professional backgrounds in Poland were tailors, weavers, shoemakers, painters, carpenters, locksmiths, typographers, goldsmiths, and salesmen. Nine of the deputies had spent the war in exile in the Soviet Union, or with *fonye*, that is, the Russians, one in Finland and one in the military. Four stated "ghetto," labour camp or Auschwitz. Almost everyone now worked in factories in Sweden as metal workers, sawmill workers and textile workers.

Reports from local groups gave a slightly different picture, with large differences in age composition, place of origin and gender composition. Of the nine members who requested membership cards for the Trelleborg Group in the summer of 1949, four were women, and almost the entire group consisted of young couples and relatives, most of whom had been born in the 1920s.[137] In Malmö, on the other hand, membership cards were ordered for eight members, one of whom was a family and all but one in their late thirties. From Landskrona, the twelve Bundists acknowledged on May 1, 1950 appear to be from five families, of whom five are women. However, on a list of members from the

[134] Greetings from Sweden began to be published in *Unzer tsait* from the Bund Jubilee in the November issue, 1947, and in the case of the First of May, from 1949. The last greeting was from an individual member to the Bund Jubilee in November, 1967.

[135] Bund's first National Assembly in Sweden took place in August 1948 in Stockholm. Groups from Stockholm, Eskilstuna, Malmö, Vetlanda, Uppsala, Trelleborg and Nässjö were represented by 25 delegates. Minutes from the National Assembly of Bund Groups in Sweden, 14–15 August, 1948. Vol. 206, ME18, 1400BA, YIVO.

[136] Ibid.

[137] Report from Vajskopf Trelleborg, July 16, 1949, to Bund's National Committee. Vol. 206, ME18, 1400BA, YIVO.

same spring, only five names are stated, with only one woman included.[138] The Vetlanda group's membership list from the spring of 1948 contains 37 names and membership numbers. Of these, thirty-one are reported by date and place of birth, as well as from where they arrived and the year of their joining the Bund. In all 17 men and 14 women are named, of whom twenty-five were in their twenties. All were born in Poland, except for one Hungarian. Several were from Łódź and Warsaw, while others were from Lublin, Kovel, Kaluszyn, Grodno, Kraków, Częstochowa and other places. Eleven stated that they had come from camps in Austria, sixteen others from Germany. With respect to when individuals joined the Bund, the list indicates that most joined *Tsukunft* in Poland as teenagers, between 13 and 16 years old, or even SKIF as 6–12-year-olds. Only four were over 19 when they joined the Bund in Poland, while eight others may have joined in Sweden (stating years of membership as 1947–48). In summary, then, it can be said that the members of Vetlanda 1948–49 were noticeably young, under 30 years of age, and had joined *Tsukunft* as teenagers, with only a handful having become members in their 30s. Almost a quarter may have joined in Sweden.[139]

For Stockholm, there are several notes and lists of members comprising of about sixty names, of which about twenty are women. The lists, however, may have been compiled at different times. The address lists are grouped by accommodation both in Kumla and in Neglinge, but also in boarding houses and apartment addresses in Stockholm and its suburbs.[140] Only a handwritten and a somewhat difficult-to-decipher list of sixteen members states age and occupations. Of these, 9 were over thirty years old (of whom one was at least forty), 5 over twenty and 1 eighteen-year-old (with one set of details illegible). The occupations were like other groups: tailors; seamstresses (at least four in the list of names were women, several names, however, are indecipherable); leatherworkers; quilters; upholsterers; drivers, plus a proofreader. They came from Kaluszyn, Kovel, Kozienice, Siedlce, Warsaw and Vilnius.[141]

[138] Orders for membership cards from the Bund group in Malmö. Membership list, Landskrona, January 7, 1950. Vol. 208, ME18, 1400BA, YIVO.

[139] The archive material contains several examples of membership applications in Sweden. For example, there was a letter to the Bund in Stockholm, March 31, 1948, from a refugee with roots in Warsaw who had spent the war in several camps and, together with his wife and children, hoped to go to America. He declared himself "completely cut off from Jewish life" and hoped that as a member he would have the opportunity to "participate in Jewish life". Vol. 209, ME18, 1400BA, YIVO.

[140] Names and address lists for members in Stockholm. Vol. 211, ME18, 1400BA, YIVO.

[141] Handwritten address list, Stockholm. Vol. 211, ME18, 1400BA, YIVO.

The reorganization

During the early summer of 1947, it appears from the fragmentary material that a more structured organization of the Bund in Stockholm had been established. Already in September the year before, Chaim Elenbogen had informed Novogrodski in New York that the Bundists in Sweden were about to try to form an organization to conduct open activities among Jews in Sweden.[142] And in the spring of 1947, the Bund had participated in the First of May demonstration in Stockholm with its own banner and slogan "Open the borders for the victims of Nazism" – in both Yiddish and Swedish.[143]

The First of May 1947

The "First of May Manifesto", written in 1947, from the "Jewish Workers' Union in Sweden" mentioned the gas chambers of the Nazi system of terror, but also the glorious Jewish uprisings in the camps and ghettos, in the spirit of "Macabe and Lekert."[144] Linking the ancient Maccabean uprising with the Bundist Hirsh Lekert's attempt to assassinate the Russian governor von Wahl in Vilna in 1902 was perhaps not very enlightening for Swedes celebrating the First of May. But for the radical Jewish participants to whom the manifesto was addressed, Lekert could stand for an indomitable revolt against the oppressors, right up to the death he himself faced before the firing squad, just as was the case now with the Bundists as the Maccabees of socialism. The manifesto expressed the spirit of rebellion that permeated the text: hundreds of thousands of Jewish survivors and martyrs were still suffering in camps. In Eastern Europe, "Nazi and anti-Semitic beasts" still "ran amok," but the Jewish masses made heroic sacrifices to rebuild their shattered Jewish lives. In "most" European countries – here the manifesto exaggerated somewhat – the war had ended with the working masses seizing power. Through fundamental social reform, the peoples of Europe were now trying to eliminate the causes of slavery and war – "that is, capitalism." However, reactionary elements were about to regroup "from [their] capitalist fortress" to defeat the working masses. It was thus important for the international working class to be vigilant and to resist the attacks of the capitalists.

[142] Letter from Emanuel Novogrodski, New York, to Chaim Elenbogen, September 9, 1946. Vol. 207, ME18, 1400BA, YIVO.
[143] See the photograph from Bund's department in the Social Democrats' First of May demonstration 1947 in Stockholm. Photo Archive, ME18, 1400BA, YIVO.
[144] First of May Manifesto "Proletarians in all countries unite" from the Jewish Workers' Union in Sweden, Stockholm, April 1947. Vol. 206, ME18, 1400BA, YIVO

The revolutionary tone in the manifesto is a little difficult to tie to the thoughts of Olberg, who usually did not express himself in slogans. But perhaps the text was a collective effort, or just strongly influenced by the intended readers. After all, the Bund were in competition with the Communists for the souls of the oppressed. At the same time, Olberg emphasized that the terrible lesson of Nazism was that the fate of the Jewish masses was linked to the destinies of both democracy and socialism: "Where reactionary and fascist forces come to power, the first victims are Jews. Where the working class comes to power, the Jewish masses have the opportunity to live their lives in freedom and as free Jews." It was therefore no coincidence that "Sweden's socialist government has shown thousands of us such a humanitarian and fraternal attitude, gotten us out of the Nazi camps and given us freedom, work and bread." And therefore, the manifesto explained, the Bundists, together with the entire Swedish working class, demonstrated for freedom and socialism, for the gates of the world to be opened for all of Hitler's victims and against the shameful camps. "Long live socialism and the First of May, long live the Bund," was the impassioned finale.[145]

Behind the proud First of May appeal and within the crowds of the Stockholm demonstration were a few individual activists who took on the task of transforming refugee care into a political organization. A handwritten report from the "board" in June of 1946 was written by Chaim Elenbogen, a treasurer's report by Max Papier, who lived with his wife Roza at Kumla Manor, and a further report from another comrade entitled, simply, "activities". A list indicates that there were seven members of the board, including Shmil Rosenberg, Sara Mehr, Elenbogen, Olberg, Papier, Paul Luxemburg and Leyzer Raukh.[146] At the end of August, the Bundists in Stockholm held a general membership meeting in the *folkshojz* – that is, the People's House (*Folkets hus*) of the labor movement – which dealt with the group's cultural work, and they decided to join the Social Democratic Party.[147] It is not clear from the material how many *khaveyrim* participated and who came to be part of the board at this stage, but what is clear is that Olberg, Mehr, Elenbogen, Papier and Rosenberg supported much of the initial activity. Here was also Aron Feiner, who during this period repeatedly signed letters from both the Swedish JLC and the Bund.

[145] Ibid.

[146] Handwritten report from Chaim Elenbogen, 28 June, 1947. Also, for the list of board member names, please see: July 23, 1947. Vol. 206, ME18, 1400BA, YIVO.

[147] Notes from August 30, 1947, at 19 *Folkets hus*, salon G, Stockholm. Vol. 206, ME18, 1400BA, YIVO.

The fiftieth anniversary

Perhaps it can be said that the formation of the Bund in Sweden into a nationwide organization took off in connection with the Bund's fiftieth anniversary in October 1947. It was celebrated around the world, from Warsaw to New York. In Stockholm, too, Bundists gathered in the cooperative housing organization HSB's hall in Stockholm for a banquet of politics and culture. Supporters from all over the country were invited, and congratulations poured in from both individuals and organizations, not just from *khaveyrim* and Bund groups out in the country or internationally. Telegrams and letters were received from the Mosaic, i.e., Jewish, congregation with the hope of "continued good cooperation." The labor educator Gunnar Hirdman, director of studies for ABF – the Swedish Worker's Educational Association – in Stockholm, sent congratulations, and the Social Democratic chairman of the city council, Carl Albert Andersson, hoped that the Bundist refugees would be "assimilated in Sweden without it losing its uniqueness."[148] A prologue by the Swedish writer Bengt Stenmark – "I can see them whenever I want to" – was performed.[149] This long piece of Swedish-language poetry wound itself around, and sprung from the Jewish socialists' struggle against the tsarist pogroms, over the "violence of the Hitlerites" which "with the support of big money" cost six million lives, to the unresolved refugee issue where thousands of displaced Jews were forced to live in camps without being admitted by the victors.

> And still in camps, over two hundred thousand are left,
> who ask where they can go, but who never get an answer.
> A few hundred have been chosen to give a good impression,
> while the others still are kept behind the fence in excruciating uncertainty.
> [...]
>
> A people who challenged Hitler and all his followers
> cannot get passports and ships, cannot have safety and free travel,
> although many countries are desperate for human arms and labor.
> Yes, that seems to be the worst problem the victorious countries have had.[150]

[148] Congratulations to Bund's fiftieth anniversary, November 14, 1947, to Paul Olberg from the Mosaic Congregation, November 15, 1947, telegram to Paul Olberg from Michaël Wächter and Edmund Rapaport, November 15, 1947, telegram to Paul Olberg from Gunnar Hirdman, and a number of letters and telegrams from Bundists in Sweden and internationally. Vol. 206 and 207, ME18, 1400BA, YIVO.

[149] "Prologue at the Jewish Social Democrats/Bund/50th anniversary in Stockholm on November 15, 1947, by Bengt Stenmark". Vol. 207, ME18, 1400BA, YIVO.

[150] Och alltjämt sitter i läger över tvåhundratusen kvar,

It was this refusal to open the borders to close to a quarter of a million Jews still in German, Austrian and Italian camps that would become a major issue for the Bund, not least in their conflict with the Zionists. As early as October 1947, and despite the Holocaust, perhaps the sentiments of the prologue reflected the resurrected hopes of some:

> …And Jewish socialists, on the basis of their old ideology,
> they meet, despite big losses, as before in the party – in the Bund.
> To allies in the struggle, their duty and their fidelity they carry.
> For the International brings happiness to all![151]

Paul Olberg emphasized the optimism in a press release through the Labour press agency in Stockholm's editorial office with the headline: "'Bund' strengthened in Hitler's storm, 50th anniversaries and world party."[152] After a long review of the Bund's history for ignorant labour press editors and readers, Olberg said that the Bund, despite the Nazi violence and the Jewish tragedy, had resumed operations, consolidated in Poland with several thousand members, but also established itself as a world party with organizations in the United States, France, Belgium and "other democratic states" – including Sweden. What Olberg was referring to was the Bund's international conference in Brussels in May 1947, where nearly sixty representatives from federations in eighteen countries came together and appointed an international coordinating committee based in New York, as well as a European secretariat in Paris.[153]

"The European catastrophe," Olberg said, had only "interrupted" the successful development of the socialist Jewish labor movement. "But the Bund is

som frågar varthän de kan resa, men som aldrig får något svar.
Man har plockat ut ett par hundra för att ha dem att peka på,
De andra får ännu bakom stängslet i pinande ovisshet gå.
[…]
Ett folk, som förklarade Hitler och hela hans anhang fejd,
kan inte få pass och få fartyg, kan inte få trygghet och lejd,
fast massor av länder blott ropar på armar och arbetskraft.
Ja, det tycks vara det värsta problem som de segrande länderna haft

[151] …och judiska socialister på sin gamla åskådningsgrund,
de möts, trots stora förluster, som förr i partiet – i Bund.
Till bundsförvanter i kampen sin plikt och sin trohet de bär,
ty Internationalen åt alla lycka bär.

[152] *A-pressens Stockholmsredaktion, Specialtjänsten* [The Editorial Staff in Stockholm of the Labour movement's Press service] Paul Olberg: 'Bund' strengthened in Hitler's storm, 50th anniversary and world party. Published no earlier than Monday, December 22, 1947, undated. Vol. 209, ME18, 1400BA, YIVO.

[153] *World Coordinating Committee of the "BUND" and Affiliated Jewish Socialist Organizations.*

alive!" And scattered in different countries, its organizations were now "everywhere compact and solid workers' collectives." The Bund was no longer just an ideological component of the international socialist labor movement but, he assured, an "active party" in the new socialist international which was under construction. Only one sentence in the press release revealed what . The "lively activities" of the Polish Bund took place "according to the specific conditions of the country" and therefore did not represent the "general principles of the Bund."[154]

Behind the words was the Soviet reshaping of Poland's political and economic conditions with the emergence of the one-party state under the rule of the Polish Workers Party – the Communist Party – and the pressure on the Polish Socialist Party and the Bund to join a "united workers' party." The year 1947 saw the worsening of contradictions between East and West, with the Truman Doctrine in March and the launch of the Marshall Plan in the autumn. In November, *Comisco* – the Committee for an International Socialist Conference – was formed, with its headquarters in London. The aim was to re-establish a socialist international after the dissolution of both the Second, Social Democratic, International and the Third, Communist, International during the war. While the Bund in Poland forcibly adapted to the new political conditions, but also in the hope of positive socialist development, which they shared with significant parts of the Polish masses during this period, the Bund organizations in the West joined what would become the new Social Democratic international. From the Coordinating Committee in New York, Olberg was urged to persuade the Swedish Social Democrats to support the Bund's membership in the new international.[155] It took a few months before the Bund in Poland broke with both Comisco and the Coordinating Committee, and the International Bund unequivocally positioned itself with the West during the Cold War. For Olberg, with his staunch anti-communism, based on his political and even personal experiences – his two sons had been executed during the Stalinist waves of terror – this was not unwelcome. That this view was not held by all his comrades would soon become evident. Now, however, it was a matter of building a strong Swedish branch of the international Bund, and from the fiftieth anniversary in Stockholm, Bundists all over the world

[154] Paul Olberg: 'Bund' strengthened in Hitler's storm, 50th anniversaries and world party… undated. Vol. 209, ME18, 1400BA, YIVO.

[155] Letter from Novogrodski to Olberg, November 13, 1947: "On November 28 there will be an international socialist conference in Antwerp, we want to get status as a member instead of a fraternal organization. It is important that the Swedish party [Social Democratic] supports our request, you know how important this is for us". Vol. 209, ME18, 1400BA, YIVO.

were congratulated by the Bund in "free Sweden" with a call to work for "the socialist idea among the Jewish masses."[156]

At the international Bund's first World Congress in Brussels in May 1947, according to the official report from Congress, the update from Sweden had been met with "special interest because no Bund organization had previously existed in the country.[157] The Swedish organization had been represented by Olberg and would, just as with other country groups, be represented on the International Coordinating Committee. The tasks provided by the World Congress to the various groups were extensive. All members would join the respective countries' socialist (read: social democratic) parties, and there form autonomous units standing for the Bund's goals. The Bundists would work either to democratize existing autonomous Jewish assemblies or establish new ones, to be elected by local Jews. Within these, they would pursue their aims on all issues of importance to Jewish life, counteract both "reactionary forces" and "assimilation" and continue the struggle for a secular, progressive Jewish culture. Wage workers would be involved in trade unions, cooperative activities would be encouraged, social activities of the kind practiced by the Bundists before the war in Poland would be developed, not least in view of the efforts to open borders for Jewish refugees and prepare them for new homes. In addition, modern Jewish culture – "literature, art, science, etc." – would be energetically supported, and special care would be given to the children. Bundists in different countries were urged to work for the establishment of state-supported Jewish schools with teaching in Yiddish, at least as supplementary education at various levels. The schools, like the *Tsysho* schools in interwar Poland, were to be guided by a progressive pedagogy that was "devoted to social justice, brotherhood and love for the Jewish people."[158]

For Jewish refugees in Sweden, some of these goals probably seemed remote, but social activities – e.g. caring for each other by offering help with housing and livelihood, as well as reuniting around Yiddish culture and understanding the Bund as an ideological hub – had been going on for at least a year and a half in Stockholm, Uppsala, Eskilstuna and Malmö. At the end of December 1947, the board of the Stockholm Group decided to establish a library as well as inviting all Bundist groups in Sweden to create a common national organization.[159]

[156] A greeting from the 50th anniversary 1947. Vol. 206, ME18, 1400BA, YIVO.

[157] *Bund Bulletin* No. 1, October 1947, p. 4. The group in Italy was also listed as new. In Stockholm, a Bundist group had existed a few years before the First World War, probably unknown to many.

[158] *Bund Bulletin* No. 1, October 1947, p. 6.

[159] Minutes. Bund Stockholm, December 29, 1947, A. Feiner. Vol. 206, ME18, 1400BA, YIVO.

The Bund's Swedish National Assembly 1948

The Bund's Swedish National Assembly – or congress – the first, and, as it would turn out, the last, was planned for August 1948. The notice was issued by the Stockholm group in June with a call to the other groups around the country to appoint one representative per ten members to convene in Stockholm in mid-August. On the agenda were international political developments, the Palestinian question, matters pertaining to the organization, and election of the party leadership.[160] It was "Comrade Mehr," chair of the Stockholm group, who opened the national meeting at six o'clock in the evening on August 14, when all thirty representatives and guests had gathered in Stockholm's *folkshojz*.[161] Representatives from Stockholm, Eskilstuna, Malmö, Vetlanda and Uppsala were present. Handwritten notes also mention "Netie" [Nässjö] and Trelleborg, but there would probably have been only individual members, at least in the case of Trelleborg, where the group was not formed until the spring of 1949.[162] Olberg and Mehr were, of course, appointed to the presidium, together with Elenbogen from Stockholm, Levkovich in Malmö and Operman from Huskvarna; the latter belonged to the Bund group in Värnamo.[163] The now 36-year-old typographer Henryk Levkovich, who according to a questionnaire had belonged to the leadership of *Tsukunft* and the youth militia, had landed a job as a founder of "a daily newspaper in Malmö," probably the leading Social Democratic morning paper *Arbetet* [Labor]. He had survived the war "in a ghetto and labor camp."[164] Born in 1906, Markus Operman was a carpenter from Borislav. He joined the Bund in 1926, where he reportedly held a chairmanship, and would end up living in the Soviet Union during the war.

[160] Letter, June 1948 (undated), from Sara Mehr and Wasserstrom "to all our groups in Sweden". Vol. 213, ME18, 1400BA, YIVO.
[161] Minutes from the first National Meeting of Bund Groups in Sweden, August 14–15, 1948. Vol. 206, ME18, 1400BA, YIVO. There is also a handwritten protocol with partially different wording, perhaps notes as a basis for the possibly more "official" minutes or report. Vol. 206, ME18, 1400BA, YIVO. Both sources form the basis for the description of the national meeting.
[162] Minutes from members' meeting 1, April 24, 1949, "Official founding of the group", notebook for board and meeting minutes, Bund group, Trelleborg, April 1949–September 1950, folder "Trelleborg". Vol. 215, ME18, 1400BA, YIVO.
[163] Minutes from the first National Assembly of Bund groups in Sweden, August 14–15, 1948, and handwritten minutes. Vol. 206, ME18, 1400BA, YIVO.
[164] Questionnaire, appendix to the Minutes from the first National Assembly of Bund groups in Sweden, August 14–15, 1948. Vol. 206, ME18, 1400BA, YIVO.

Politics

They met just after that juncture in history, when the great alliance of the war years between the Soviet Union and the Western Allies collapsed definitively, and the emerging Cold War began to shape both world politics and the states' internal political situations. Under the pressure of the Truman Doctrine, the May Crisis of 1947, and the great strikes in France, the Communists had been expelled not only from the French but the Italian government. In the same autumn, the *Kominform* was established as a kind of successor to the dissolved Communist International. By the following February, the Communists had seized power in Czechoslovakia. Around Eastern Europe, Social Democratic parties were forcibly merged with Communist parties. Comisco condemned the Social Democrats, who did not break with the Communists, in both the East and the West. In March 1948, Social Democratic parties, led by the British Labour Party, gathered in Sanderstead to support the Marshall Plan. The world, including the labor movement, was torn apart.

In Sweden, radicalism during the final stages of the war had characterized the Social Democrats' post-war program, which, with the support of the Communists, pushed for a planned economy and nationalization. The metal workers' strike in 1945 gave the Communists momentum. Already, in the 1944 parliamentary elections, the SKP had attained over 10 percent of the vote; by the end of the war, it had more than fifty thousand members. However, the advent of the Cold War would quickly reverse its fortunes. Opponents of a planned economy among liberals and conservatives mobilized in the spring of 1948 as a non-socialist alternative. In the autumn election, the Social Democratic government survived by a hair's breadth. Communist representation was almost halved, and Sweden became part of the Marshall family. It was during the dramatic summer weeks of 1948 that Bundists from different parts of the country met.

Cold War

After having observed a moment of silence for the Bund's fallen comrades, Olberg began with a full two-hour speech on the world political situation and Jewish issues.[165] From the minutes, it appears that Olberg gave an overview of both the causes and consequences of the world war, referring to the agreements

165 Minutes from the first National Assembly of Bund groups in Sweden, August 14–15, 1948, and handwritten minutes. Vol. 206, ME18, 1400BA, YIVO.

in Yalta and Potsdam, to the peace and the formation of the UN. A great mistake, he said, had been made in giving the great powers a veto and the power to decide on "the fate of all the smaller nations." He discussed the Marshall Plan and the economic and political struggle between the United States and the Soviet Union, with the development of an Eastern and Western bloc in world politics and the Berlin blockade, which had already begun in June. The risks of military confrontations and a new world war could not be ruled out, said Olberg, who, in line with criticisms of the decline of democracies in the 1930s, used phrases such as "anti-war policies will plunge countries into war because of dishonest action and conflicting goals," but the notes are unclear.[166] He went on to talk about the Swedish labor movement's preparations in cases of war and Sweden's neutrality during both world wars. It was a direction, he continued, which Swedish Social Democracy maintained despite the criticism of non-socialists and the Norwegian and Danish social democratic parties' accession to the Western bloc. Without passing judgment, the minutes move on to present the Swedish Social Democrats' policies ahead of the autumn general elections.

By the spring of 1948, the development that many Bundists feared had become a reality. At its Central Committee meeting in March and a national conference in Wrocław in early April, the Polish Bund decided to break with both Comisco and the Bund's International Coordinating Committee.[167] It was in the wake of the so-called "Prague Coup" in February, when the Czechoslovakian Communist Party took power. The party leader of the Polish Bund, Michal Shuldenfrei, explained that while the Polish Bundists were clinging to revolutionary socialism, the rest of the Bund had converted to reformism. There was no *driter koyekh*, third power, in world politics, but the Bund in the West had united with the anti-Soviet alliance, which constituted a weapon of the international bourgeoisie against socialism.[168] While the Polish Bund condemned the Truman Doctrine and the Marshall Plan, and while a few months later they merged with the Polish Communist Party, the Bundists within the International Coordinating Committee sought to integrate into Western social democratic parties. "There is not a single Bund organization in the world that does not deeply regret the circumstances that led the Polish Bund to sever all its ties with the Bund family and with the independent socialist movement in general," the Coordinating Committee declared.[169] But

[166] Ibid.
[167] Slucki, 2012, pp. 68–74.
[168] Ibid.
[169] *Bund Bulletin* No. 8–9, August–September, 1948, p. 5.

at the same time, the international Bund could now speak openly. In order not to harm their Polish comrades, it was said that the movement had sometimes been forced into a painful silence regarding the Soviet Union and communism. Now, though, the situation had changed radically. The Bundists could take their place among the socialist parties that defended democracy and the rights of the individual against "the totalitarian variant of socialism."[170]

Olberg had been reached by information from Novogrodski immediately after the Polish Central Committee decision in March and been urged to speed up attempts to obtain transit visas for Polish Bundists, who " now run the greatest risk."[171] The Polish Bund was said to be in a state of panic, and they were "cutting all ties with the West."[172] Shuldenfrei and party secretary Fishgrund were wrongly accused of representing only a small number of members at the Wrocław conference, "the vast majority distancing themselves." The Bund can be "destroyed, but not swallowed," Novogrodski assured him.[173] At the same time, Olberg was urged to work through the Swedish Social Democrats to ensure that the Bund gained a regular place in Comisco, despite the Polish Bund having distanced itself. "This is a matter of life or death" for us.[174]

A "lively discussion" at the National Assembly in Stockholm reflected a significant difference of opinion surrounding the conflict between East and West. "Both blocs stand for a fraudulent policy [illegible]; America contented itself with sending weapons to the Soviet Union, biding its time until crushing both Germany and the Soviet Union with one blow," said one speaker whose name was not noted. Heniek Bornstein, a young carpenter and former secretary of *Tsukunft* in Łódź who worked at a textile factory in the small industrial town of Vetlanda, criticized Olberg for being too close to the Western bloc. The Bund must "stand for an independent line." That the Soviet Union rejected the Marshall Plan, he believed, was due to fear of Western influence among the Russian people and in the "Eastern democracies." Chaim Elenbogen also emphasized that "the Western bloc is our opponent," the Bund must strive for a "third power" that could withstand "both imperialist blocs." The resolution later adopted by the National Assembly warned of the risk of a

[170] Ibid.
[171] Letter, March 21 and March 30, 1948, from Novogrodski to Olberg. Vol. 209, ME18, 1400BA, YIVO.
[172] Letter, April 5, 1948, from Novogrodski to Olberg. Vol. 209, ME18, 1400BA, YIVO
[173] Letter, April 14, 1948, from Novogrodski to Olberg, Vol. 209, ME18, 1400BA, YIVO. For safety's sake, it seems that Olberg wrote to Fishgrund on May 30, 1948, requesting "authentic information" about whether the Polish Bund had really split. Vol. 209, ME18, 1400BA, YIVO.
[174] April 22, 1948, circular from Novogrodski. Vol. 209, ME18, 1400BA, YIVO.

third world war that would lead to the downfall of human civilization.[175] As global antagonists the two blocs stood, armed to the teeth; on the one hand, the Soviet Union and its client states – representing the abolition of private capitalism but doing so within a totalitarian system that had been established with the help of communist parties and police methods, and that resulted in the working masses experiencing a newer and worse slavery. On the other side was the highly developed but capitalist America, which, with the help of the Marshall Plan, had tried to aid, but also influence, other countries. "The international working class must be vigilant in the face of the dangers that threaten humanity from both sides of the conflict," the resolution concluded, saying that only a united socialist Europe could serve as the counterforce that would prevent a new catastrophe from happening.[176]

Having said all of this, it was not issues surrounding the Bund in Poland, or the antagonistic relations between East and West, that dominated discussions at the assembly, but Israel.

Israel

By November 1947, the UN General Assembly had decided on the partition plan for an Arab and Jewish state, with warfare between Jewish and Arab forces the result. When the British mandate expired on May 14th of the following year, the independent Jewish state of Israel was quickly proclaimed, and was immediately recognized by the Soviet Union and the United States. The ensuing Israeli "war of independence," or al-Nakba – the "catastrophe" – in Palestinian history, erupted in full force as the Bundists in Sweden held their National Assembly. The notes from Olberg's speech on the topic of "Jewish problems" read as follows: "Jewish society in Palestine and its significance after the World War. [illegible] and historical significance. Its influence on the Jewish people. Zionist politics. UN partition resolution. Its effect on various non-political [illegible]. Bund's position; opinions of various members on the new situation. [illegible] the possibilities of a Jewish society in Palestine. The prospects for an end to the civil war." The minutes from this "especially heated discussion" reflected the different views present as the assembly. As for "our view of a Jewish state," Heniek Bornstein argued that the armed struggle was meaningless, and that Jews and Arabs must reach a consensus. Elenbogen, on the other hand, took a stand to support the existence of a Jewish state. He was

[175] "Resolution" from the first National Assembly of Bund groups in Sweden, August 14–15, 1948. Vol. 207, ME18, 1400BA, YIVO.
[176] Ibid.

supported by "Comrade Lojke," who said that the reality that Jews were now experiencing in Palestine was "stronger than any theory"; yes, perhaps here lay "the solution to the Jewish problem." "If our sons and daughters are fighting there, we must look after them." Shmiel Rosenfeld had the same view and urged all comrades to rethink the matter: "We must change our attitude toward the [illegible] Jewish state." "Comrade Tshishnik" agreed. Bundists faced a *fait accompli*, the Jewish state was established and internationally recognized. "We cannot stand by and refrain from taking a political stand." That position was to support the Jewish state, but at the same time oppose "Zionism as such."

The 43-year-old veteran and shoemaker Leib Gnacik from Eskilstuna believed quite the opposite, and tried to split the difference. He had belonged to the Łódź movement since his teens and had survived the ghetto and the concentration camps; he thought that the Jewish struggle should be supported, though not the creation of a Jewish state. For Ber Perelemuter from the small town of Vingåker, also from an older generation, it was an impossible position. A Jewish state was, he emphasized, "an illusion" that Bundists simply had to oppose. The Jewish people could survive without a Jewish state. He was supported by 39-year-old Khayem Borenstein from Malmö. Despite "the tragedy experienced by the Jewish people," a Jewish state was no solution; "only the victory of socialism" could solve the Jewish problem. Jankel Obranshka held the same opinion. He represented Vetlanda, though lived in the village of Mullsjö. According to archival information, he was forty years old and a shoemaker. He had joined the Bund in 1924, and had been chairman of a *Tsukunft* department and for a few years was party secretary, though it is unclear at what level he held this particular position. Obranshka spent the war years in the Soviet Union.[177] According to the minutes, he gave a "fiery speech on socialism and internationalism" and considered that the Palestinian Jewish community was no answer to the "Jewish problem." On the contrary, the Palestinian Jews had distanced themselves from the Jewish diaspora, not least through their struggle against the British Labour Party, "which is close to us." And most agreed with Obranshka. Sara Mehr believed that a Jewish state had no chance of surviving. Henryk Levkovich from Malmö was of the same opinion. Now it was up to the Bundists to double their efforts to propagate their views and spread the word in Yiddish. The 40-year-old Getsl Lustgartn from Siedlce, Poland, a party member for nearly twenty-five years, agreed.[178]

[177] Document in Box 46, Vol. 207, ME18, 1400BA, YIVO.
[178] Minutes from the first National Assembly of Bund groups in Sweden, August 14–15, 1948, and handwritten minutes. Vol. 206, ME18, 1400BA, YIVO.

One can imagine that it was a rather tired conference. Proceedings were called to a close just before midnight, after a resolution committee – comprising of Obranshka, Elenbogen, Tshishnik and Olberg – had been appointed. It is unclear whether the committee formulated its own motion for a resolution on the Palestinian issue or whether it was content to present the two resolutions – from the majority and the minority within the Bund's International Coordinating Committee – which were presented to the Bund's Second World Congress in October 1948.

International Bund and Israel

In June 1948, the Coordinating Committee had met in Brussels to discuss the new state of Israel, and did not change the Bund's established position one inch; quite the contrary. The proclamation of the Jewish state was strongly condemned as an expression of the worst form of nationalism, a threat to Jewish society in Palestine and even to world peace.[179] According to the opinion of those assembled in Brussels, the unreasonableness of a Zionist state was also shown by the country's artificial division with impossibly long borders, corridors and islands with Jewish and Arab minorities, "ports without inland and inland without ports." The whole thing is a source of irredentism – separatism – and war. The establishment of a Jewish state had also led to the Jewish population being dragged down by "poisonous chauvinistic tendencies":

> Deeply despairing and shaken by the murders of six million of their co-religionists, the masses of the Jewish people have been swept away by strong nationalist sentiments that have been skillfully exploited and fueled by Zionist propaganda, causing a psychosis of Zionist and messianic illusions among Jews.[180]

Now many Jews, the statement said, came to despise the diaspora in an atmosphere that favored "political street robbery, terror and extreme expressions of domestic Jewish fascism, nationalism and reactionary currents."[181] The tendency was growing, the Bundists in Brussels stated, to regard all Jewish communities in the world as a "second-rate hinterland" for the state of Israel. But the Jewish people, through their two-thousand-year development, had become a "world nation" that can only safeguard its national and cultural interests once

[179] The statement is reproduced in full under the heading "The Jewish Labor Bund and the State of Israel" in *Bund Bulletin*, No. 8–9, August–September, 1948, pp. 1–4.
[180] Ibid.
[181] Ibid.

freedom, equality and economic security are developed through democratic socialism. Instead, both Zionists and Communists tried, the Bundists argued, to win over Jewish communities by offering terroristic and totalitarian solutions. Yes, the support of the Soviet Union and the whole communist camp for the "Zionist cause" was not about the interests of the Jewish people, but about imperialism, with catastrophic consequences for Jewish life. American support, for its part, was merely an expression of ongoing power struggles between Democrats and Republicans, as evidenced by the discrimination against Jewish immigration to the United States in new refugee legislation. The solution for the Jewish people in Palestine must be guided by the "universal humanist principles of justice, democracy and international solidarity." Real peace could only be achieved in an independent, democratic, and socialist Palestine with equal rights for both Jews and Arabs, all monitored by the UN, as well as guarantees for Yiddish in Jewish society. At the same time, the Bund criticized the new Jewish state for the treatment of what were believed to be four hundred thousand Arab refugees who were prevented from returning to their homes. Two thousand years of deportations and suffering, and over two hundred thousand Jews still in European camps, seemed to be "completely forgotten" when part of the Jewish population itself came to exercise state power. "Nationalism is short-sighted, and Jewish nationalism is no exception to that sad fact."[182]

The statement from the meeting in Brussels had led to a storm of condemnation of the Bund from widely differing Jewish camps: Zionist, Communist and others. The influential *Jewish Daily Forward* in New York, once the flagship of Jewish socialism in the United States with many collaborators from the Bundist milieu, published the Bund's statements about Israel, but with the editorial comment that the Jewish labor movement in America did not share the Bund's position. "The American Jewish workers' movement: The Workmen's Circle, the Jewish Labor Committee, the major Jewish unions, and the *Forverts* have all congratulated the Jewish state and committed themselves to doing everything in their power to help the state of Israel in its fight against its enemies and achieve membership in the world's family of nations."[183] It was precisely these milieux and mass organizations, which had so far constituted the Bund's strongholds, that now took a stand in support of the new state. There was a veritable flood of condemnatory articles printed. "The entire

[182] "Arab Refugees", *Bund Bulletin*, No. 8–9, August–September, 1948, p. 4.
[183] *Forverts*, July 20, 1948.

Jewish press, newspapers, weekly magazines and numerous other publications united to appoint the Bund traitors to the Jewish cause," the *Bund Bulletin* wrote under the defiant headline "We will not be bullied ."[184]

When the Bundists' small National Assembly in Stockholm's People's House gathered at eleven o'clock on Sunday, August 15, it would be clear that the majority, thirteen members, took a stand for the majority resolution that reflected those attending the Brussels meeting, while six other representatives voted for a less condemnatory position toward the new Jewish state. From the notes and reports of some local groups, it appears that it should have been a position that corresponded to the prevailing mood. In Vetlanda, the members repeatedly discussed the Palestinian issue and took a stand for the majority resolution.[185] At a regional conference in Malmö in early July, with Bundists from Malmö, Trelleborg and Landskrona, where both Olberg and Mehr were present, the notes read: "Saturday discussion on Palestine: against political Zionism. Illusions. Endangers the Jewish community in Palestine. Draws attention away from the German camps. The unwavering outlook of the Bund: continue along the same path for a more secure Jewish future. Resist the wave of nationalism sweeping across the Jewish streets."[186] In Eskilstuna, the votes were more evenly cast: seven members voted for the majority resolution, while six supported the minority, with the other four abstaining.[187] Where Paul Olberg stood on the issue was no secret. He represented the Coordinating Committee's majority proposal and was outraged that the representatives of the minority resolution sent out their proposal before the forthcoming World Congress to individual Bundists in Sweden, especially to someone who Olberg did not think was reliable and "almost a Zionist."[188]

It should be mentioned here that the minority resolution stopped short of directly supporting the formation of the new state of Israel. The Jews were, as the minority resolution emphasized, a world people, and its issues could only be solved through international socialism.[189] But the organized and national-conscious Jewish community in Palestine, with its seven hundred thousand

[184] "We Will Not Be Bullied", *Bund Bulletin*, No. 8–9, August–September, 1948, p. 4.

[185] Letter from Chezes in Vetlanda to Olberg, July 5 (possibly June 5), 1948, about planned Palestine discussion. Notes from a meeting on June 20, 1948 where Operman and Obranshka gave a lecture on the "Palestine problem". Notes: July 17, 1948, from the Vetlanda Regional Assembly discussing the Palestinian question; "The members were for the majority resolution". All from Vol. 213, ME18, 1400BA, YIVO.

[186] Report from regional Bund conference in Malmö, July 3–4, 1948. Vol. 206, "Malmö", ME18, 1400BA, YIVO.

[187] Report from Kaptchuk in Eskilstuna to Sara Mehr, August 5, 1948. Vol. 206, ME18, 1400BA, YIVO.

[188] Letter from Olberg to Pinkus Schwartz, July 10, 1950. Vol. 208, ME18, 1400BA, YIVO.

[189] *Bund Bulletin*, No. 11, November, 1948, pp. 4–5

inhabitants, was, the resolution said, a particularly important part of the Jewish people. They had no choice but to resist "foreign Arab armies," which represented "pro-Nazi feudal groups that politically dominate the lives of Arabs." The Bund should stand on the side of the Palestinian Jews in the struggle for national rights and self-determination, but at the same time oppose Zionism and all plans for an expansion of Jewish society at the expense of the Arab peoples. The Jews of the world must be warned of the illusion that the formation of Israel would solve the "Jewish problem" on a world scale. The establishment of the state of Israel was only a "palliative solution." Jewish society in the state of Israel could not be based on "petty nationalism and chauvinism." Not only because "such a course would be anti-democratic," but it would also be in direct opposition to Jewish society, which "at best" would constitute a small island surrounded by Arab neighbors.[190] The peace, economy and political future of the Jews in Palestine could only be secured through a Jewish–Arab agreement on the basis of a voluntary federation or a "bi-national state," plus a "socialist victory in the world."[191] Gnacik from Eskilstuna had probably understood the minority position quite correctly.

Conflicts with Zionists

Conflicts with Zionist groups, so common in interwar Poland, had already been going on for some time in the Swedish context. From Gislaved, a small town in southern Sweden, a female Bundist wrote to Olberg and appealed for a visit: "We are very unhappy here, surrounded by Zionists who are constantly visited by emissaries from Palestine. We are really desperate when no one visits us."[192] How a Bundist who arrived in Sweden from ghettos and camps could look any Swedish Jew who advocated migration to Palestine in the eye was expressed bitterly by the female camp prisoner from Halmstad, in the south. A point underlined in a long letter she wrote about the Nazi terror and her arrival in Sweden.[193] "May the Swedish Jews, the representatives of Zionism, not be afraid that we Jewish refugees are causing anti-Semitism. [...] May the Aronsons, Kaplans [unreadable] and Lapiduses, the big manufacturers and stockholders, know that we refugees, who for six years had the right to suffocate under the fascist boot, also have the right to stay in Sweden..." On the hypothetical question why she did not travel to Palestine, she replied: "You can take

[190] Ibid p. 5
[191] Ibid.
[192] Letter from Sala Ditenfeld to Paul Olberg, March 6, 1946, Box 36, folder 24, reel 105, see. III, JLC, TAMWAG.
[193] Letter from Hella Rudnitska to Olberg, Halmstad, February 22, 1946. Vol. 207, ME18, 1400BA, YIVO.

everything with you, you are strong, during the six years when your brothers burned, you just sighed and said how good we are here, you felt the heat of the fire and [unreadable] warmed yourselves, did business and put more money in your safes... You should travel and build a new home for your broken sisters and brothers." If Jews belonged to the pioneer movement *Hechalutz*, it was for fear of assimilation, not primarily for the sake of Zionism. But the risk was that the "missionary party," that is, the Zionists, would capture many Jewish souls with "promises of peace and tranquility." Why couldn't the Swedish Jews instead take a few thousand lonely people under their wings and help them? "A large proportion of us want to travel to America because there, among Jews, we can recreate our Jewish culture." A sizable number, she thought, wanted to stay in Sweden, while a few would move to relatives in Palestine. Instead of Zionism, all Jewish organizations should demand that Jewish victims be allowed to travel and settle wherever they wished.[194] That the Bundists felt that the Swedish Jewish establishment took a stand for the Zionists is evident from recurring mistrust, including against the Jewish congregation in Stockholm.

From Eskilstuna, the Bund group reported that it tried to get support from the "Mosaic congregation," (*Mosaiska*) in Stockholm for an event commemorating the uprising in the Warsaw ghetto, but was refused when the congergation learned that Bundists were arranging it.[195] This problem recurred during the Yiddish actress Chayele Grober's tour of Sweden in the autumn of 1947. After the war, Grober was a renowned artist in the Yiddish context and performed songs and recitals around the world.[196] In September, she arrived in Sweden for several appearances in Stockholm and elsewhere. In Stockholm, tickets were sold through the World Jewish Congress as a benefit concert for "the sick and needy among the 1945 survivors."[197] But of the concerts that were held in other parts of the country, two were organized by Bundist groups – at least if we are to believe an indignant letter from Sara Mehr about the lack of

[194] Ibid. Pontus Rudberg *The Swedish Jews and the victims of Nazi terror, 1933–1945*, Uppsala University, Uppsala, 2015, discusses the role the Mosaic congregation in Stockholm was given by Swedish authorities regarding the reception of Jewish refugees. Rudberg criticizes and nuances notions that the congregation would have been restrictive, made selections on arbitrary grounds and discriminated against poor Jews from Eastern Europe. On the other hand, the congregation functioned "in practice as a kind of filter" (p. 355) for control based on Swedish regulations. For the previously more negative perspective towards the congregation, see Svante Hansson *Flykt och överlevnad – flyktingverksamhet i Mosaiska församlingen i Stockholm 1933–1950* [Escape and survival – refugee activities in the Mosaic congregation in Stockholm 1933–1950], Stockholm 2004.

[195] Report from the Bund group in Eskilstuna to the International Coordinating Committee, without year, but probably 1948. Vol. 207, ME18, 1400BA, YIVO.

[196] http://yleksikon.blogspot.com/2015/09/khayele-chayele-grober.html

[197] *Dagens Nyheter*, October 11 and October 14, 1947.

financial compensation from the Jewish community, which apparently financed the tour.[198] The whole thing was more serious than the comrades might have realized, she explained. During a visit to "Mosaiska" in order to sort out compensation for the two concerts arranged close to "where we have Bund groups," the congregation did not want to hear about the matter despite the promise of an agreement. The person to whom she spoke was a "Zionist and a German Jew." When asked about the reason for the non-payment, he had answered that "it is the Bundists who are responsible." The reason why *Arbeter-Ring* in Malmö, to which Sara Mehr's letter was addressed, was not informed about the concert tour, was that, according to one man, "these people are boycotted by all organizations in Malmö – no one wants to deal with them." According to her own account, she read the riot act to the man, explaining to him that she herself, a well-known Swedish Social Democrat, had in fact been involved in the founding of *Arbeter-Ring* in Malmö, and that a group of comrades who were working under the auspices of the Jewish Labor Committees should not be treated as criminals. On the representative's declaration that he was only a simple official, Sara Mehr had called him a "right-wing Zionist" to whom the word "socialist" was foreign.[199]

The conflicts over Yiddish events in Malmö escalated during the same autumn when *Arbeter-Ring* invited the couple Josef Glikson and Tsipojre Faynsilber-Glikson, who had a background in theater in Warsaw, to perform. The Association for Surviving Jews, founded in 1945, tried, according to local Bundists, to recruit the artists for their own competing event the same day, if not the day after.[200] When this was not possible, the Association for the survivors, according to the Gliksons, called for a boycott of *Arbeter-Ring's* cultural evening, arranging a competing dance event. The proceeds would go to the camps in Cyprus where Jews on their way to Palestine were detained by British authorities. For the Malmö Bundists and the Gliksons, the Association's actions were acts of sabotage against *Arbeter-Ring's* events. In an angry letter to the Association, the artists explained that after being in Sweden for eight months, they now had the opportunity to perform in Malmö for the first time.[201] Not only did the artists now feel personally hurt, they said, but above all it was not as though Sweden was overflowing with Yiddish culture. "Is this not a reminder of the most hostile, petty political disputes in the most remote

[198] Letter from Sara Mehr to the Malmö branch, October 17, 1947, Vol. 216, ME18, 1400BA, YIVO.
[199] Ibid.
[200] Correspondence about the conflict over Glikson's appearance, including programs, is in Vol. 216, ME18, 1400BA, YIVO.
[201] Letter from Josef Glikson and Tsipojre Fajnsilber-Glikson to the board of the Association for the 1945 rescued Jews in Malmö, October 2, 1947. Vol. 216, ME18, 1400BA, YIVO.

small towns, from which we have come so far and from which we are separated by the horrific tragedies the Jewish people have experienced during the last few years?" The two artists emphasized that they had no interest in either politics in general or the Association's "holy war" against the Bundists. That they were both living in the Bund home at Kumla Manor outside Stockholm was possibly not known to the Association.[202]

The disagreement between the Malmö Bundists and the Association for Surviving Jews had its own history. In the autumn of 1946, Khayem Borenstein, in a letter to the board of the Association, had accused them of protecting black market traders and those receiving stolen goods, as well as illegal immigrants.[203] The whole thing seems to have initially touched on a personal matter where Borenstein claimed that one of the Association's protégés, "like a Shylock," stole his apartment and sold it at a profit. But the accusation was formulated in political terms: Borenstein wrote that the Bundists were Jewish Social Democrats, and that the Swedish Social Democratic government has "helped us regain life and made people who were 99 percent dead alive again, giving them the opportunity to live, work and find a place in this country." Therefore, it was the duty of all Jews and Jewish organizations to follow the laws of the land, while the board of the Association was protecting "*déclassé* elements." Unless the Association changes its mind on the issue of the apartment and stops covering up the "scandalous crimes," then the entire board will be made responsible "for these crimes and suffer the consequences."[204]

The matter seems to have developed into an endless schism. When Borenstein threatened to publish the accusations and scandalize the Association before Malmö's Jews, the Association's board in turn demanded an apology and that it should in fact be Borenstein who is brought before a party court and made responsible for his actions.[205] This ongoing tug-of-war over cultural events can be traced back to a statement in September 1947 from the then completely newly formed *Yidishe Kulturfarband Arbeter-Ring* in Malmö.[206] The Association was accused of having sunk into such demoralization that its meetings turned into circuses, and comradely discussions were replaced by

[202] Letter from Josef Glikson to Genye Borenstein, Malmö, September 18, 1947. Vol. 216, ME18, 1400BA, YIVO.
[203] Letter from Khayem Borenstein to the board of the Association for the 1945 rescued Jews in Malmö, September 17, 1946, Vol. 206, ME18, 1400BA, YIVO.
[204] Ibid.
[205] Letter from the board of the 1945 rescued Jews in Malmö, September 14, 1948. Vol. 216, ME18, 1400BA, YIVO.
[206] "To the public" from the board of the Yiddish Cultural Association *Arbeter-Ring* in Malmö, [undated] September, 1947. Vol. 216, ME18, 1400BA, YIVO.

"arguments of violence" in the form of glasses, bottles, chairs, and benches. While *Arbeter-Ring* intended to try to create a healthy cultural life for Jewish workers, its members, it was claimed, were attacked verbally once the Association had "declared war" on *Arbeter-Ring*. The Bundists would not "use their methods against them," but would rather "reveal the Association's harmfulness to the rebirth of Jewish cultural life in Malmö."[207]

For the Bund group, the whole thing should have been stressful. After all, politics was mixed with personal accusations. A members' meeting in the autumn of 1948, two years after the original accusation, unanimously decided to criticize Borenstein for his personal letter to the Association; the whole affair should be handled by the group as a whole, it was declared.[208] The conflicts in Malmö hardly seem to have diminished after the advent of Israel. At the commemoration ceremony in April 1949 for the uprising in the Warsaw ghetto, the Bundists, in their own view, had succeeded in bringing about a broader and more inclusive plan for the event, which, however, was disrupted by a battle over banners in the meeting room. According to the Bund group, the agreement was: no flags. And yet when a Zionist flag was held aloft, the Bundists sought to hang their own, with "serious tumult" the result. "If it had not been for the provocation of the Zionists, the evening would have been a fond memory of respect for our fallen heroes," summed up the Malmö group's minutes.[209]

Although the fighting in Malmö from time to time seems to have been particularly malicious, contradictions against Zionists were also experienced elsewhere. In Stockholm, the Bundists' *Arbeter-Ring* in the spring of 1948 had addressed the Polish Jews' Association with a proposal to jointly commemorate the anniversary of the uprising in the Warsaw ghetto.[210] To their possibly feigned astonishment, they received answers from the Zionist World Jewish Congress, WJC, that the Polish Jewish Association was not interested. The letter prompted a sharply condemnatory response from *Arbeter-Ring's* Aron Feiner, who said he was "shocked" that the WJC was responding on behalf of the Polish Jewish Association. The day of remembrance was not the concern of a single organization; the uprising in Warsaw had been organized by the Jewish Defense Committee ZOB where "all factions of Jewish life were included," and

207 Ibid.
208 Minutes, Bund Malmö, September 23, 1948. Vol. 216, ME18, 1400BA, YIVO.
209 Minutes, Bund Malmö, April 19, 1949. Vol. 216, ME18, 1400BA, YIVO.
210 Invitation by Mr A Feiner, March 17, 1948, to a meeting on a commemoration of the Warsaw Ghetto Uprising. Vol. 206, ME18, 1400BA, YIVO.

the commemoration therefore concerned everyone. If it split into two, "you are responsible," Feiner concluded.[211] A toxic answer was not slow in coming. WJC considered the letter from *Arbeter-Ring* to be most "strange."[212] The WJC was not involved at all, the Polish Jewish Association considered the memorial service to be their thing – something they had announced to *Arbeter-Ring* by telephone. Why, then, did *Arbeter-Ring* raise this with WJC at all, "we are not interested in your view of collaborations." In addition, "We want to remind you that your party, which since its inception has separated you from Jews in general, should be a little more considerate of those who do not want to cooperate." And, "who took responsibility for your separate memorial service last year and every single year?" With the addition: "We consider the matter closed." The confusion did not only provoke the ire of the Bundists over what they perceived as the WJC's usurpation of the Polish Jewish Association. When Feiner had originally opened up for cooperation for the memorial, it was not on behalf of *Arbeter-Ring*, but the Jewish Labor Committee on Wallingatan 21 (i.e. the Social Democrats' premises within the People's House), where the coordinating meeting was intended to take place.[213] *Arbeter-Ring's* premises were the same, and Feiner performed both roles with changing addressees. This mess probably undermined the serious character of the invitation. In Uppsala, as we will see later, the schism with Zionism would penetrate deep into the Bund group, ultimately destroying it.

Folke Bernadotte and "Jewish fascism"

The assassination of the Swedish UN mediator Folke Bernadotte in September 1948 further intensified, if this was even possible, the conflict between Bundists and Zionists. "This crime," condemned the Bund in Sweden, "has excluded the fascist Stern Gang, along with its supporters and defenders, from civilized humanity."[214] Aggressive nationalist and chauvinist currents within the Zionist movement had, continued the condemnation, systematically spread intolerance and violence throughout the movement. As a leader in the Swedish Red Cross, Folke Bernadotte had been responsible for the "white buses" that in the final stages of the war also transported Jewish prisoners to Sweden, among

[211] Letter from *Kulturfarband Arbeter-ring*, A Feiner, to the World Jewish Congress in Stockholm, April 5, 1948. Vol. 206, ME18, 1400BA, YIVO.

[212] Letter from WJC to *Arbeter-ring*, April 7, 1948. Vol. 206, ME18, 1400BA, YIVO.

[213] Invitation by Mr A Feiner, March 17, 1948, to a meeting on a commemoration of the Warsaw Ghetto Uprising. Vol. 206, ME18, 1400BA, YIVO.

[214] Declaration from the Social Democratic Association 'BUND' in Sweden, undated. Vol. 206, ME18, 1400BA, YIVO.

them several Bundists.[215] His mandate for the UN partition plan and the negotiation of a ceasefire in the fighting was perceived by the most militant Zionist groups as a hostile obstacle to eliminate. For the Bund in Sweden, the murder was not just an assassination of a UN mediator, but an almost existential issue. The fact that Jews murdered a famous Swede in the service of world peace – who was also considered to have saved Jews from Nazism – made the condemnation more urgent and the line of opposition more pronounced. The Bund in Sweden was also one of the very first contributors to the memorial fund for peace and humanity established in the name of Folke Bernadotte, a detail also mentioned in the Swedish press.[216] For the Bundists in Sweden, the assassination was an attack on socialism, in the form of Swedish social democracy and the British Labour government. The "Stern Gang," or *Lohamei Herut Israel*, was an underground, right-wing guerrilla group, which had been waging an armed struggle against British rule since the war years. According to the Bundists, Clement Attlee's Labour victory in 1945 had brought British socialism to power, which was now seeking to abolish the UN mandate of Palestine in as peaceful and just manner as possible. Against this endeavor stood an anti-socialist triangle of Soviet communism, Western capitalism and Zionism, whose openly fascist spearhead now showed its naked face. Perhaps the Bund's vulnerable position in the Swedish context was reflected in the fact that the statement made to the Swedish public was blunter than the version published in the international Bundist press. There, the characterization of the "Stern Gang" as "fascist" had been replaced by "terrorist."[217] Or had something been lost in translation? The Bund's mouthpiece was otherwise hardly low-key when it came to Menachem Begin's Zionist battle group *Irgun Zvai Leumi* (from which the Stern group had split). When Begin was overwhelmingly welcomed by Jewish organizations in New York during a visit in the late fall of 1948, the Bund criticized them for praising a Jewish fascist as a hero.[218] Terrorist attacks involving civilians, the murder of captured British soldiers, and the massacre in the Arab village of Deir Yassin, where women and children were killed "for the Zionist dreams of a Greater Israel," placed Begin among figures such as Hitler and Mussolini, the Bund said.

[215] Interview with Marek Webb at YIVO, New York (20140513).
[216] "50 kronor to the Folke Bernadotte Memorial Fund, Swedish European Aid from the Jewish Social Democratic Association 'BUND' in Sweden", September 21, 1948, Vol. 206, ME18, 1400BA, YIVO. See, for example, *Dagens Nyheter*, September 23, 1948.
[217] *Bund Bulletin*, No. 11, November 1948, p. 7.
[218] *Bund Bulletin*, No. 12, December 1948, pp. 1–2.

A softening of attitude towards Zionism, or at least Israel, of the kind that several delegates at Bund's National Assembly in Stockholm cautiously hinted at, was unthinkable. In addition, the Bund's press began to be filled with reports of Zionists in camps and Jewish communities beginning to push for material support for military struggle and for the new state. "A wave of Zionist terror in Argentina," the *Bund Bulletin* headlined in September 1948.[219] The Zionists were said to have started collecting 50 million pesos for Israel as a mandatory tax on the Jewish community. Anyone who "opposed the demands of the Zionist terrorists" and refused to pay was, the article claimed, denied access to synagogues, excluded from prayer on Yom Kippur, wedding ceremonies, circumcision of children and Jewish burials. They were also excluded from Jewish institutional boards, the Bund Bulletin claimed.[220]

Documents from DP camps in Germany were said to show how Jewish camp residents, regardless of political views, were forced into the Israeli military in order not to lose their ration cards and livelihoods. The camps were also said to being emptied without giving its inhabitants any alternative to moving to Israel.[221] At present, according to the Bund Bulletin, the majority of the remaining 115,000 Jews in German and Austrian camps refused to become citizens of the State of Israel. Most of them had spent the war in Soviet gulag camps and were tormented by communist guards. They wanted to reunite with relatives in democratic countries such as the United States, Canada, and Australia to live a normal life, and they refused to become pioneers in the Negev desert or wage war against Arabs. Convinced Zionists, the Bund's organ claimed, had traveled to Israel long ago, while Zionist leaders of the DP camps also forced Jews who had already been granted work permits in the United States to go to Israel.[222]

Conditions in the new state were also described as difficult, with a new camp existence for the unhappy Jewish masses, who having been forced to endure the oppression of the war years, were now denied access to democracies. Later, it was alarmingly described how Jewish refugees, now on their way from Israel to Italy, arrived with shocking stories about barbed wire-fenced camps for tens of thousands of people with catastrophic health care, high child mortality, corruption, and bribery. Those who tried to leave Israel were only allowed to bring with them 5 pounds, were deprived of other assets, were seen as "traitors

[219] *Bund* Bulletin, No. 8–9, August–September 1948, p. 8.
[220] Ibid.
[221] *Bund Bulletin*, No. 12, December 1948, p. 6 and No. 14, February 1949.
[222] *Bund Bulletin*, No. 16–17, April–May 1949.

of the Jewish cause," and were denied support from the major aid organizations that raised millions of dollars for "humanitarian and politically independent aid."[223] The historian David Slucki believes that the reporting of these events by Bundists included agitational exaggerations in their fierce struggle with the Zionists.[224] At the same time, there is, in the correspondence between Bundists, evidence of some arm-twisting, which was not intended for public viewing.[225] Nonetheless, the reports ensured that all bridges were burned, meaning that a less hostile attitude toward Israel was, for a time, unfeasible.

The Second World Congress

The Bund's Second World Congress in the first week of October 1948 was, in a sense, the zenith of international regeneration. When a thousand members and guests took over the Hotel Pennsylvania's large conference hall in New York, the Bund seemed to represent an impressive force, both within the socialist movement and the Jewish world.[226] From the American Socialist Party, the meeting was greeted with great approval by its legendary chairman Norman Thomas, and greetings flowed in from Comisco and European Social Democratic parties – including the Swedish one. American Jewish organizations that had taken a different stance on Israel, such as JLC, Workmen's Circle, and trade unions, were among the well-wishers. The fact that the congress took place during a time of strong hostility from Jewish public opinion, even "hatred of Bund ideology," was considered by the congressional report to be merely an expression of the typical blindness within "all extreme nationalist movements."[227] But this hatred had not been able to prevent, the report continued, the congress being carried out very successfully and constituting a further step

[223] *Bund Bulletin*, No. 1–2 (22–23), January–February 1950, p. 8.
[224] Slucki 2012, pp. 47–56.
[225] Letter from Vetlanda to Olberg, June 20, 1948: "We have received letters from Austria, comrades in camps who have visas but are still in camps. They are forced to travel from Austria to Palestine." Vol. 213, ME18, 1400BA, YIVO.
[226] See congressional report in Bund Bulletin No. 11, November 1948, pp. 2–3. The actual negotiations took place in the socialist Tamiment Institute (formerly Rand School) with 60 representatives from 18 countries, including Sweden and "Palestine". Officially, the Bund represented between twenty and fifty thousand members around the world in the early 1950s, but according to Slucki 2012, p. 11, the real number should have been around five thousand. An internal report showed that only 2,480 participated in the election of representatives and votes in the local sections before the World Congress in 1948. 1,909 were stated to have voted for the majority resolution on Israel, 549 for the minority while 31 abstained (slightly more than in the representative elections). See Emanuel Novogrodski's report from the International Coordinating Committee, October 21, 1948. Vol. 207, ME18, 1400BA, YIVO.
[227] *Bund Bulletin* No. 11, November 1948, p. 2.

along the path of Bund's "glorious achievements."[228] And surely many Bundists around the world were encouraged to step up their efforts in all areas where the World Congress made decisions, from mutual aid and organizational reconstruction to the struggle for secular Yiddish culture, socialist politics, and Jewish rights. However, a letter from Emanuel Novogrodski to the Bund in Sweden a few weeks after the congress warned of what was now required. "As expected, the Zionist wave has now poisoned the 'Jewish street'", Novogrodski began.[229] As a result, the financial situation of the International Coordinating Committee had deteriorated. In the budget for 1949, the Swedish group was therefore expected to contribute five hundred dollars. With the exchange rate of that time, it meant close to two thousand Swedish crowns, or in today's money around forty thousand Swedish crowns. The daily wage for an industrial worker in Sweden in 1949 (the employment of many Bundists), was just over 21 Swedish crowns, but many of the members received only refugee benefits. So, the sum needed was significant, but, Novogrodski continued, "we are convinced of the needlessness of reminding you of the enormous significance of this thing. It is no exaggeration to say that our very existence depends on it."[230]

[228] Ibid., p. 3.
[229] Letter from E Novogrodski to Bund organization in Sverige, December 10, 1948. Vol. 206, ME18, 1400BA, YIVO.
[230] Ibid.

Paul Olberg. YIVO photo archive.

ÖPP
NSERNA
OFFER

Bundist contingent in Stockholm First of May demonstration 1947. "Open the borders to the victims of Nazism", in Swedish and Yiddish. YIVO photo archive.

Top: The Bund group in Stockholm 1949. Second from the left on the floor is Zenia Larsson. On the second row, second from the left is Roza Klepfish (beside Paul Olberg). Fourth from the left is Fanya Feiner beside Sara Mehr, Aron Feiner and Eda Rak's mother Guta. Standing in the third row, second from the left (with glasses) is Zelig Wasserstrom, Avrom Sobol, Mayer Rak (the father of Eda), Sziah Szechatow with his wife Eta Szechatow. YIVO photo archive.

Bottom: Celebration of the opening of the Bund home in Mälarbaden 1946. Standing in the back is Markus (Motl) Kshienski. YIVO photo archive.

Top: Paul Olberg, Faygele Falz and Markus Kshienski during the celebration in Mälarbaden 1946.

Bottom: The Bund group in the industrial town of Eskilstuna. Standing, from the right: Nute Kaptchuk, Leib Ozholek and Meyer Tromka. Standing on the far left Leib Gnacik. Sitting, from the left "wife Tromka". YIVO photo archive.

Top: The Bund group in the textile city of Borås.

Bottom: Celebration of the opening of the Bund home in Mälarbaden 1946. The sign on the wall in Swedish reads: "Welcome!!! Long live socialism", with the portrait of Hjalmar Branting, the pioneer of Swedish social democracy, below. Fifth from the left on the second row is Sara Mehr, to her left, with glasses, Jacob Pat. from the Jewish Labor Committee, Markus Kshienski and Paul Olberg. On the floor to the right, Faygele Falz. YIVO photo archive.

Top: The choir at the opening celebration in Mälarbaden in 1946. Second from the left is Leib Gnacik. Among the women standing, from the right, is Rifke Weinberg, Esterke Silberberg, "wife Leffler", Jadwiga Zilberstein, Shaye Rozntsvayg, Malke Zilberstein and Sara Leib. YIVO photo archive.

Bottom: Sara Mehr celebrating her 60th birthday. To the left, her son Hjalmar Mehr and to the right, the leader of Stockholm social democracy Zeth Hög-lund. Photo: Riwkin/ARAB.

The Stockholm Bund marching in the social democratic first of May demonstration 1946. The man to the left is Chaim Elenbogen (Bolik). YIVO photo archive.

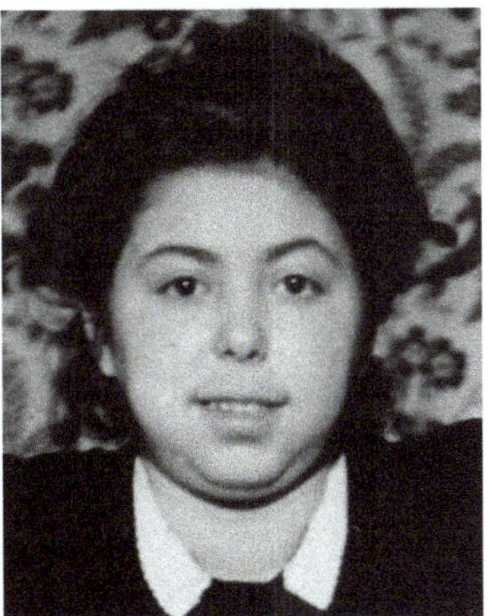

Top: Bundists on the steps to the Bund home at Kumla mansion. Photo: Eda Rak.

Middle: Eda Rak. Photo: Håkan Blomqvist.

Bottom: Faygele or Fayga Falz. YIVO photo archive.

Top: Over many years Paul Olberg received post cards expressing gratitude from bundists who had passed through Sweden.

Bottom: A celebration card from the bundists in Neglinge to Paul Olbergs 70th birthday.

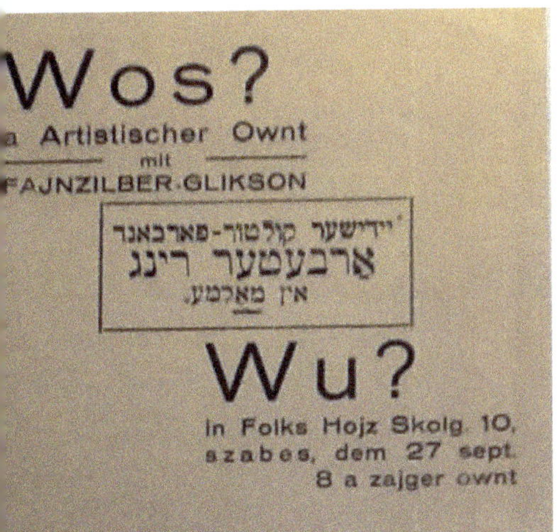

Wos?
a Artistischer Ownt
mit
FAJNZILBER-GLIKSON

יידישער קולטור-פארבאנד
ארבעטער רינג
אין מאלמע.

Wu?
in Folks Hojz Skolg. 10,
szabes, dem 27 sept.
8 a zajger ownt

Jidiszer Kultur Farband
ARBETER RING
in Malmö.

Ale kumen szabes,
dem 27 september
punktlech 8 a zajger ownt
in Folks Hojz, Skolgatan 10
ojf
A ARTISTISCHEN OWNT
mit dem ontajl fun die cwaj szoj-
szpiler fun warszewer Jungteater
CYPORA FAJNZILBER u. JOSEF GLIKSON
[illegible]
programen.
[illegible]

Top: Leaflets for Arbeter Ring's cultural event with Cypora Fajnsilber and Josef Glikson in Malmö, 1947.

Bottom: Irena Klepfish visiting her old primary school in Neglinge, 2019, holding a school photo from the late 1940s. Photo: Håkan Blomqvist.

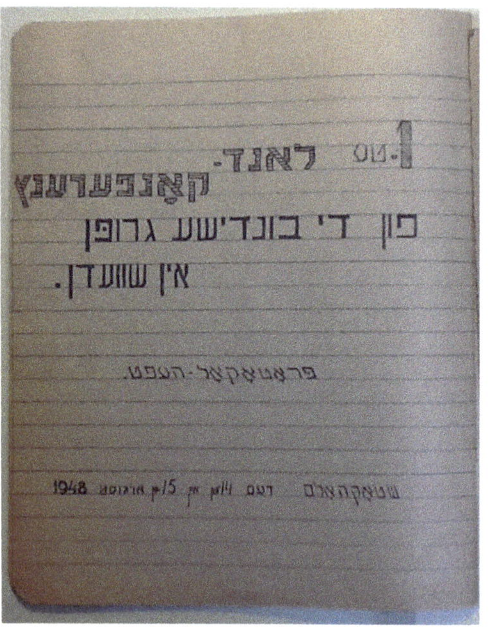

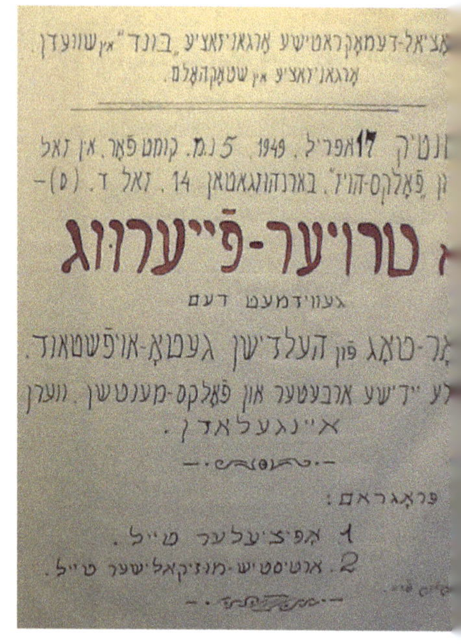

Top (left): Minutes of the first national assembly of the Bund groups in Sweden, August 14–15, 1948. Top (right): Poster from the Stockholm Bund to commemorate the heroic Warzaw ghetto uprising at the People's house (Folkets hus) in Stockholm April 17. "All Jewish workers" and the public invited.

Bottom (left): Tobias Amster in the late 1970s. Photo: Harry Amster. Bottom (right): Minutes from the Bund group in Trelleborg.

Top: Ber Perelmuter. On his right, wearing glasses, Zenia Larsson. Photo: Susanne Levin.

Bottom (left): Sara Ferdman (later Tauben) skiing with her father Nuson in Sweden early 1950s. Bottom (right): Eta and Sziah Szechatow. Photo: Sara Ferdman Tauben.

The Ferdman family, Nuson with wife Ruchla arrived in Sweden 1948, here with the daughter Sara and son Benny, both born in Sweden. Photo: Sara Ferdman Tauben.

I. Ekstein Lidköpingsvägen 19 Hammarbyhöjd

Sz. Perl Ch. Makowski Pens. Johansson III tr.
Sveavägen 70 Stockholm

L. Rauch Hantwerkargatan 80 Stockholm

A. Ajzensztajn

I. Cukier Białygłowski. Niwinski.
villa Lillhem. Rönninge BOX 23

Ch. Sojke Ängsvägen 1 Stockholm

Sz. Seper Brännkirkagatan 87 Stockholm

A. Sobol Strindbergsvägen 9b Södertälje

N. Ferdman Wallenbergsvägen 13 Näglinge

Sz. Szechatow Wallenbergsvägen

Tankus F. Bromma

N. Wiszub Inteckningsvägen 63
Midsommarkransen

I. Wergewajg Pensionat St. Eriksgatan 25 V tr.
Stockholm

Top: Handwritten membership lists (with among others Sobol, Ferdman and Szechatow).

Bottom: Children's birthday celebration at the Kumla mansion.

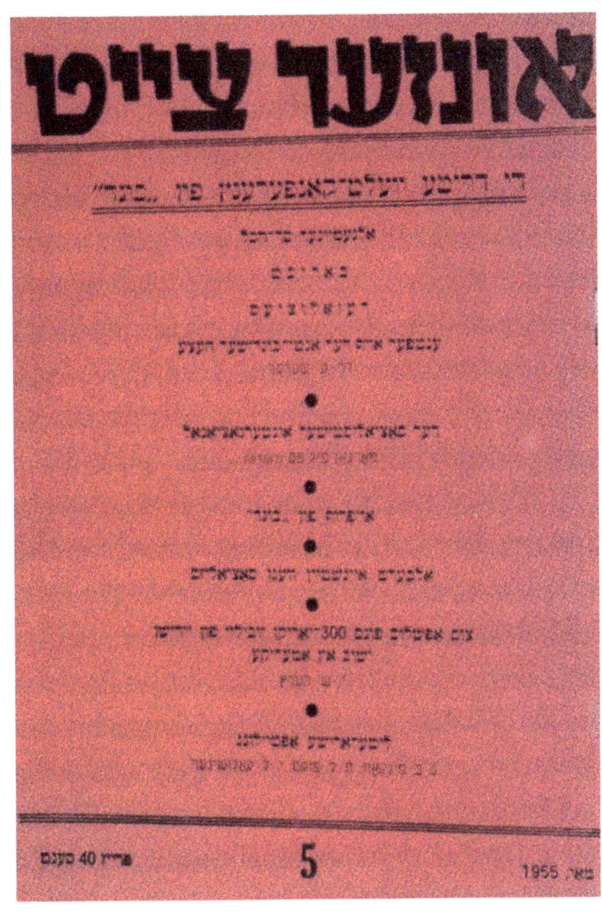

אונזער צייט

מאי, 1955 — 5 — פרייז 40 סענט

NOTRE VOIX

QUOTIDIEN
20e ANNÉE

Banque Nationale pour le Commerce et l'Industrie
Agence Turenne 11.987

אונזער שטימע

יובל־נומער

32 זייטן

REDACTION : 20, Rue Ferdinand-Duval, Paris-4e · Tél. : ARC. 39-09 · ADMINISTRATION : 110, Rue Vieille-du-Temple, Paris-3e · Tél. : ARC. 23-08

צוואנציק יאר

לעבן זאל „אונזער שטימע"

Top: Unzer Tsayt.

Bottom: Bund's daily paper Unzer Shtime published from Paris. Paul Olberg was the Swedish correspondence.

יידישע סאָציאַל־דעמאָקראַטישע אַרבעטער־פּאַרטיי
„בונד" אין שוועדן

פּאַרטיי־לעגיטימאַציע נר. 2

נאָמען שרה מעהר

עלטער 1897

פּאַרטיי־גרופּע אין סטאָקהאָלם

פּאָרזיצער:

סעקרעטאַר:

סטאָקהאָלם, ד. סעפּט. 1949 י.

Judiska Socialdemokratiska Förbundet
»BUND» i Sverige

MEDLEMSKORT Nr.

Namn S Mehr

född

Avdelning i

Ordförande:

Sekreterare:

, den 19

Top: Leib Gnacik with wife Sara Gitla. Photo: Hanna Cohen.

Bottom: Membership card of Sara Mehr for the social democratic association Bund in Sweden, in Swedish and Yiddish.

Activities in Sweden

At the Swedish National Assembly in August, the local Bund groups had reported on their activities.[231] From Vetlanda in the southern forest region, "Comrade Obranshka" reported that the group had about forty members, which also included some comrades in the nearby industrial town of Huskvarna and some in the region's central city of Jönköping. They had all arrived in the past year from German and Austrian camps. In Vetlanda, regular regional meetings were held with discussions on political and cultural issues. However, closer contact with Stockholm and other groups was needed. Obranshka wrote about the difficulties comrades faced when they arrived in Sweden: "They are spread all over the country and separated from each other." It was important to concentrate comrades in certain places where they could carry out lively activity; in larger groups, Jewish children's activities and cultural associations were needed.[232] The careful booklet with minutes of local activity states that the Vetlanda group's first meeting was held in March 1948 with members also from nearby Nässjö, Sävsjö, Mullsjö, Huskvarna and Hövik (spelled Hevik). The founding meeting of the group had included extensive discussions about the need to gather comrades and break the "sad fact that we are isolated from general cultural Jewish life in the world."[233] It ended optimistically: "The members were assembled at set tables until late in the evening and sang workers' and folk songs," and 27 kronor was collected for *Unzer Shtime*. "The first meeting for new arrivals to Sweden ended with joy at being able to see each other often."[234]

The Bundist group in the "large industrial city of Eskilstuna," not far from Stockholm, belonged, Leib Gnacik announced, to those formed back in 1945. The group comprised of twenty members with lively activity among the approximately one hundred newly arrived Jewish families. In a report to the International Coordinating Committee, the city is believed, with slight exaggeration, to have 66,000 inhabitants, of which "most work in metal factories." Immediately after the war, the report continued, some forty Jewish families had arrived from Hungary, Romania, and Poland. "The experiences of each of them

[231] Minutes from the first National Assembly of Bund groups in Sweden, August 14–15, 1948. Second session at 11 am, August 15, 1948, and handwritten minutes. Vol. 206, ME18, 1400BA, YIVO.
[232] Ibid.
[233] Contribution by Operman, notes from the meeting on March 28, 1948, in the booklet for the Bund group in Vetlanda, March 1948, Vol. 213, ME18, 1400BA, YIVO
[234] Ibid.

are the story of a tormented people, both from those who were enslaved by Hitler and sent to the death camps and those who were sent into exile on the Siberian tundra." Among the members was a Bund group from Vilnius that still held together both socially and politically, "but without forgetting their comradely duties."[235]

For the Malmö group, which was also founded in 1945, Henryk Levkovich reported on twenty members in the city itself, plus fifteen in the region. Cultural and political activities were conducted among Malmö's "about four hundred Jews" who "took the Bund group seriously." Attempts were made to establish children's activities for about forty children whose parents, while busy at work, wanted for their children, a Jewish upbringing in a Jewish children's home. Given the strenuous conflict with the Association for the Surviving Jews of 1945, Levkovich may have surprised the other delegates with the information that the Bundists in Malmö had been invited to join the Association's board. But the "social life" for Jews in Malmö was concentrated, he explained, around the association for the survivors.

Tobias Amster, from the early Uppsala group, and Ber Perelmutter, from the small town of Vingåker, listed a number of activities they had help set-up since the start: lectures; cultural events and dance performances; participation in a Jewish council in Uppsala (actually a Jewish association)[236] "with a Bundist as chairman," he added; memorial services for the Warsaw ghetto uprising; the establishment of a library, "an evening with Swedish friends," artistic performances and lectures by Comrade Olberg on Sweden's aid to Jewish refugees.

Stockholm was represented by Elenbogen, who, doubtless to the surprise of many, spoke about how the traditions of Bundism in Sweden went all the way back to 1904, even though its current organizational form had begun after the end of the war. In Sweden, he explained, there were about six thousand assimilated Swedish Jews. But thanks to the "initiative of the workers' government and the Red Cross," about ten thousand Jews had been transported here from German camps for rehabilitation. The thousands of Eastern European Jews who arrived in Sweden were almost exclusively from the working class, and if they were not before, "ninety percent were now." The whole thing was "a dream for Bundist work." But there were also great

[235] Report from the Bund group in Eskilstuna to the International Coordinating Committee, without year, but probably 1948. Vol. 207, ME18, 1400BA, YIVO.

[236] By "Jewish councils" the Bundists probably meant the twenty or so Jewish associations that were formed during the period in various parts of the country for Jewish refugees through the Jewish congregation in Stockholm. See memorial article in *Forvert's*, February 15, 1969.

difficulties here. The new arrivals were, as Obranshka pointed out, scattered across the country. Zionist sentiments prevailed, and money was lacking.[237] The Bund in Stockholm had in practice functioned as a national center for contact with the groups in the country and with the International Coordinating Committee and JLC. Here was located a library named after the late Bundist leader Shloime Mendelsohn, who had died a few months earlier.[238] The library lent Yiddish literature to comrades elsewhere. Speakers from Stockholm traveled around, though only a few could do so. There was no economy to support the local groups, and these had to rely mainly on their own efforts. But a stronger organization was needed. Heniek Bornstein believed that a central organization was required for more regular activities in the country. He called for instructions and a central circular, preferably a hectographed bulletin. Elenbogen had suggested that the Bundists would try to form Jewish sections in the unions, but Eskilstuna's Gnacik considered that the members must first and foremost start by joining the unions. He also emphasized, like previous speakers, the need to concentrate newcomers within larger cities, a question that constantly hindered their efforts.

Olberg, for his part, emphasized the importance of uniting the activities with local social democratic organizations, but he also realized the difficulties, not least the problem of language. The seemingly intense discussion finally led to the National Assembly's election of a joint national board for the "Jewish Social Democratic Association 'BUND' in Sweden." The elected board members were: Olberg (18 votes), Mehr (17), Elenbogen (17), Amster (15), Obranshka (15), Gnacik (13) and Levkovich (11).[239] The Board's task was through letters and tours – including an organized party structure with regular membership meetings (at least every fortnight), election of local boards (with chairman, secretary and treasurer) – as well as a press committee responsible for member subscriptions to *Unzer Shtime* and *Unzer Tsayt*. In addition, collection of money was organized for the Bundist press, the International Coordinating Committee, and comrades in need of help in various countries. Mutual assistance, with refugee reception, housing, work, childcare, and sup-

[237] Minutes from the first National Assembly of Bund Groups in Sweden August 14–15, 1948, and handwritten minutes. Vol. 206, ME18, 1400BA, YIVO.

[238] During the 1920s and 1930s, Shloime Mendelson was one of the leaders of the secular Jewish school system *Tsysho* in Poland and managed to get to the United States after the outbreak of war, where he became one of the Bund's leading figures. He died of a heart attack at the age of 51 in February 1948. See https://www.jta.org/1948/02/11/archive/shlomo-mendelson-jewish-writer-and-socialist-leader-dies-in-los-angeles (20190612).

[239] Minutes from the first National Assembly of Bund Groups in Sweden, August 14–15, 1948. Second session, 15 August, 1948, and handwritten minutes. Vol. 206, ME18, 1400BA, YIVO.

port was an obvious priority. The task of spreading the Bund's political ideas and socialist Yiddish culture to Jews in Sweden was central. If possible, the groups, such as those in Malmö, Stockholm, and Uppsala, would form cultural associations, with a Yiddish library, theater, and music activities.

Memory culture

Socially, the Bundists were held together by their political *mishpokhe*, the family culture built around the responsibilities of the movement's members to one another. Culturally, Jewish holidays such as Purim and Rosh Hashana in secularized and socialist form constituted a glue. To bind the groups together, activities were also planned around a cohesive political memory culture, with several Bundist commemorations at the center. These were mainly about the Warsaw Ghetto Uprising, the suicide of Shmul Zygielbojm, the assassinated Bundist leaders, Erlich and Alter, and the anniversaries of the founding of the Bund; the fiftieth anniversary in 1947 was the highlight, but then annual gatherings followed.

The Warsaw Ghetto Uprising and Shmul Zygielbojm

That April 19 was one of the Bundists' most important memorial dates was a given. The uprising in the Warsaw ghetto in April 1943 was not only one of the most acclaimed actions and acts of heroic of Jewish resistance in the face of Nazi genocide. In the furious and hopeless battle, the Bund and the young activists of *Tsukunft* played a central role. Some survived and continued the fighting as partisans or managed to stay hidden until the end of the war. A number were among those who eventually left Poland. One of them, the legendary Bundist leader "Comrade Bernard," or Bernard Goldstein, emigrated to the United States; in 1947, he published through *Unzer Tsayt's* publishing house several testimonies from the ghetto and the uprising, entitled *Di Shvue: Eydes vel zayn di likhtike shtern*. The testimonies were published a few years later in English, under the title *The Stars Bear Witness,* and became part of the Bundists' literary and political canon.[240] For all local groups in Sweden, April 19 was the most important mobilization of the spring, at least as important as the First of May. How the commemoration could look is stated in a report from the fifth anniversary in Stockholm in 1948.[241] The hall in the People's house was described as heaving, with three invited "ghetto fighters" in the presidium, the two widows, Roza Klepfisz and Channa

[240] Bernard Goldstein *The Stars Bear Witness*, The Viking Press, New York 1949.
[241] Fifth anniversary. Report. Vol. 206, ME18, 1400BA, YIVO.

Fryszdorf, from the Bund home in Neglinge, and Borech Spiegel. Paul Olberg opened the meeting with a moment of silence for the fallen and then spoke about the significance of April 19. Shmiel Rosenfeld gave a speech on the background and the "political and psychological aspects" that led Jews in the ghetto to take up arms against the German war machine. The decision to fight for human dignity despite the inevitable outcome, Rosenfeld explained, was linked to the "political and revolutionary training that the Jewish workers have received from the Bund for decades."[242] Joy Granditsky recited "*khaver* Zygielbojm's" suicide note.

Shmul Zygielbojm (1895–1943), also known as Artur, was the trade unionist leader who represented the Bund in the Polish government-in-exile in London from 1942.[243] When his cry for help over the fate of the Polish Jews and the destruction of the Warsaw Ghetto did not stir the Allies into action, he took his life in protest on May 11 with the words: "I cannot continue to live and be silent when the remnants of the Polish Jews, whose representative I am, are murdered. My comrades in the Warsaw ghetto fell with weapons in hand in one last heroic battle. I was not allowed to fall like them and with them, but belong to them in their mass grave."[244] This was followed at the commemoration by personal reminiscences of the uprising by Borech Spiegel, after which "Professor Ernst Wasserfogl" performed piano pieces from Peer Gynt and Chopin before the gathering jointly sang the Partisan anthem – "*Zog nisht keyn mol az du geyst dem letstn veg*" (Never say you are going the last mile) – and *Di Shvue*. [245]

The Trelleborg Group's archives describe a meeting "in memory of Artur Zygielbojm" on May 15, 1949.[246] Comrade Fajgenbojm from the local board spoke to the six-year memory of Zygielbojms "heroic death" – unfortunately, the world did not listen to his desperate cry for help for Europe's Jews. Several members of the group recounted their meetings with Zygielbojm in the Bund before concluding with *Di Shvue*.

Local groups adapted the programs to local conditions. In Vetlanda, the memorial service in 1948 was already arranged on Sunday, April 18, for then a

[242] Ibid.

[243] In the minutes and reports of the Bund in Sweden his name is transcribed in many ways. See also http://www.yivoencyclopedia.org/article.aspx/Zygielbojm_Shmuel_Mordkhe.

[244] Translation here from Irena Klepfisz, Daniel Soyer *The Stars Bear Witness – The Jewish Labor Bund, 1897–2017*, YIVO, New York, 2017, p. 25.

[245] Fifth anniversary. Report. Vol. 206, ME18, 1400BA, YIVO.

[246] Minutes taken at a meeting with the Bund group in Trelleborg, May 15, 1949, Bund group, Trelleborg, Sweden, Vol. 215, ME18, 1400BA, YIVO.

regional board meeting could be held in the morning. The ensuing celebration was reported in the minutes: "All Jews in Vetlanda and from the region were there, the hall was decorated with appropriate posters and pictures of our heroes. Comrade Operman gave the lecture, the memory of the fallen was honored with a moment of silence. Music: Zheni sang two ghetto songs that brought tears to our eyes and brought back memories of our martyrs, which was received with gratitude. It ended with the Partisan anthem, and everyone sang along."[247] From Eskilstuna, it was reported that "most Jews in the town participated" at the memorial.[248] The orphaned girl Zitka lit six candles according to the appeal of the newly formed *Alveltlekher yidisher kultur-kongres* – World Congress for Yiddish Culture (see below). A moment of silence followed "in memory of our martyrs and heroes," whereupon "Comrade Fekher" declared that these April days would forever be "a sacred memory for us." Comrade Morocco recited poems by, among others, Chaim Nachman Bialik*; Leib Gnacik and Sara Mehr, who was invited from Stockholm, also spoke. Chopin's funeral march and Yiddish music were performed, after which the celebration ended with the singing of the Partisan anthem, in unison.[249]

Erlich and Alter

The Polish Bundist leaders Henryk Erlich (1882–1942) and Victor Alter (1890–1943) played a prominent role in the Bundists' culture of memory. They both belonged to the generation that was active in the Bund, both within the Russian Empire before the First World War and in interwar Poland. Originally from Lublin, Erlich studied law in Warsaw and economics in Berlin. He was imprisoned as a young Bund activist, and had taken part in the 1905 Russian Revolution. As a member of the Bund's Central Committee, he belonged to those who, after the October Revolution of 1917, opposed joining the Bolshevik Party.[250] In independent Poland, Erlich, as the editor of *Folkstsaytung*, became the Bund's central leader in the 1930s, together with Alter. The latter, born in Mława, had, in contrast, a working-class background and belonged to the

[247] Minutes, Vetlanda, April 18, 1948. Vol. 213, ME18, 1400BA, YIVO.

[248] Report from the Bund group in Eskilstuna to the International Coordinating Committee, without year, but probably 1948. Vol. 207, ME18, 1400BA, YIVO.

* Chaim Nahman Bialik (1873–1934), a leading figure in Hebrew poetry who also wrote a large number of folk poems in Yiddish. http://www.yivoencyclopedia.org/article.aspx/Bialik_Hayim_Nahman (20190617).

[249] Handwritten report where other points could not be read, and Report from the Bund group in Eskilstuna to the International Coordinating Committee, without year, but probably 1948. Vol. 207, ME18, 1400BA, YIVO.

[250] http://www.yivoencyclopedia.org/article.aspx/Erlich_Henryk (20190617).

organizers of the Bund's trade union activities among the Polish Jewish working class.[251] As Secretary General of the Central Council of the Jewish Trade Unions in Poland, he worked with Erlich to secure the Bund's accession to the Socialist International, and was one of the harshest critics of the Stalinist terror and Moscow trials of the 1930s. After the outbreak of war in 1939, both Erlich and Alter entered the Soviet occupation zone, and were arrested by the security police for anti-Soviet activities. After years of interrogation and torture, they were sentenced to death in the summer of 1941, just as the German war machine was rolling into the Soviet Union. Hoping to mobilize Jewish resistance and international support against the invasion, they were suddenly released, together with Jewish cultural activists and others, to organize the Soviet Jewish Anti-Fascist Committee. It was a short reprieve. After giving their names to the initiative, they were once more arrested. In 1942, after brutal interrogations, Erlich hanged himself; Alter was shot in February 1943, accused of being a Nazi agent.

For the Bund, the fate of the two leaders reflected the very essence of the bestial nature of the communist project and the irreconcilable contradiction between what the Bundists saw as socialism and communism. Articles, brochures, posters, and memorial ceremonies on the theme "Erlich and Alter" were integral parts of pointing out the profound ideological differences. Naturally, the national meeting in August 1948 began with a moment of silence for those fallen members of the Bund, with Erlich and Alter the main names. The Bund regarded the death sentences of 1941 as the starting point for the policy of remembrance, and by the tenth anniversary of 1951, great efforts had been made to draw international attention to the murdered Bundist leaders. *Unzer Tsayt's* publisher republished a book of remembrance which, according to Sara Mehr, all Bundists should read: "it should be as sacred to Bundists as the Bible is to the religious."[252] The Swedish Bundists even seem to have planned to publish their own volume, including personal memoirs from Bundists in Sweden, but apparently without success.[253] Olberg sent a memoir by the Socialist International's Secretary General Julius Braunthal to about thirty Social Democratic newspapers in Sweden, with the hope of getting the leading social democrats Gustav Möller, Zeth Höglund and Ture Nerman to write

[251] http://www.yivoencyclopedia.org/article.aspx/Alter_Wiktor (20190617).

[252] Letter from Sara Mehr to Novogrodski, November 27, 1951. Vol. 93, ME18, 1400BA, YIVO. The book was the third edition of *Henrik Erlikh and Viktor Alter, a lebn fun kemfer, a toyt fun martirer* (Henryk Erlich and Viktor Alter, a life of struggle, a death of martyrdom), New York, 1943.

[253] "Erlich-Alterboken", layout and content. Vol. 93, ME18, 1400BA, YIVO.

responses. They belonged, Sara Mehr remembered, to the generation that knew, and even had met, the Bundist leaders, unlike most leading Social Democrats who were in their forties and knew little about international issues. For her part, Mehr had tried to contact Möller, but "unfortunately" managed only to get as far as meeting his wife; "she watches over him like a hawk."[254] So, from Möller nothing happened. Mehr was, however, able to send to New York an article by Zeth Höglund and one by Ture Nerman.

Specific activities that structured the organization's memorial work were, of course, the First of May celebrations, and other events that were connected more generally to the international workers' movement's holidays, and, not infrequently, the birthdays of leading comrades.

Paul Olberg's seventieth birthday

One such occasion was Paul Olberg's seventieth birthday, at the end of November 1948. It became a matter not only for the Bund in Sweden but also for the International Coordinating Committee and JLC. In letters to her foreign comrades, Sara Mehr urged them to provide greetings, articles for the Bund's and other Yiddish press, as well as financial support.[255] In local Swedish groups, fundraisers were held, and congratulations were sent. The intention was not only to honor Olberg, but to make a political impression through as broad and massive a tribute as possible to the Bundist chairman in Sweden, who also represented several Jewish organizations such as the JLC, the Congress for Jewish Culture and ORT, the international organization for the promotion of Jewish vocational training.[256] To say that the celebration was successful would be an understatement. The celebration of Olberg brought together not only the Swedish and international Yiddish community, but a broad spectrum of Swedish social and political life.[257]

[254] Letter from Sara Mehr to Novogrodski, November 27, 1951. Letter from Novogrodski to Sara Mehr, November 19 and 30, 1951, with thanks for articles from Nerman and Höglund. Vol. 93, ME18, 1400BA, YIVO.

[255] Letter from Sara Mehr to Yankev Pat, October 21, 1948, with information about Olberg's upcoming 70th birthday and the need for financial support for the reception, which was estimated to cost 4–500 Swedish crowns. Letter from Sara Mehr to Novogrodski on November 5, 1948, about "major preparations for the 70th anniversary" with information about planned participants, also from the government and about an article in *Forverts*. Letter from Sara Mehr to Rafal Ryba about an article for *Unzer Shtime*. Letter from Sara Mehr to the International Coordinating Committee November 12, 1948, on Olberg's birthday and article to *Unzer tsait*. All letters in Vol. 206, ME18, 1400BA, YIVO.

[256] For ORT see https://www.ort.org/ (20190612). During these years, Olberg was ORT's Swedish representative. In Paul Olberg's personal archive, PO 435, ARAB contains a large number of ORT's Swedish archive documents during some of the post-war years.

[257] Greetings in Olberg's archive. Vol. 25 PO 435, ARAB.

First of May

Eskilstuna reported to New York on the First of May demonstration of 1948: After the demonstration, "in which our members participated," the Bundists gathered "for a traditional Swedish cup of coffee in a friendly atmosphere." Comrade Morocco spoke of the First of May tradition and the threat of war, and stated that socialism meant peace – but not at any cost. "If freedom is at stake, we will be on the side that defends freedom." He believed that the Jewish people could only have equal rights in a free socialist society. "Bundist stubbornness and honest belief in the victory of socialism give us the courage to continue our Bundist work," Morocco concluded.[258]

In Vetlanda, about forty members from the region gathered in a private apartment for the May celebrations of 1948. Comrade Operman spoke about how the Bund had celebrated the First of May in Poland before the war and Obranshka about the history of the celebrations. Vetlanda's new Bundist banner was unveiled by Comrade Chezes, who said that, in 1939, *Tsukunft's* flag had to be buried in Grodno so that the Germans would not get hold of it. Throughout the war, he dreamed of returning there and digging it up. Finally, when he did manage to return, no one was left to help him. Now his dream had partly come true. What followed these talks was a dinner with entertainment, with the evening ending with a rendition of *The Internationale*.[259]

In Trelleborg, a report from the newly formed Bund group's First of May banquet in 1949 noted a fine atmosphere with a speech by Comrade Borenstein from Malmö about the importance of the day for the labor movement as a whole and for Jewish socialists in particular. The eleven assembled *khaveyrim* sang revolutionary Bundist songs "that took us back to the old atmosphere."[260] The following year, the groups in Trelleborg, Malmö and Landskrona held a joint First of May celebration in Malmö, perhaps in the People's house; the place is not noted, only that the large hall was decorated with banners for a free socialist world. About sixty Bundists listened to the opening speech by Comrade Schneidman and to Borenstein's speech on the history of the First of May celebrations. Comrade Sukienik from Landskrona recited poetry, after

[258] Report from the Bund group in Eskilstuna to the International Coordinating Committee, without year, but possibly 1948. Vol. 207, ME18, 1400BA, YIVO.

[259] Minutes, Vetlanda, May 1, 1948, Vol. 213, ME18, 1400BA, YIVO. Report in *Unzer shtime*, April 14, 1948.

[260] Minutes taken at a meeting with the Bund group in Trelleborg, May 1, 1949, Archives of the Bund group, Trelleborg, Sweden, Vol. 215, ME18, 1400BA, YIVO.

which dinner was served, and then a dance "to a phonograph" took place before everyone went home "in good spirits."[261]

After the May Day celebrations in Stockholm in 1949, the Bundists began discussing their participation in the day's demonstrations. The Stockholm Bund group had, through contact with the Social Democrats, been given a good place, almost in front of the demonstration; their comrades from Uppsala had also been invited to attend.[262] The group had gathered outside the People's House with a banner with the text *Zol lebn di yidishe shprakh un kultur* – Long live Yiddish Language and Culture – in both Yiddish and Swedish. After the demonstration, as at previous May Day celebrations, the members would gather for tea. But this year would be different. At a subsequent board meeting, it was established that fewer people participated in both the demonstration and the tea.[263] "The slogan on the banner was not such a good choice," criticized one of the members. On the contrary, another said, it was precisely the question that was now "the most important thing in our work," while Olberg stated that the support largely corresponded to the group's ability. However, he also mentioned the "indescribable fact" that some young members had refused to carry the banner and just stood by and watched![264]

One year after the advent of Israel, the loss of the Polish Bund and the deepening of the Cold War, Bundists experienced how their ranks, which had previously been so energetically organized, were already beginning to thin. "Our numbers are 'systematically' dwindling", said one of those who had most recently arrived from Poland, Avrom Sobol, but a *Tsukunft* group had to be established to inform the young. "Can we try to gather Bundists from the country in Stockholm in order to keep the Bund home in Kumla?" Wasserstrom asked. "No, we cannot expect more people to come to Stockholm," Olberg replied. Even in Vetlanda, it was noted after the First of May, 1949 that "our work has become weaker."[265] The banquet had admittedly been successful. Representatives of the Swedish Social Democrats and the trade union movement had participated, and one of the Bundists, Comrade Rosenblum, had even given a speech in Swedish! After several hours at set tables, everyone

[261] Minutes, meeting No. 36 with the Bund group in Trelleborg, May 1, 1950, Archives of the Bund group, Trelleborg, Sweden, Vol. 215, ME18, 1400BA, YIVO.
[262] Minutes, Bund Stockholm Board, April 22, 1949. Letter from Olberg to Bund Uppsala, April 27, 1949 with an invitation to the First of May celebration in Stockholm. Vol. 211, ME18, 1400BA, YIVO.
[263] Minutes, Bund Stockholm Board, May 13, 1949. Vol. 211, ME18, 1400BA, YIVO.
[264] Ibid.
[265] Minutes, Bund Vetlanda Board, June 5, 1949. Vol. 213, ME18, 1400BA, YIVO.

sang *Di Shvue*.[266] A problem was that fewer comrades had attended, albeit only a slight decline to thirty-five from forty the year before, but, perhaps more worryingly, the board was concerned about "passivity," as was the case for example in Huskvarna. In a report to Rafal Ryba at the Bund's European Secretariat in Paris, which had been urgently requested since the past summer, Olberg gave a rather gloomy picture.[267] The delay in the report, he explained, was because the organization's secretary, Elenbogen, had become politically enervated. In recent months, the "old guard," the comrades who arrived during the first year after the war, had left Sweden, most of them for Canada. Elsewhere in the archival material, there are invitations to farewell parties.[268] In a subsequent report to Ryba just a month later, Olberg was even gloomier.[269] After giving an account of several important efforts by the Bund and JLC in Sweden, he raised several problems in an almost depressed tone. Most members were only interested in emigrating as soon as possible. Even though some had been living in Sweden for three years, they had not tried to place their roots there, or to learn Swedish, and because they did not know the language, it became difficult to get a job. In addition, some had declared themselves Bundists "without really believing in Bundism." Therefore, they did not pay their membership fees, so it was difficult to finance activities and manage fees to New York. Quite a few of the supporters, Olberg said, "only stay in our organization as long as they get something out of it." He himself preferred a smaller organization of real and committed socialists, of people who could be trusted.

As in other countries, there were, Olberg continued, only a few comrades who had a good socialist education, but even they felt that their stay in Sweden was temporary, thus not devoting enough time and effort to party work. What was missing was idealism and – money! Now three more experienced Bundists from Poland had arrived, Wolf Goldberg, Avrom Sobol and Sziah Szechatow. "Most comrades here do not like them, but they are actually the only ones I can trust to get things done." Latecomers could sometimes be met with suspicions of communist sympathies. The forty-five-year-old tailor Sobol, who was part of the leadership of a clothing union in Warsaw, had fled to the Soviet Union

266 Minutes, Vetlanda, May 1, 1949, Vol. 213, ME18, 1400BA, YIVO.

267 Letter from Olberg to the Bund's European Secretariat in Paris, March 9, 1949. Vol. 207, ME18, 1400BA, YIVO.

268 Minutes, Bund Stockholm, March 16, 1949, farewell party for Klepfisz and Feiner, Vol. 211, ME18, 1400BA, YIVO, and invitation form to the farewell meeting at the ABF (Association for Labour and Adult Education) building in Stockholm, March 26, 1949, Vol. 207, ME18, 1400BA, YIVO.

269 Letter from Olberg to Rafal Ryba, Paris, April 29, 1949, Vol. 206, ME18, 1400BA, YIVO.

after the Germans attacked, but was placed in a camp.[270] Despite his and others' many years of activities in the Bund, Olberg added, as in all emigration, people continued to fight unnecessarily with each other. Writing letters to them was not enough; "if I could just take the time to talk to them, I might be able to calm them down." But worse was, he said, the pressure from Zionist organizations and the Swedish Jewish community, who could hardly wait until they had to stop supporting Jewish refugees. Now that JOINT – the American United Jewish Distribution Committee for Emergency Relief – had reduced its contributions, the Jewish community had also reduced its assistance, and the "first victim was Yiddish culture." Still, most of the members had jobs and were members of trade unions; they earned a good living, and had all the rights that Swedish social policy offered.[271]

The experienced new comrades who arrived from Poland brought with them "heated discussions" and sharp criticism of the Polish Bund's development, a critique that apparently also hit some of the later arrivals.[272] In Stockholm, one of them refused to be elected to the board, as those who arrived earlier "think that the newcomers from Poland are bad."[273] As an explanation for the lack of optimism, Olberg explained: "Everywhere, our groups must take into account the fact that the Zionists have the upper hand, they have large sums of money and the ability to run broad campaigns."[274] He himself hoped that the World Congress for Yiddish Culture would send a well-known representative and ally on a visit to Sweden; after all, the Zionists had large gatherings with international representation "every week and even twice a week!"

World Congress for Yiddish Culture

The *Alveltlekher yidisher kultur-kongres* – the World Congress for Yiddish Culture – initiated by the international Bund in 1948, took an important place in the Bundists' local activities in Sweden as well.[275] The organization was

[270] Information from *Lebns-fragn* 1982, by Leo Greenbaum, YIVO.

[271] Letter from Olberg to Rafal Ryba, Paris, April 29, 1949, Vol. 206, ME18, 1400BA, YIVO.

[272] Letter from Olberg to the Bund's European Secretariat in Paris, March 9, 1949. Vol. 207, ME18, 1400BA, YIVO. In the spring of 1949, the Bund in Stockholm held several party meetings on the Bund in Poland, for example on April 9, 1949, where the debate was settled with the first speech in 10 minutes and the second speech in 5 minutes. Minutes, Bund Stockholm, April 9, 1949. Vol. 211, ME18, 1400BA, YIVO.

[273] It is Avrom Sobol that is referenced. Protocol Bund Stockholm, February 25, 1949. Vol. 211, ME18, 1400BA, YIVO.

[274] Letter from Olberg to the Bund's European Secretariat in Paris, March 9, 1949. Vol. 207, ME18, 1400BA, YIVO.

[275] For the World Congress of Yiddish Culture, see: http://congressforjewishculture.org/ (20190623).

officially formed by Jewish writers and intellectuals, but behind the project was the Bund's efforts to defend and spread Yiddish against assimilation, as well as the Hebraization that accompanied the success of Zionism and the establishment of the state of Israel. Olberg reported to Ryba in Paris that all work in Sweden prior to the formation of the Culture Congress had been carried out "under the leadership of our organization."[276] Local cultural associations, such as *Arbeter-Ring* in Malmö and Stockholm or *Kultur-Vinkl* in Uppsala, like the Bund group's cultural activities in general, were linked to the Culture Congress, whose Swedish chairman was none other than Paul Olberg.[277] Their activities included concerts, theater performances and poetry evenings, with readings of the greats of Yiddish literature, such as Y. L. Peretz, Mordkhe Gebirtig and Sholem Aleichem.[278]

Contacts with the Swedish labor movement

For the international Bund, it was obvious that the Bund groups in different countries would join the parties of the re-created Socialist International. In the Swedish context, as we have seen time and time again in circulars and at membership meetings, it was emphasized that the groups must contact the local Social Democrats and the trade union movement to foster collaborations and to exchange experiences. The difficulty, however, was the language, "so they cannot attend the meetings," Olberg explained in a report.[279] It was mainly through Olberg's, and to some extent Sara Mehr's, connections with leading Social Democratic circles that the Bund in Sweden could be legitimized in the eyes of local labor constituencies and trade unions. Olberg put in a great deal of effort to getting the International Coordinating Committee in New York to send congratulatory telegrams to the Swedish Social Democratic party's anniversaries and its leaders' birthdays – as well as, by the same token, reminding Swedish Social Democratic leaders to send greetings to international Bund events, not to mention supporting the Bund's membership applications to both Comisco and the Socialist International. Locally, some basic contact was

[276] Letter from Olberg to the Bund's European Secretariat in Paris, March 9, 1949. Vol. 207, ME18, 1400BA, YIVO.

[277] In a letter from the World Congress for Jewish Culture in April 1950 [undated], the activities are presented with Paul Olberg as chairman of the Swedish department. Vol. 213, ME18, 1400BA, YIVO.

[278] See, for example, undated program sheet with readings from YL Perets ("Three Gifts"), Mordkhe Gebirtig, ("It Hurts", "Krakow Ghetto" and "Motele"), Simkhe-Bunem Shayevitsh ("Get Out"), Leyb Olitski ("The Brown Porridge"), Yisroel Ashendorf ("Cyprus" and "Monologue from an Arrival in Sweden"), Menachem Mendl ("Emigrant"), Motl Peysye ("Kantorn's son") and more. Vol. 206, ME18, 1400BA, YIVO.

[279] Letter from Olberg to Rafal Ryba, Paris, April 29, 1949. Vol. 206, ME18, 1400BA, YIVO.

maintained. The groups were able to demonstrate with the Social Democrats on the First of May, hold meetings in the People's House, and sometimes they managed to invite representatives of local labor organizations to some memorial events.

Perhaps the most extensive local cooperation, setting apart contacts within Stockholm, probably took place in Trelleborg, the furthest south. The young Bundist group in Trelleborg, which was formed by former members of *Tsukunft* and where everyone worked at the rubber factory, seems to have been particularly active. In particular, the group tried to forge ties with the Social Democratic Youth Association, SSU (*Sveriges Socialdemokratiska Ungdomsförbund*), in this case with Trelleborg's SDUK (*Socialdemokratiska ungdomsklubb*). In the minutes about membership and board meetings, they would relay information about their close contacts in the following way:

> October 30, 1949, Anniversary celebration in the presence of SAP [the Social Democratic Party], SSU and the Swedish Public Employment Service
> February 19, 1950, Planning a meeting with SAP
> March 4, 1950, Rubinowich reported from the meeting with SAP
> March 18, 1950, Swedish comrade has been invited to lecture about SAP's history
> April 19, 1950, Article about Bund published in Arbetet [daily Social Democratic paper "Labor" in Southern Sweden].
> May 27, 1950, Greetings from Henry Nilsson [chairman of Social Democratic youth group Frihet, "Freedom"] to Vajskopf [representative of the Bund group].
> Undated Greetings from our group at a meeting to honor SSU Trelleborg before the international youth camp.
> May 28, 1950, Proposal from SSU for a joint board meeting.
> June 17, 1950, Report from our last meeting with SSU.
> June 21, 1950, SSU wants joint meetings.
> July 2, 1950, Cooperation with SSU was discussed.
> July 29, 1950, Impressions from the international youth camp in Stockholm.

However, notes in the minutes about cooperation with Swedish organizations were considerably sparser. There are, for example, no entries in the minutes of the social democratic youth club in Trelleborg during the period.[280] The youth club's annual report for 1950, however, states that some discussions had been held during the summer at the "summer home" – a colony cottage in a communal allotment garden in the northern part of Trelleborg – "including with

[280] According to archivist Christel Winberg at Arbetarrörelsens Arkiv [Workers' Movement's Archive] in Trelleborg, February 22, 2016.

the Jewish soc. dem. group 'Bund.'"[281] A telegram from the "Jewish Social-Democratic group 'Bund' in Trelleborg" on the occasion of the SSU club's thirtieth anniversary is also preserved with the text: "For your thirtieth anniversary, we wish you success in your activities for the good of the entire socialist world."[282] In the minutes of Trelleborg's labor constituency board, a meeting with the Bundists in February 1950 is mentioned: "A committee from Polish Soc.Dem. group at Trelleborg's rubber factory had requested a meeting with the municipal board. This committee reported in a longer speech about the social democratic movement 'Bund' in Poland, the organization to which they belonged, i.e. the branch now functioning in Sweden. They wanted cooperation with the labor constituency because they felt isolated."[283] The chairman of the local Social Democrats had welcomed them to the meetings, "when they, as friends of the party and solidarity trade union members, could count on support from the constituency."[284] There is no mention in the minutes that the Bund was a Jewish organization, nor are there records of any continued contact. It thus seems to be mainly the Social Democratic youth club with which a certain collaboration developed.

The local page for Trelleborg in the newspaper *Arbetet* mentions the greeting from "Trelleborg's Jewish Social Democratic Group" to the Social Democratic youth club's thirtieth anniversary celebration, and that discussion evenings at the club's summer home were held on two occasions with "the Jewish comrades."[285] From the Social Democratic youth club's inaugural meeting in Trelleborg before the youth association's large international socialist summer camp in Stockholm in July 1950, *Arbetet* reported that a "Polish refugee" had given a "captivating speech."[286] Some members of the Bund group in Trelleborg also participated in the huge Stockholm camp as representatives of *Tsukunft*, with signs in Yiddish and active participation in

[281] Trelleborgs soc. dem. youth club FRIHET [Freedom], Annual Report 1950, p. 5. Arbetarrörelsens Arkiv [Workers' Movement's Archive], Trelleborg. Information about the colony cottage from Christel Winberg, February 22, 2016.

[282] Telegram to SDUK *Folkets hus* [People's House] Trelleborg, April 1, 1950 from the Jewish Social-Democratic group "Bund" in Trelleborg, Arbetarrörelsens Arkiv [Workers' Movement's Archive] in Trelleborg.

[283] Minutes kept at a meeting with the Board of Trelleborg's labor constituency on February 20, 1950, Arbetarrörelsens Arkiv [Workers' Movement's Archive] in Trelleborg.

[284] Ibid.

[285] *Arbetet*, April 3, 1950 "SDUK Frihet in Trelleborg celebrated a magnificent 30th anniversary party" and *Arbetet*, June 1, 1950 the notice "Trelleborgs SDUK Frihet" which states that the discussion evenings were arranged on June 13 and 19, 1950.

[286] *Arbetet*, May 27, 1950 "SDUK Frihet had a successful opening meeting".

discussions.[287] Just before the international youth camp, the Bundists had been particularly pleased with a political effort in Trelleborg. The Swedish Communist Party held a large meeting in the city with a leading communist as speaker.[288] "After listening to his speech about the father of the people," that is, Stalin, the Bundists resolutely intervened, according to a report to New York. "With our weak knowledge of Swedish, we told the truth and received applause." The applause may have come from members of the Social Democratic youth, who, according to the report, were happy that the young people of *Tsukunft* wanted to help them study communism and Soviet Russia and democracy in the East and West.[289]

[287] Report from the Social Democratic youth camp to Bund Trelleborg. Vol. 215, ME18, 1400BA, YIVO.
[288] Report from the Bund Trelleborg to the International Coordinating Committee, July 10, 1950. Vol. 215, ME18, 1400BA, YIVO.
[289] Vajskopf also contacted Olberg and asked for literature on communism and the Soviet Union for the meetings. Letter from Vajskopf to Olberg, June 21, 1950, letter from Olberg to Vajskopf with tips on books, 23 June, 1950. Vol. 215, ME18, 1400BA, YIVO.

Ordeals

Personal difficulties

Behind the Bundists' intense political and cultural activities were at the same time difficult personal experiences, often with both mental and physical consequences, illnesses, sorrows, and worries. In addition to the refugee community's often fatiguing everyday worries. Through letters and minutes, there is hope for help and support with everything from contacts with family and friend to health care, jobs, housing and other things besides.

"Two of our families in Gränna [a small town in the south] are hungry because the hotel wants to get rid of them, Comrade Mehr must intervene personally," was an appeal made directly to Olberg.[290] "Dear Comrade Mehr," wrote another, "perhaps you remember our talking when you were here about my employer, who did not pay for my vacation, and my wife, who sewed for his pregnant wife, but did not get paid. [...] We ask you, if possible, to help us with things for the children. With my current income, it is not possible."[291] From the small town of Tyringe, further south, a woman wrote to the Stockholm group that she was in a desperate situation. "We have no money for food for our son. We were robbed at the Polish border, and everything was taken from me." She was disappointed in Sweden: "We would have been better off in a Polish prison," and hoped to get money for a trip to Stockholm.[292] "We have two sick comrades whom we must help, and we cannot afford to pay *Unzer Tsayt*," was an emergency call from Vetlanda. The wife of a man who had undergone surgery must work to earn a little, and asked, "What do we do with the children?."[293] From Vetlanda, comrades also appealed for help with housing for several members who managed to find work at a factory, but the employer's attempt to sort things out was hampered by rumors spreading "that our comrades are cheating" and reflecting badly on all Bundists.[294]

Avram Stolar, editor of *Unzer Tsayt*, hoped to get Sara Mehr's help for a comrade in Łódź.[295] He had had his foot amputated and needed a prosthesis from Stockholm. But Olberg explained that the comrade then had to travel to

[290] Letter from Obranshka, Mullsjö, April 28, 1948 to Olberg. Vol. 209, ME18, 1400BA, YIVO.
[291] Letter from Spiro and his wife in Vetlanda, June 29, 1948 to Sara Mehr. Vol. 209, ME18, 1400BA, YIVO.
[292] Letter from K in Tyringe to Zelig Wasserstrom in Stockholm. Undated. Vol. 206, ME18, 1400BA, YIVO.
[293] Letter from Obranshka to Olberg, May 23, 1949. Vol. 206, ME18, 1400BA, YIVO.
[294] Letter from Chezes in Vetlanda to Sara Mehr, June 5, 1948. Vol. 206, ME18, 1400BA, YIVO.
[295] Letter from A Stolar to Sara Mehr, December 28, 1948. Vol. 206, ME18, 1400BA, YIVO.

Stockholm; how would he pay for it? This also applied to travel and subsistence for wife and children. The American JLC had promised to provide fifty percent, but, explained Stolar, the Bund in Sweden must account for the other half. "Most of our members in Sweden have work and income, so it is their duty to regularly contribute the appropriate amount to help a comrade in such a tragic situation." In New York, Stolar announced, the Bundists had created a support fund to help comrades in dire need by deducting 2 percent of each working member's income.

Loneliness

However, the overriding problem that recurs in both personal letters and from local group discussions, is loneliness; the lack of a sense of community belonging to Jewish communities, and the difficulty for members to move together into larger communities. As a representative of both the JLC and the Bund, Olberg could not possibly respond to the exorbitant number of letters at the pace for which desperate comrades hoped. "Your silence upsets me. If I have hurt your feelings, please forgive me ," wrote a sick friend from Filipstad, in western Sweden, who said that in receiving a letter from Olberg, he could forget the nightmares of yesterday and the unhappy present for at least a few minutes.[296] He was in a foreign land, estranged from his family and friends, physically and morally broken. But then the letter had arrived, and Olberg's warm words filled him with both joy and courage. The letter was accompanied by newspapers in which political issues were discussed in the spirit of socialism and "our dear Bundism." But then he added: "This little ray of light has disappeared from my sad life… All that remains is the gray, monotonous reality."[297]

At the same time, another comrade from Malmö, the then recently arrived Henryk Levkovich, who was to become a leader in the Swedish Bundist organization, wrote: "I cannot understand why I did not receive an answer from you. Are you really so busy that you do not have ten minutes to write a letter to me?"[298] He was the only one in his family who survived; he suffered from water in his lungs and could not work: "I have no family, all I have is you." He appealed for more letters, and for a greeting on his name day. From the village of Bjärnum in the south, a Bundist expressed despair in a letter to comrades in Trelleborg, writing that he and his wife had participated in the Warsaw ghetto uprisings, were sent to Majdanek and then to Auschwitz. Now

[296] Letter from Filipstad, March 3, 1946 to Paul Olberg. Box 36, folder 24, reel 105, ser. III, JLC, TAMWAG.

[297] Ibid.

[298] Letter from Levkovich, Malmö, March 1, 1946 to Paul Olberg. Box 36, folder 24, reel 105, ser. III, JLC, TAMWAG.

for two years they had been "stuck" with a small child in Bjärnum, and were the only Jewish family in the area. "My wife and I are young people, not yet thirty, we have always lived in big cities with party members in a Jewish environment, and now we simply live in a prison without bars." He appealed for help in moving in with comrades elsewhere. "Dear comrades, believe me, I will lose my mind out of loneliness without my own people around me, without familiar surroundings," and signed with "Your comrade in desperation."[299] Paul Olberg and the management in Stockholm were severely criticized for not working hard enough for such a move.

"There is a large group of Bundists in Sweden who are spread across the country," underlined a resolution from the young group in Trelleborg, who probably did not know the extent of the work that rested on so few shoulders. "They all live with memories of their past. They are not allowed to move together to just a few cities, so they are far apart, far from comrades who could comfort them in moments of grief and spur them on to act. Bundists feel orphaned. Nothing has been done to establish contact so that we can exchange ideas. This is the result of your work so far, comrades!"[300] For Olberg and Mehr, such criticism must have felt painfully unfair, and Olberg referred to Swedish rules for refugees that did not allow such relocation.[301]

For some, life itself and hopes ended in Swedish sanatoriums and the wait for recovery. "Honor the memory of the seventeen-year-old Mariem Frank from Romania," wrote a female Bundist from the sanatorium in Halmstad, where many Jewish women were cared for after arriving in Sweden.[302] The girl had been torn away from her parents and relatives in Auschwitz, and survived nineteen months in Bergen-Belsen until liberation. "I sat by Mariem's bed and stroked her sweaty forehead to comfort her." Ten minutes before her death, "she asked me to sing a song of freedom and said [...], 'I can forget the hold that death has on me, sing'... 'We are building a new world, the old one no longer exists.'" Mariem Frank, in the words of the letter writer a silent intelligent and innocent child who was no longer afraid of anything, was forced to unite with hundreds of sisters who did not survive. "May her childlike face with

[299] Letter from YV to Vajskopf, December 7, 1949. Vol. 215, ME18, 1400BA, YIVO.
[300] To the Bund's National Committee in Sweden from meeting with the group in Trelleborg, October 5, 1949. Vol. 215, ME18, 1400BA, YIVO.
[301] See letter dated September 18, 1948, from Olberg to Levkovich in Malmö about negotiations with the Ministry of Labor and the "strict order" that "our members" from Germany and Poland may not stay in Stockholm, Malmö or Gothenburg. It is, Olberg emphasizes, the county labor boards who decide on a place where the refugees can live and work. Vol. 216, ME18, 1400BA, YIVO.
[302] Letter from Hella Rudnitska to "Dear Comrades", February 22, 1946. Vol. 207, ME18, 1400BA, YIVO.

the sad smile become a reflection of the world from the great catastrophe of the war. May the image of her last minutes in life, her emaciated legs, ravaged skin, the long skinny face with all the wrinkles of a centenarian, [...], the blue lips, the long narrow nose and the big beautiful dark eyes, never be forgotten!"[303]

Sara Mehr sent obituaries to *Unzer Shtime* in Paris with texts about comrades who had died "after a long illness." Among the Stockholm group's documents are letters to "all members", with stock phrases such as: "We are sorry to announce that the wife of...", stating the time of the funeral and where the Bundists would gather.[304] One autumn day in 1948, Olberg had to announce to the Bund groups around the country that "Our dear comrade Faiga Falz died on Wednesday, November 10, in Västerås at the age of twenty after a long illness." All comrades were urged to show the young *Tsukunft* comrade their deep respect by attending the funeral at the Jewish cemetery in Stockholm.[305]

Organizational difficulties

The organizational difficulties for the Bund in Sweden were, of course, almost insurmountable. Virtually all activities took place through the voluntary efforts of refugees who had been through catastrophic events who lacked not only material resources but roots in a foreign society. Only Paul Olberg, Sara Mehr and, it seems, one other comrade mastered Swedish.[306] A number were probably able to communicate in German, while opportunities for speaking Yiddish were rare. Through contacts with the Swedish Social Democrats, the People's House could be booked cheaply or, it seems, often free of charge. The financing of housing, as well as some emergency aid did not come from the Bund, but from JLC, which also financed Olberg's refugee work.[307] The Bundists in Sweden would, however, contribute five hundred dollars annually to the International Coordinating Committee, carry out subscription and fundraising campaigns for *Unzer Tsayt* and *Unzer Shtime* and to support comrades in

[303] Ibid.

[304] Letter from Sara Mehr to *Unzer Shtime* in Paris, July 28, 1949. "Please publish these three obituaries...". Circulars to "all members", July 1949. Vol. 206, ME18, 1400BA, YIVO.

[305] Circular November 1948. Vol. 206, ME18, 1400BA, YIVO.

[306] "*Khaver* Rosenblum" in Vetlanda also seems, according to archive information, to have mastered some Swedish.

[307] According to Olberg's self-declarations for taxation 1946–49, he was remunerated as secretary of JLC with 500 kronor a month (about $1100 in today's value) plus pension contributions at least during the period October–December 1945 up until 1948. "General self-declaration for taxation" 1946, 1947, 1948, 1949. Vol. 26 and 30, PO 435, ARAB.

difficulty both in Sweden and in other countries. The demands for collections and assessments became increasingly high into the 1950s.

The International Coordinating Committee appealed not only for increased support, but above all for payment of what was already budgeted. The committee attached its entire international budget to show what needs must wholly be met.[308] *Unzser Tsayt* announced that the newspaper now completely lacked the support of American Jewish organizations and therefore was entirely dependent on its subscribers. "Even though published in rich America, it is a publication without funds," wrote the editor Avram Stolar in a call to Mehr asking her to collect four dollars from each subscriber.[309] *Unzer Shtime* in Paris announced that support from readers – through an extensive subscription and fundraising campaign – was literally about the newspaper's survival. "It's not a cliché, but the absolute truth. *Unzer Shtime* can only continue to be published if the campaign is successful. For years, we have struggled to save money, but our finances have never been as bad as they are now."[310] In addition, aid was collected for Bundists in the DP camps and, from 1951, for comrades in Israel, who were in dire need for support.[311] Members were also expected to contribute to the Swedish Social Democrats' election fund, Folke Bernadotte's memorial fund, Olberg's birthday, and the many local cultural and memorial events.

Who is a member?

The financial pressure on members who at the same time were struggling with everyday expenses could not have been insignificant. As a result, the issue of membership fees was an object of discussion. In Vetlanda, the group's founding meeting in March 1948 decided on one Swedish crown per member per month.[312] A year later, the Trelleborg group doubled the fee, though decided at

[308] Letter from Novogrodski to the Bund in Sweden, January 17, 1951 with the World Coordinating Committees budget for 1951. Vol. 210, ME18, 1400BA, YIVO.

[309] Letter from A Stolar to Sara Mehr, December 28, 1948. Also, letter from *Unzer Tsaits* E Sherer and Stolar, February 11, 1949: "Unzer Tsait no longer receives subsidies from American organizations because we are independent of American organizations and of Israel. That is why we are dependent on our comrades around the world". Vol. 207, ME18, 1400BA, YIVO.

[310] Circular from *Unzer Shtime*, Paris, October, 1952: "Campaign for Bund's only daily newspaper". Vol. 207, ME18, 1400BA, YIVO.

[311] See, for example, the call from Novogrodski to the Bund in Sweden, June 29, 1949 "Dear friends! In Israel, there are now several hundred Bundists from DP camps. We set up cultural homes for old and new members. Help our comrades in Israel financially!" Vol. 211, ME18, 1400BA, YIVO. The Circular to the Bund in Sweden in 1951 urges: "Over 600 Bundists go hungry in Israel. We Bundists in Sweden can help, 25 kronor per package". Vol. 210, ME18, 1400BA, YIVO.

[312] Minutes, Vetlanda, March 28, 1948. Vol. 213, ME18, 1400BA, YIVO.

the same time that "active participation" should be the basis for membership, not fees.[313] When, in the autumn of 1949, printed membership cards – copied from the Social Democratic Party' but with text in Yiddish for the "Jewish Social Democratic Union 'BUND' in Sweden" – were dispatched, Olberg insisted that the cards could only be issued to paying members.[314] Olberg had membership card number 1, with stamps on the cards designating fee payments – though only a few months into the 1950s, the routine of stamping the card might have stopped.[315] From time to time, the registers were cleared of members who were neither active nor paying their membership fee. The issue of comrades' passivity was a constant source of irritation and board criticism.

"Everything is on me, from the smallest task to the largest," Obranshka in Vetlanda complained to Sara Mehr. "The other members are doing me a favor if they even come."[316] And for some, everyday life and family took over completely. "Especially now, when they have a nice apartment, what do they need us for?," Obranshka sighed.[317] In addition, there were questions about reliability. Who was the person, what did he or she do during the war? Was it an honest Bundist or just someone who sought financial help from JLC? The source material contains several examples of mistrust of membership applications, suspicions of treason during the war years: some were alleged to have been a policeman in the ghetto, some a communist.[318] Such was the recurring ambiguity in the relationship between the Bund and the JLC.

Members were repeatedly informed that they must distinguish between the two addressees in letters.[319] After the American JLC's position on Israel, this became even more important, especially since the JLC supported not only Bundists but also other Jewish socialists, such as the Labor Zionist Left, Linke

[313] Minutes, Bund Trelleborg, Meeting No. 1, April 24, 1949. Vol. 215, ME18, 1400BA, YIVO.

[314] Letter from the Bund group in Trelleborg to the National Committee, February 28, 1950: "Our delegate to the National Committee tried to convince you that payment of membership fees cannot constitute a basis for membership without activity, participation. We hope that the decision does not apply to us." Vol. 215, ME18, 1400BA, YIVO. The Vetlanda group had a different attitude: "We think that those who do not pay should not get a membership card either because everyone who works here can afford it." Letter from Obranshka to Sara Mehr, August 2, 1949. Vol. 211, ME18, 1400BA, YIVO.

[315] Membership card No. 1. Vol. 1, PO 435, ARAB.

[316] Letter from Obranshka to Sara Mehr, August 2, 1949. Vol. 211, ME18, 1400BA, YIVO.

[317] Ibid.

[318] Paul Olberg's personal archive contains documents from the so-called "Masur case", when Olberg warned of a refugee from *Linke Poalei Zion,* accused by a woman of collaboration during the war years. Strong demands were made from the leftwing Zionists that the refugee should be cleared of false accusations, and that Olberg should rescind his earlier accusations or alternatively be brought before a party court. Olberg maintained however that the information was trustworthy. Vol. 9, PO 435, ARAB.

[319] For example, letter from Sara Mehr chairman and Wasserstrom secretary to the local groups, July 9, 1948, "Separate letters to the Bund and JLC – until now, the Bund and JLC have worked closely together, now we hope there will be a clearer separation." Vol. 209, ME18, 1400BA, YIVO.

Poalei Zion. However, this distinction was not the easiest to maintain. The address of the two organizations was, as noted, the same. Olberg was employed by JLC, but at the same time was chairman of the Bund in Sweden; he even mixed up the letterheads. The fact that he was also chairman of the Swedish section of the World Congress for Yiddish Culture and ORT's representative, as well as an influential Social Democrat and diligent publicist, did not diminish the uncertainty about his role – perhaps not even to himself. When was Olberg performing tasks for JLC and the Bund, and when was he fulfilling his other responsibilities?

His great work in mediating contacts, seeking visas, arranging work and housing, visiting sanatoriums and camps, at the same time as he led the Bund's operations in Sweden, conducting correspondence and speaking at meetings, keeping in touch with local groups and New York and the European Secretariat in Paris, working for *Unzer Shtime*, as well as his writing for the Social Democratic and other press, as well as in book form … in what capacity did he do what, and when? Having said this, in practice, many members perceived the JLC and the Bund as roughly the same thing; others though were annoyed by the lack of separation. As a source of conflict, role confusion was an especially contentious issue.

The decay

With the Korean War and the threat of a third world war, there followed almost a panic among Bundists in Sweden. One report claimed: "Everyone wants to leave and go as far away from Europe as possible."[320] For most Jewish refugees, Sweden had been considered a transit country on the way to relatives and friends in other countries – that is, exactly what the granted transit visa had required. At the same time, new US legislation in 1950 on the reception of displaced persons from Europe outside the current migration quotas seemed to open a door to the United States.[321] Olberg traveled around to the Bund groups to talk about international developments, informing them about the migration situation. The new opening also applied to Scandinavia, but it was difficult to be recognized as a "DP," and each candidate had to fill in a form with someone who certified the person's identity and guaranteed residence in the US (a so-called affidavit), and state their political opinion, i.e., swear they were not a communist.[322] Many tried to seize the opportunity.

The members drifted away to the United States, Canada, Argentina, Australia, and in some cases Israel. From Vetlanda, Obranshka wrote to Olberg back in the autumn of 1949 that only five families remained in the region, and that he himself was trying to get to Australia.[323] A friend from Poland, "a sensible man who knows what it is like in Sweden," had managed to get there. His cousin in Landskrona would also try, "but did not dare to bring it up with you, who have done so much to help us to Sweden." Obranshka thought it was a bit childish and was convinced that Olberg very well understood "what we are going through when we think about how close we are to that wolf," that is,

[320] Report from Perel, September 21, 1950, to *Facts and Opinion* in New York. Vol. 206, ME18, 1400BA, YIVO.
[321] US immigration legislation underwent several changes during the first post-war years. The "Displaced Persons Act" of 1948 introduced an immigration quota for a few hundred thousand adults and more than fifteen thousand orphaned children from war-torn Europe; a number that doubled in the summer of 1950, on the condition that the immigrant could present an affidavit for support in the United States. Through the so-called McCarran-Walter bill or the Immigration and Nationality Act two years later, American immigration policy moved to a more restrictive phase.
[322] Report from Perel, September 21, 1950, to *Facts and Opinion* in New York. Vol. 206, ME18, 1400BA, YIVO.
[323] Letter from Obranshka to Olberg November 4, 1949. Vol. 208, ME18, 1400BA, YIVO. A report from Obranshka and Chezes to the National Committee on March 12, 1950, on the activities in Vetlanda in 1949 states that several members have moved, and the group has been reduced to five families. Vol. 208, ME18, 1400BA, YIVO. An undated report on the financial year 1949 in the Vetlanda Group's archive material states that the group decreased "when members left for other cities" and that only 10 members remained in Vetlanda and 16 in the region. Vol. 213, ME18, 1400BA, YIVO.

the Soviet Union. In September 1950, the Bundists held their last meeting in Trelleborg; it was the forty-first recorded member meeting since the group had been formed the spring before.[324] In a resolution adopted by the six members present, to be sent to the national leadership in Stockholm, it was announced that only two members would now remain, and that this last meeting solemnly ended the activities there: "To the tune of *Di Shvue* we now sing, we promise you and all the other allies around the world that wherever we may be, we will stand by your side in our common struggle against our enemies, until the sun of freedom and justice shines. The names of those who sacrificed their lives for a better and brighter world will always be etched in our hearts."[325] In a separate letter to Olberg, Vajskopf wrote: "I'm sure you understand and are not angry at us," and in a postscript, he added: "Comrade Bornstein is leaving today, and we have sent our entire archives to New York."[326]

In the spring of 1950, the Malmö group reported that activity had stopped: "we have been doing almost nothing lately."[327] The remaining nine members were said not to be so interested in political meetings anymore, but all subscribed to *Unzer Shtime* and received another fifteen copies of *Unzer Tsayt* each month. A leading comrade had left "without giving reasons," and "unless the members become more active, we will have to close down the group." At a members' meeting, help was requested from the national leadership; "until then, we will not be active."[328] Some kind of temporary help was however forthcoming. Olberg, and Rafal Ryba from the European Secretariat, who planned to visit the Bund in Sweden, would come to the First of May festivities. So until then, at least some comrades could be involved in organizing a banquet.[329]

In the summer of 1950, Sara Mehr explained to Novogrodski that several comrades had left, so neither the Stockholm group nor the National Committee were functioning anymore. During his short visit, Rafal Ryba had seen

[324] Minutes, Bund group, Trelleborg, Meeting No. 41, September 17, 1950, Vol. 215, ME18, 1400BA, YIVO.

[325] Letter from Trelleborg to the national National Committee, September 17, 1950, with 6 signatories. Vol. 206, ME18, 1400BA, YIVO.

[326] Letter from Trelleborg to Olberg, September 24, 1950. In a letter from Olberg and Perel to Vajskopf, September 15, 1950, they regretted that they could not attend the closing meeting: "We are very sorry that your group is disbanded due to emigration. When you were active, you contributed a lot to deepening our work in Sweden". Vol. 206, ME18, 1400BA, YIVO.

[327] Report from Borenstein, Malmö, to the National Committee, March 26, 1950. Vol. 208, ME18, 1400BA, YIVO.

[328] Ibid.

[329] Letter from Perel in the National Committee, to Schneidman in Malmö about Olberg and Ryba's visit. Letter from Schneidman in Malmö. Vol. 208, ME18, 1400BA, YIVO.

that "the situation here is very serious."[330] A few months later, Perelmutter from Uppsala announced that only two comrades were left there, and that "most have left, not much remains in Sweden."[331] At the same time, Sukienik in Landskrona explained to *Unzer Tsayt* why there were so few subscribers: "With so many Jews leaving, it is increasingly difficult to conduct party work in Sweden. It is possible that I myself will leave for North America within a year." He had arranged for work and an apartment in Kansas City, and he wondered: "Are there many Jews there, and a Bund group, or something similar?"[332] From Gnacik in the Eskilstuna group, it was later reported that the local board had a meeting with only two members, "because a comrade is 'tired'."[333] The situation in Eskilstuna was "very serious." Members who were previously only slightly active have now become entirely passive. It was not, Gnacik thought, a question of politics, but rather it is about private circumstances, and "it is an incurable disease." He had written his letter with a heavy heart; he wanted the Bund group in Eskilstuna, "which was almost the best in Sweden," to survive. Now he wanted to try to convene the members one last time so that they themselves could decide what to do.[334] In New York, Novogrodski gradually received more and more Bundists from Sweden after the first generation of refugees had arrived. "We are happy to tell you that we are finally leaving Sweden to settle in New York," wrote a female comrade from Malmö on the way with MS *Gripsholm* and with thanks for all the help with the trip: " were it not for you, we would still be staying in Sweden."[335] And Novogrodski promised: "You will find a warm environment in New York."[336]

With the increasing flow of Bundists leaving Sweden, of course, the small Swedish organization weakened at a corresponding rate. Membership fees, subscription payments and fundraising results were affected. In addition, new collections from creative forces were added. In the late autumn of 1949, the Bundist *Arbeter-Ring* in Paris began work on a monument to honor the fallen

[330] Letter from Sara Mehr to Novogrodski, October 29, 1950. Vol. 93, ME18, 1400BA, YIVO.
[331] Letter from Ber Perelmutter to Novogrodski, April 24, 1950. Vol. 93, ME18, 1400BA, YIVO.
[332] Letter from Sukienik to Stolar, April 10, 1951, Stolar forwarded the question to Novogrodski who replied to Sukienik, April 24, 1951, that Kansas City was a large city but without a Bund organization. However, there were some Jews there, "once you are there, maybe you can form a Bund group." Vol. 93, ME18, 1400BA, YIVO.
[333] Letter from Gnacik to the Stockholm Board, October 9, 1952. Vol. 207, ME18, 1400BA, YIVO.
[334] Ibid. Olberg replied on October 13, 1952 that he understood the problems and that Goldberg would be sent to Eskilstuna for a meeting on October 18 to discuss the group's situation and the campaign for *Unzer Shtime*. Vol. 207, ME18, 1400BA, YIVO.
[335] Letter from Pesl Bernstein to Novogrodski, December 22, 1951. Vol. 93, ME18, 1400BA, YIVO.
[336] Letter from Novogrodski to Pesl Bernstein, December 27, 1951. Vol. 93, ME18, 1400BA, YIVO.

fighters of the Bund against Nazism.[337] The working group had received a suitable offer from a Swedish company specializing in granite. "We have asked you to raise money so that you can give us the granite as a gift. We are responsible for engraving, etc., which is also expensive," wrote Rafal Ryba to Olberg, and he wondered why Olberg did not answer.[338]

In Landskrona, five members had left the Malmö group in January 1950 due to a general sense of apathy within the branch.[339] In the autumn of 1950, a new group had been formed in the textile city of Borås, which included eleven members, most of them from Łódź, who seem initially to have been active.[340] But it was precisely in the autumn of 1950 that the number of members leaving and organizational difficulties increased. By the end of 1949, Obranshka had already reported from Vetlanda how difficult it was to campaign for *Unzer Shtime* with so few comrades left.[341] And Chezes responded to Olberg's calls to pay for more copies of the newspaper: "In Vetlanda, there are no other Jews."[342]

Novogrodski sent the increasingly strained and reduced budget of the International Coordinating Committee to the local Bundist organizations, emphasizing that the bulk of the costs simply had to be covered by sacrifices from members. It was not just Jewish organizations in the United States that had stopped contributing. June 1952 brought the death of the multimillionaire Frank Atran, who had donated a five-story building, the Atran Jewish Cultural House, to the JLC; the building also housed the Bund. Now that opportunity was endangered. "We ask you not to underestimate your obligations," the Bund in Sweden was urged, recalling the $500 annual fee that had long been set.[343]

Novogrodski's letters to Olberg became increasingly impatient. "I'm surprised that someone like you has cleared his conscience about not sending

[337] Letter about fundraising campaign for a monument in Paris to the fallen of the Bund, February 7, 1950. Vol. 208, ME18, 1400BA, YIVO.

[338] Letter from Rafal Ryba to Olberg, January 9, 1950, "Why have you stopped writing". Vol. 208, ME18, 1400BA, YIVO.

[339] Letter, January 1950, from Sukienik in Landskrona to the National Committee about the first meeting with the Bund group in Landskrona, list of members and report from the commenced activities. Vol. 208, ME18, 1400BA, YIVO.

[340] Report from Borås to Olberg, September 27, 1950. Vol. 206, ME18, 1400BA, YIVO.

[341] Letter from Obranshka to Olberg November 4, 1949. Vol. 208, ME18, 1400BA, YIVO.

[342] Letter from Chezes to Olberg, October 23, 1949. Vol. 208, ME18, 1400BA, YIVO.

[343] Letter from Novogrodski to the Bund in Sweden, January 6, 1950 with the International Coordinating Committee's budget for 1950 with a deficit of ten thousand dollars and carefully specified revenues and expenses. Vol. 208 ME18, 1400BA, YIVO. Letter from Novogrodski to the Bund in Sweden, January 17, 1951, with the International Coordinating Committee's preliminary budget of 51,730 US Dollars in annual cost. Vol. 210, ME18, 1400BA, YIVO.

money to the Coordinating Committee."[344] He said he understood that a lot of other things required fundraising, not least regarding the emergency call from *Unzer Shtime*, but finally he appealed: "You have not sent money to the Coordinating Committee for several years. We do not want to compete with *Unzer Shtime*, and so on, but it is an old rule to first and foremost support the center. You give to everyone except us."[345] At the same time, Olberg was pressed for payment from subscriptions to *Unzer Tsayt*. He was asked how many subscribers were left, and when will the payments come? "In your letter from April, you promised to send money for subscriptions, it is very important, our work is in a generally difficult situation," wrote Stolar in August 1952.[346] There were still, he reminded Olberg a month later, about thirty subscribers in Sweden "even after we removed non-payers, so it was quite a lot of money. The few Bundists in Sweden earn decently, so it would be good if you could contribute." And then there were recurring attempts to reconcile the number of active subscriptions: "Should I still send sixteen copies to Eskilstuna?"[347] From Olberg came the answer: "We cannot send money until the end of the month."[348]

The background to Gnacik's depressing letter about the situation in Eskilstuna was precisely the pressure for payments for fundraisers, subscriptions, and membership fees. This is how the crisis could appear, so to speak, on the ground: The Eskilstuna group had decided to send in a certain sum from sixteen members to *Unzer Tsayt* for the annual First of May greeting.[349] However, the national leadership had set a slighter higher quota. A minor matter? Certainly, but not in this high-pressure situation. In a furious letter from the treasurer Wolf Goldberg, Gnacik and the Eskilstuna group were scolded severely. "I do not understand what is happening. Your group has not become smaller. Why is the number of subscribers decreasing and why do you not send money?."[350] Apparently, Goldberg wrote ironically, the Eskilstuna group had decided to "be the navel of the world and ignore the decisions of the National Committee." The group had also "ignored" the April 1 deadline for First of May greetings, "so you can be happy that they arrived at all." Likewise

[344] Letter from Novogrodski to Olberg, August 27, 1952. Olberg replied on September 5, 1952, that at the same time as all the campaigns for *Unzer Shtime*, the comrades in Israel and more, it was not possible to collect for the International Coordinating Committee. Vol. 207, ME18, 1400BA, YIVO.

[345] Letter from Novogrodski to Olberg, November 8, 1952. Vol. 207, ME18, 1400BA, YIVO.

[346] Letter from Avram Stolar to Olberg, August 8, 1952. Vol. 207, ME18, 1400BA, YIVO.

[347] Ibid. Letter from Avram Stolar to Olberg, September 16, 1952. Vol. 207, ME18, 1400BA, YIVO.

[348] Letter from Olberg to Avram Stolar, September 24, 1952. Vol. 207, ME18, 1400BA, YIVO.

[349] Letter from Bund in Eskilstuna to Olberg, April 15, 1952. Vol. 207, ME18, 1400BA, YIVO.

[350] Letter from Wolff Godlberg to Gnacik in Eskilstuna, July 10, 1952. Vol. 207, ME18, 1400BA, YIVO.

the library: "All readers in Sweden pay 1.50, but Eskilstuna intends to pay 50 öre! And you do not even pay that." Moreover, only four members in Eskilstuna had contributed to "our suffering comrades in Israel." Goldberg said he was surprised that the Eskilstuna group could ignore the leadership's decision, and rebuked the members in perhaps not an entirely reasonable manner: "We must insist that you do not act as your own state in the future. Eskilstuna is not on Mars."[351]

Under pressure from world events and political developments, the Bund in Sweden withered. The British Labour's narrow election victory in 1950 presaged its defeat the following year and marked the end of "British socialism," which many Bundists saw as a third way between East and West. Owing to departures and creeping apathy, the Bund in Sweden gradually became an empty husk. Hence the increasingly unreasonable pressure placed on those who had significant responsibilities within the organization, though who could no longer fulfill their commitments. Olberg sought to keep up the appearances of a functioning party organization for as long as he could, not least for the eyes of the Coordinating Committee in New York. However, growing irritation over these difficulties would soon find expression in complaints, personal conflicts, and disputes.

The conflicts

In the archival material, discliplinary matters tended to become more numerous with the passing of time. Not that they were absent before. When the first Bundists arrived in 1945, Olberg had already warned about introducing conflict into the organization by accepting what he saw as too ambitious people: "We have had enough conflicts already." Friendly and disciplined behavior was essential, so that the organization could be kept together, and things could be achieved. In order to maintain party discipline and resolve disputes, the Bund set up, among other things, a system of party- or comrade trials.

Comrade courts

Comrade trials or *partey-gerikhtn* could lead to mediation, reprimands, and, in the worst cases, expulsion. The procedure would involve disputants presenting their case to a trusted comrade, or several, appointed by the local or national leadership, and accepted by all parties involved in the case. This, though, was easier said than done. In some instances, the jury was rejected as biased, on

[351] Ibid.

other occasions, one of the contending parties simply failed to appear, because either they had already chosen to leave the organization or had emigrated from Sweden before the trial took place.

Trying to resolve disciplinary issues, even the more difficult cases, within the movement rather than calling the police and going to court was an obvious choice for revolutionary and socialist movements. For those who had worked under authoritarian and repressive regimes such as tsarist Russia, it was especially important not to let the opposing state machinery into its own, often underground, movement – the case with, for example, the existence of subsequent dissident movements within dictatorships.[352] In the Jewish context, there was the additional tradition of Jewish courts, *Beit din*, which resolved disputes internal to the community. We have already seen that the Association of Surviving Jews in Malmö demanded that Khayem Borenstein be brought before a party court for his behavior. In that case, no action seems to have been taken other than criticism at a members' meeting. However, party trials would be relevant in other cases. A female comrade in Malmö was accused of gossiping about members to outsiders and talking publicly about internal affairs; she was expelled.[353] In Stockholm, a couple of members were summoned to court having allegedly insulted a third member, who in turn was accused of stealing and allowing communists to infiltrate Bundist circles in Poland.[354] With frustrations growing within the party, trials were requested in several cases due to insults, lack of discipline and uncomradely behavior.

Malmö

The background to the increasing apathy in Malmö was an escalating and destructive personal conflict between a few leading members, on the one hand, and Henryk Levkovich and the group's treasurer, on the other.[355] The whole episode gives a claustrophobic impression of the powerlessness of the diminishing presence of the Bundists and a growing sense of resentment.

[352] How "revolutionary morality" and social control were maintained in Chilean radical refugee groups in Sweden during the 1970s and 80s – not unlike the order within the Bund in Sweden – has been studied by Beatriz Lindqvist in *Drömmar och vardag i exil. Om chilenska flyktingars kulturella strategier* [Dreams and Everyday Life in Exile. On the cultural strategies of Chilean refugees], Carlsson Bokförlag, Stockholm 1991.

[353] Borenstein to the Comrade Court on the case of a comrade, September 18, 1948. Borenstein criticized the Comrade Court's decision not to expel the accused. Olberg wrote to Levkovich on September 18, 1948, that certain things are only used by opponents if they become public, but thought that the Comrade Court was right. Vol. 216, ME18, 1400BA, YIVO.

[354] Minutes, Bund Stockholm, February 25, 1949 and March 1, 1949. Vol. 211, ME18, 1400BA, YIVO.

[355] Documents from the Bund group in Malmö contain many letters about the conflict. Vol. 208, ME18, 1400BA, YIVO.

Levkovich was accused of using physical force against the treasurer in connection with a dispute over accounts. "The whole town knows about it and talks about it, it hurts us," the Malmö group's secretary wrote to Olberg as a justification for why Levkovich, one of the group's central figures, had suddenly been expelled.[356] Olberg said that he was shocked by the whole matter, and that the leadership would investigate what happened. In a long letter to Olberg, Levkovich tried to defend himself.[357] After a period of "anger directed against me" by a couple who had lost a board election (which apparently did take place), "they smuggled in a person as treasurer who does not know Yiddish and does not know how to keep books." Because Levkovich wanted to keep the group together, he took time off from work to help the treasurer with the bookkeeping. However, when a discrepancy was discovered, according to Levkovich, the treasurer did not want to understand the error, but the "narrow-minded little man, or shall we say the instrument," began to "insult me, using offensive language," and finally "spat in my face, it's true, believe it or not." So Levkovich opened the door and threw him out. But it was "a damn lie" that Levkovich had hit him. At a subsequent membership meeting, where there were " more important things to talk about," the entire time was devoted to this matter. Levkovich declared that it was all an incitement campaign against him that must be dealt with by people from another group, through a "commission" or party trial. Upset, he had left the meeting, whereafter, in his absence, he was expelled. So, he appealed to the national leadership to treat the matter democratically and humanely: "It is inconceivable in a democratic organization to punish someone behind his back without me having the opportunity to defend myself."[358]

However, no such trial took place, despite the Trelleborg Group's setting up a motion for such a proposal.[359] Levkovich had accepted the process, but the treasurer refused to participate without a decision by Olberg in Stockholm; such a decision never came. The National Committee decided the matter a couple of months later by approving the expulsion. Levkovich's criticism was

[356] Letter from Siegelman to the National Committee, October 3, 1949. Vol. 208, ME18, 1400BA, YIVO.
[357] Letter from Levkovich to Olberg, October 2, 1949, "Sorry if this letter upsets you…" Vol. 208, ME18, 1400BA, YIVO.
[358] Ibid.
[359] Letter from Bornstein in Trelleborg (not Malmö) to A. Fajgenbom in Stockholm, October 18, 1949. Vol. 208, ME18, 1400BA, YIVO.

"unfounded," and the leadership gave their full backing to the group's decision.[360]

Uppsala

In Uppsala, a comrade-led trial took place in the spring of 1950, with obviously devastating consequences for the small organization. The case concerned a dispute between two members over the cost of an apartment. The comrades involved in the dispute promised to obey the "court's" ruling. Nonetheless, questions were raised afterwards by both parties, to the chagrin of Perelmutter, who erupted and told several comrades to go to hell.[361] The whole matter was complicated by the fact that the disputants were on different sides of another disagreement that had emerged around *Kultur-Vinkl* and its library. It fundamentally concerned the relationship with the Zionists and the unclear division of roles between the Bund and the JLC. Until February 1950, activity in Uppsala, by Bund's standards, seems to have been quite successful. A couple of major events had been held, including the Bund's anniversary party in November and a public meeting including film screenings, socials, and the participation of Sara Mehr. Some co-operation took place with the local Social Democrats and the Trade Union Central Organization.[362] Three new families had arrived in the autumn of 1949, and Perelmutter had arranged apartments for them: "I did my comradely duty and think that they are happy." Some of the members had already gotten a job. But Perelmutter felt exhausted: "Unfortunately, I do almost all party work myself."[363]

The Uppsala Bund's initiator, Tobias Amster, was chairman of *Kultur-Vinkl*, and Perelmutter was responsible for the library. *Kultur-Vinkl* was open not only to Bundists, but to all Jews in Uppsala, and included, approximately,

[360] Letter from Olberg to Schneidman, January 7, 1950. Perhaps the National Committee could not have acted differently. In a private formulation from Bornstein in Trelleborg to Fajgenbom in the National Committee October 18, 1949, it was emphasized that the conflict between Levkovich and one of the leading wives was unbearable: "Hatred is so strong that if Levkovich's membership is regained, the Bund group in Malmö will be destroyed." At a meeting in November 1949, Khayem Borenstein was appointed chairman and Pesl Bernstein the new treasurer, according to a report from Khayem Borenstein, Malmö to the National Committee March 26, 1950. All these documents in Vol. 208, ME18, 1400BA, YIVO. However, Pesl Bernstein left the group the following year and left for New York in December 1951. Letter from Pesl Bernstein to Novogrodski, December 22, 1951, ME18. Vol. 93, ME18, 1400BA, YIVO.

[361] Bund Uppsala minutes of March 11, March 13 and March 20, 1950 with a composition of the "member court", promises to follow the decision, the presentation of the case and criticism of Perelmutter's actions. Vol. 212, ME18, 1400BA, YIVO.

[362] See, among other documents, letters from Perelmutter to Olberg, December 13 and 31, 1949, January 23, 1950. Vol. 208, ME18, 1400BA, YIVO.

[363] Letters from Perelmutter to Olberg, January 23, 1950, October 7, 1949, February 7, 1950. Vol. 208, ME18, 1400BA, YIVO.

forty members. To Perelmutter's growing annoyance, even Zionists could join. In letter after letter to Olberg and the National Committee, Perelmutter and those closest to him pointed out what they considered unbearable misconduct, accusing Amster of betraying the Bund's ideals.[364] It all developed into personal disagreements, where the original accusations over the cost of an apartment seemed to set in motion a chain reaction. Without, here, attempting to sort out the course of events in any detail, some points are worth mentioning. In his protest against Zionist participation in *Kultur-Vinkl*, Perelmutter apparently locked the library and took the key and lending stamp. He was expelled from *Kultur-Vinkl* by eighteen voting members, including Amster and two other Bundists – but according to Perelmutter, some of the names were forged. Amster was thrown out of the Bund's Uppsala branch by the other ten members. Amster and his two comrades were forbidden to attend a meeting in Uppsala with Boris (Baruch) Shefner, from the Bund leadership in New York, who was on a visit to Sweden… and so it went.[365] The whole matter developed into a very bitter, almost hate-filled entanglement, with countless letters back and forth mostly happening behind the backs of those involved.

The split was exacerbated by the battle over the book collection of *Kultur-Vinkl's* Yiddish library: it had more than two hundred books, and Olberg considered it an affiliate to the organization's Mendelsohn Library in Stockholm. But to which organization did the books belong? For the Uppsala Bundists, of course, the organization was the Bund, although JLC was formally responsible for the donations. After the split, Perelmutter shipped about twenty-five books from *Kultur-Vinkl* to the Bund group. For Amster, the books belonged to *Kultur-Vinkl*, and the Bund group had no say. Olberg and the Bund's national leadership, with the support of JLC in New York, emphasized that the books belonged to JLC, and so they initially took Amster's side.[366]

[364] Letter from Perelmutter and Praw to the National Committee, March 27, 1950, that Amster was deprived of his party rights until the Committee decided. Letter from Praw and Perelmutter to the National Committee, April 2, 1950: "We have not yet received an answer about the Amster conflict". Letter from Perelmutter to the National Committee, April 4, 1950: "Amster helps the Zionists […] I have been expelled from Kultur-vinkl. […] At the next meeting with our Uppsala group, we will expel Amster." Vol. 208, ME18, 1400BA, YIVO. The Uppsala Group's minutes deal with the conflict over *Kultur-Vinkl* and the library and the expulsion of Amster in detail on March 25, 1950 and March 27, 1950. Vol. 212 "Uppsala", ME18, 1400BA, YIVO.

[365] Letter from Praw to "Dear Comrades", April 3, 1950, with a list of comrades to attend the meeting with Shefner. Letter from Perelmutter, April 3, 1950 without addressee: "You cannot let Amster come to the meeting." Vol. 208, ME18, 1400BA, YIVO

[366] Letter from Olberg and Perel to Novogrodski, June 23, 1950: "Comrade Perelmutter's behavior has damaged JLC in Uppsala […] Comrade Perelmutter does not have our trust. I agree with Amster. The library belongs to *Kultur-Vinkl*." Letter from Tabachynski, JLC of America, June 16, 1950: "We note that

Rumors even seem to have circulated that Perelmutter would be reported to the police for theft. But two years later, when *Kultur-Vinkl* merged with the Jewish association formed in Uppsala by the famous Swedish historian Hugo Valentin, Olberg requested that all books from *Kultur-Vinkl's* library be restored to JLC or perhaps transferred to the Bund. The books however, had apparently been given away as "memorial gifts" to members who left Sweden or were deposited with certain individuals so as not to end up in the hands of "antagonists." Olberg also now mentioned the possibility of taking the matter up with the police, but Valentin seemed to have received a reasonable explanation from Amster that he really did not think he needed the police, but rather retraining, "as his nerves could no longer tolerate factory work."[367]

For Perelmutter, the lack of support from Olberg and the National Committee was a betrayal; it thus marked the end of their previous personal and close friendship. Forlornly, he wrote of his ill feeling toward Olberg's actions. Things became so hard to cope with that he had to see a doctor: "I can no longer bear this stress within me."[368] And the threat of going to the police? He had spent the war in Finland and fought against the Bolsheviks. "For me, the police mean that you want to send me back to Poland. It is not worthy of a democratic humanist and socialist. And I do not bow to the orders of the NKVD," i.e., the Soviet secret police. What had he done to deserve this? He had read through all their old letters from when they were friends, and he had done everything Olberg had asked; he had endured insults "for your sake" and acted as a Bundist and socialist; he had even put in a lot of work and even money into the party. Unfortunately, he had survived "when all my loved ones perished"; Olberg had given him hope, but now with one hand had destroyed it. "I have now lost everything, including faith in myself."[369] In the spring of 1951, the formerly active Bund group in Uppsala passed away.

Conditions of exile

With the lack of activity, departures and increasing pressure on those remaining, personal clashes increased. There was nothing uncommon in this within settings of political exile as Olberg himself pointed out. Few have discussed the conditions of exile – the "incurable rift" between the "self and its true home" –

Kultur-Vinkl is the right institution and that all books sent should go there." Vol. 93, ME18, 1400BA, YIVO.

[367] Letter from Hugo Valentin to Olberg, April 28, 1953, from Olberg to Hugo Valentin, May 5, 1953, from Hugo Valentin to Olberg, June 2, 1953 and from Hugo Valentin to Olberg, June 22, 1953, all letters in Vol. 22, PO 435, ARAB.

[368] Letter from Perelmutter to Olberg, April 18, 1950. Vol. 212, ME18, 1400BA, YIVO.

[369] Ibid.

more strongly than Edward Said, whose description of exile could have applied to the Bundists in Sweden: exile as loneliness, as the feeling of being deprived of a sense of "commonal belonging" and fellowship with others, a fundamentally incoherent and "jealous" state, with the need not only to recreate broken lives, but also to re-emerge from the confusion – in something, such as perhaps a state, a movement, a party.[370]

For exiled Bundists, this foothold was first and foremost their own movement, their political *mishpokhe* scattered around the world in an archipelago of small groups, where the remnants of the Bund met on their way from exile to exile. Cut off from their social roots and political milieu, exiled activists, Said writes, tend to be both filled with defeat – "What went wrong?" "Whose fault was it?", etc. – and to repeat the formulas based on a different reality. They remain outsiders in their new setting, because of language, experience, and difficulties in understanding the politics and culture of the new place. It is about loss, not only about what was once familiar and recognizable, but about the loss of what is now often called political, cultural, and social capital: the former union leader for large groups of co-workers; the writer with a reputation among readers; the politician with friends and enemies, has turned into … a nobody, without yet having the ability to stand one's ground, or perhaps even to orient him- or herself in the new situation; from the severance of old ties comes the experiencing of phantom pains. Moreover, they were faced with the necessity of rebuilding their lives, of arranging a functional existence, of learning new things and initiating an unknown phase of life, where their previous ways of living are transformed into memories, while a new life pattern begins only tentatively to take shape. The writer Zenia Larsson formulated her anxiety in the face of the dawning love she experienced with a Swedish man who would one day become her husband. What would such a relationship risk?

> It would mean crossing an invisible boundary, abandoning my entire former world, alienating myself from our past, our tradition and culture, and stepping into something completely different to me – a foreign world with a spirit that is incomprehensible to me and a culture with which I have nothing in common, which I neither love nor know.[371]

[370] Edward W. Said "Tankar om exil" [Thoughts on exile] in *Från exilen* [From exile], Ordfront, Stockholm 2006.
[371] Larsson 1972, p. 86, "Den 4 september 1947" [September 4, 1947].

On the side of the West

The intensification of the Cold War from the autumn of 1947 seemed to be leading toward a new world war, just months after the previous one. The upheavals and confrontations of 1948 were followed by ever greater contradictions. At the Bund's National Assembly in Sweden in August, Olberg warned of a new war.[372] The following summer, the US' monopoly on nuclear armaments was broken after the Soviet Union detonated its first atomic bomb. At the same time, the Chinese Communists were on their way to power in the most populous state on earth, and on October 1, 1949, the People's Republic was proclaimed. The fighting on the Korean Peninsula between the Communists in the north and the nationalists in the south would lead to the Korean War in June 1950, with the United States and the United Nations on one side, and the Soviet Union in alliance with China, on the other. McCarthyism in the United States and the cold war atmosphere within the blocs soon wiped out the space for some "third power" in world politics. On the Soviet side, repression intensified as the Stalinist regime's initiated a new mobilization against external and internal enemies, not least after the break with Tito's Yugoslavia in the autumn of 1948. During the Stalinist show trials, which swept across Eastern Europe, a communist leader such as Laszlo Rajk was accused and executed for "Titoism" in Hungary in 1949, and Rudolf Slansky was executed in Czechoslovakia in 1950 for "Trotskyism-Titoism-Zionism." The wave of terror coincided with the Soviet Union's change of view surrounding Israel. Communists who had engaged in cooperation with Israel were identified as Zionist nationalists and enemies of socialism. The campaigns played on anti-Semitic sentiments in societies where the Holocaust had just taken place, often with the support of large segments of the population. In the Soviet Union itself, Stalin's last wave of terror was directed at Jewish intellectuals, including members of the Jewish Anti-Fascist Committee, and was to culminate in the infamous "Doctors' Plot."

Korea

With the outbreak of the Korean War, the International Bund obviously sided with the West. "Democracies have learned since Munich 1938 that

[372] Minutes from the first National Assembly of Bund groups in Sweden, August 14–15, 1948, and handwritten minutes. Vol. 206, ME18, 1400BA, YIVO.

appeasement is not the way to stop an aggressor seeking world domination," said the Bund's Jewish Labor Bund Bulletin, condemning the "evil and false" communist propaganda associated with the fighting.[373] When in late summer, 1950, the Bund in the United States and Canada met for a large joint conference at the Riverside Plaza Hotel in New York, UN military intervention was hailed as a defense of the Asian peoples' struggle for freedom from communist aggression.[374] The Bund's line was that democracies must stop communist expansion even, when required, by military means, but at the same time to oppose colonialism and dictatorship – such as the Franco regime in Spain or "various reactionary leaders such as Chiang Kai-Shek," the leader of Nationalist China. In order to counter brutal aggression in the future – which could lead to the greatest human catastrophe in history, a third world war – not only did the "democratic camp" and the UN have to be strengthened, but above all, the millions of working people around the world needed to be convinced of the harmfulness of communism; only a democratic liberal socialism could give all people, regardless of race, religion or nationality, equal rights and opportunities.[375]

The Bund therefore opposed the US Anti-Subversive Act enacted in Congress in 1950 by "reactionary forces", who exploited public opinion against communist aggression in Korea. The deep-rooted democratic spirit of the American people and the legislation in general were sufficient protection against communist propaganda and Moscow's actions, the Bund said.[376] In line with that attitude, the Bund would support the verdicts against Ethel and Julius Rosenberg in the espionage scandal characteristic of the anti-communist atmosphere in the US in the early 1950s. The Rosenbergs, according to the Bund, had been given a fair trial and were found guilty. The Communists' accusations of witch-hunts and anti-Semitism were just hypocrisy. On the other hand, the death sentences should have been changed for humanitarian reasons, for the sake of the Rosenbergs' children and in order not to imitate Soviet "justice."[377]

[373] *Bund Bulletin* No. 5–6, May–June, 1950, p. 1 "World Peace – But No Appeasement".

[374] *Bund Bulletin* No. 7–12, July–December, 1950, p. 10, "War in Korea".

[375] Ibid.

[376] Ibid.

[377] *Bund Bulletin* No. 25–27, January–March, 1953, p. 4, "The Rosenberg Case". The Rosenbergs were executed in June 1953 for spying; among other things, for handing over information about the American nuclear bomb program to the Soviet Union. The verdicts have been hotly debated in both the public and in academic research.

In the Swedish context, Olberg came to typify the explicit anti-communism of the West. According to a report from one of Olberg's speeches, he had claimed that Russia's goal was to take over the whole of Asia, Europe, and America. The United States had been unprepared for Russian expansion, but with the support of forty-seven countries in the UN, a storm of protests had surprised the Russians after they attacked Korea. It was the task of the international socialist labor movement to prevent Russian aggression and a new world war.[378] According to Olberg, the American labor movement was at the forefront here. The AFL-CIO trade union movement, with its 16 million members, supported "its government" against communist expansion.[379] Here, too, the JLC, with its half a million members, played an important role that had won recognition from "all layers of American democracy" for its struggle against totalitarianism, racism, and oppression. For JLC, "the fight against Bolshevik oppression," Olberg explained in line with the Bund's position, was that dictatorship increased the risks for the Jewish people, while democracy made life safer. "The fate of the Jews in the world relates to the state of democracy in Europe. Only democracy protects the Jews ," was his point.[380] At a rally at the Astor Hotel in New York with two thousand union representatives, Olberg told of how the renowned leader of the International Ladies Garment Workers' Union, David Dubinsky, demanded resistance against communist aggression and called the Russian regime a "terrorist dictatorship." As a representative of the Jewish working class in the United States, Olberg continued, Dubinsky said that Russian rulers under the red flag would turn the Jews into scapegoats. "Stalin will not stop at anything in his quest to establish Soviet imperialism and tyranny everywhere." Only through a systematic struggle for political and economic democracy could the communists' imperialist plans be stopped. The head of the JLC's study department had added before the big mass meeting: "The situation of the Jews under Stalinism was a thousand times worse than under Tsarism."[381] Olberg thus opposed any idea of any kind of "third position." His attack on the "shameful Stockholm appeal" for peace and that of the Nobel laureate and anti-Nazi Thomas Mann, who advocated relaxation of tensions between the blocs, attracted attention.[382]

[378] Report from Perel September 21, 1950, to *Facts and Opinion* in New York. Vol. 206, ME18, 1400BA, YIVO.

[379] Manuscript on the Korean War by Paul Olberg. Vol. 210, ME18, 1400BA, YIVO.

[380] Ibid.

[381] Ibid.

[382] In an open letter to Thomas Mann, originally published in the Swiss Social Democratic newspaper *Volksrecht* on September 9, 1949, Olberg harshly criticized the author for excusing the Soviet dictator-

The focus of Olberg's involvement increasingly became the critique of what he saw as Soviet imperialism and anti-Semitism.[383] In the Bund's fight against anti-Semitism, members had been urged to anchor the issue in each country's Socialist Party. Rafal Ryba at the Federal Secretariat in Paris came close to berating Olberg about reports on the matter from Sweden and the actions of the Swedish Bundists.[384] In turn, Olberg sent an abrasive response; you cannot seek anti-Semitism "where it does not exist."[385] Olberg became preoccupied with the threat from the Soviets.

The Israeli Bund

As for the view of Israel and Zionism, the Bund's attitude did not really change in principle after the state was established and the war of independence ended. A Jewish state would not solve the "Jewish problem" – that is, the right of the world Jewish people to their own language, culture, and autonomy in a society with democratic and social rights for all. It could only happen through socialism. The bourgeois nationalist ideology of Zionism, as defined by the Bund, was still regarded as an illusory dead end. Israel could never become the

ship by advocating relaxation, disarmament, and compromise between the blocs. In March 1950, the Stockholm appeal for peace and disarmament against nuclear weapons was launched, initiated the year before by the Soviet-backed World Peace Council. The campaign for the appeal, which gathered millions of signatures worldwide, was run in Sweden by the Swedish Peace Committee with the support of the Swedish Communist Party. For Olberg's polemic with Thomas Mann see Enerud pp. 177–179.

[383] Olberg published a number of articles on the topic and a controversial monograph, Paul Olberg, *Antisemitism i Sovjetunionen* [Anti-Semitism in the Soviet Union], Natur och Kultur, Stockholm 1953. An obvious source of inspiration for Olberg's book was the Menshevik leader Solomon Schwarz's book *The Jews in the Soviet Union*, Syracuse University Press, Syracuse 1951. Schwarz hoped that Olberg could publish it in Swedish, but Olberg wrote his own version instead. See letter from Solomon Schwarz to Olberg, May 30, 1951. Vol. 31, PO 435, ARAB.

[384] For example, letter from Rafal Ryba, European Secretariat, November 16, 1948, to Bund I Sverige: "I am surprised that you did not send reports on the situation in Sweden, the new arrivals and the Bund groups. We need a closer relationship between the European Secretariat and the Confederation in Sweden." Vol. 207, ME18, 1400BA, YIVO.

[385] Letter from Olberg to Ryba, April 7, 1948, with an answer to Ryba's question as to why Olberg was not informed about the anti-Semitic Einar Åberg's activities. "He is an isolated case", Olberg replied and "has no influence", people laughed at the anti-Semites and the Swedish parliament had passed a law banning anti-Semitic expressions. Vol. 206, ME18, 1400BA, YIVO. In a later detailed report from June 13, 1951, possibly to the Bund's European Secretariat, Olberg describes in detail a Nazi conference in Malmö, May 13–14, 1951 organized by well-known fascist Per Engdahl where Nazi organizations from eight countries are said to have participated with a subsequent demonstration that gathered five hundred participants. According to Olberg, Engdahl had requested 30 visas from Germany, but only one of the participants had received it "by bluffing". The entire Swedish press responded, Olberg claimed, in silence "perhaps because they see the Nazis as insignificant, but also because they do not want to show that such things exist in Sweden." Demands to ban the Nazis would be problematic, "then you must also ban the Communists." Vol. 210, ME18, 1400BA, YIVO.

home of all Jews, and building a state on what we today would call ethnic grounds – disregarding the Arab population – would lead to endless conflicts and feed the worst sides of nationalism. At the same time, the Bund represented the position that Jews – and others – should not be prevented from crossing borders and settling wherever they wished – through free movement in a free world.

By the early 1950s, many Bundists had reunited with relatives and friends in Israel, where they had formed a local branch of the international Bund. It was under the leadership of, among others, Yisachar Artuski, a supporter of the international Bund's minority position on Israel, that the Israeli Bundist Yiddish magazine *Lebns-Fragn* was founded in 1951.[386] According to the Bund's organizational pattern, the cultural organization *Arbeter-Ring*, children's groups, *kinderheym* and cooperatives were formed. *Brit Haavoda Arbeter-Ring*, the Bund building in Tel Aviv, became a gathering place, with libraries, political meetings, cultural events and the celebration of Jewish holidays in secular socialist form, as well as memorials. Culturally, the Israeli Bund fought against what was seen as the stigmatization of Yiddish and "ghetto Jews" by the Zionists. Politically, the Bundists sought to perpetuate the memories of the Jewish resistance struggle against fascism – and fought what they saw as Zionist militarization and confrontational policies against the Arab peoples. In short, *doikayt* was practiced on Israeli territory. The Bund even ran candidates for election to the Knesset in 1959, but without success.[387]

The International Bund campaigned against discrimination against Yiddish in Israel and to help Israeli comrades: "Dear friends! In Israel, there are now several hundred Bundists from DP camps. We set up culture houses for old and new members. Help our comrades in Israel financially!"[388] When the Trelleborg group was disbanded in the autumn of 1950, the minutes concluded: "We are scattered all over the world and constantly on the move. Decision: the money that is left over will be sent to the comrades in Israel."[389] Fundraising lists were gradually circulated among the Bundists in Sweden, who for 25 kronor could finance an aid package for vulnerable comrades: "Over six

[386] For Artuski and *Lebns Fragn* see Slucki 2012, pp. 192–201. *Lebns Fragn's* last editor who took over after Artuski's death in 1971, was Yitskhak Luden (1897–2017), the magazine was closed in 2014.

[387] In the 1959 Knesset election, the Bund received only about 1,300 votes out of nearly one million, of which over 370,000 were for the Mapai Zionist Workers' Party (formerly Poalei Zion) and nearly 70,000 for the left-wing Zionist Mapam (including former Linke Poalei Zion).

[388] Letter from Novogrodski to the Bund in Stockholm, June 29, 1949. Vol. 211, ME18, 1400BA, YIVO.

[389] Minutes from membership meeting No. 41, Bund group in Trelleborg, September 17, 1950. Vol. 215, ME18, 1400BA, YIVO.

hundred Bundists are going hungry in Israel, we Bundists in Sweden can help."[390] The Bund in New York thanked the Swedish Bundists for seventy packages they managed to put together.[391]

At the same time, the Bund was forced to realize that most countries, as well as the UN, recognized Israel as a sovereign state, that the largest Jewish organizations and most congregations supported Israel, as did the re-established Socialist International of which the Bund fought to be members. Olberg could only state that the Swedish Social Democratic government recognized Israel in 1949 and that the Social Democratic Party, the trade union movement, and the cooperative movement donated large sums to Israeli aid. A few years after the recognition, Olberg informed Novogrodski in a resigned tone that the Swedish trade union central LO and consumer cooperative association KF had donated 100 000 Swedish kronor to Israel (the equivalence of about $230 000 today), and how difficult it was to get a hearing for the Bund's perspective.[392]

The experience of the international youth camp in Stockholm in 1950, where the young *Tsukunft* members of the Trelleborg group were invited and participated with signs in Yiddish, had been overwhelming. But it also spoke in clear language on the Israeli question. The huge camp, with perhaps thirty thousand participants from thirty countries in a camp town with hundreds of tents, cooperative shops, a post office, cinema and amusement park, made a big impression on the participants – not to mention the final demonstration, with sixty thousand participants in a Stockholm draped with red flags. The Bundist press reported that during the camp's *Festspiel*, each group had presented something emblematic of their home countries.[393] What was not mentioned was that the Jewish element in the camp, which received a lot of attention in the Social Democratic youth paper *Frihet,* was not the Bundists from *Tsukunft*, but the young Labor Zionists from Israel, the Bundists' most bitter competitors.[394]

This was no fleeting nationalistic storm that swept along the Jewish street. The Jewish state had become a fact of Jewish life.

[390] Circular to Yiddish Culture Vinkl, Uppsala, 1951. Vol. 210, ME18, 1400BA, YIVO.
[391] Letter from Avram Stolar to Olberg, September 16, 1952. Vol. 207, ME18, 1400BA, YIVO.
[392] Letter from Olberg to Novogrodski, December 7, 1951. Vol. 207, ME18, 1400BA, YIVO.
[393] See undated reports by "our Stockholm correspondent" Sh Perel to *Unzer Tsait* and *Unzer Shtime*. Vol. 93, ME18, 1400BA, YIVO.
[394] "Vi kommer från Israel" (We come from Israel), *Frihet* No. 15–16, 1950.

The split

In the autumn of 1950, difficulties for the Bund in Sweden worsened when a painful, sharply critical settling of accounts was initiated against Olberg's leadership. As we have seen, many Bundists in Sweden were frustrated by their isolation and the difficulties they had in moving to larger cities with established Jewish communities. This sense of frustration was compounded by the idea that this was because of Olberg's negligence, along with the JLC and the Swedish Bundist leadership. In addition, there was irritation over the lack of communication and work plans, as well as disappointment that Stockholm could not support local groups more. "It simply could not go on like this. All the work is on Olberg's shoulders. This unhealthy situation must end," young comrades in Trelleborg had written to the National Committee back in the autumn of 1949, in a long and somewhat condescending letter.[395] That same autumn, Novogrodski had visited Stockholm to see the situation for himself, and to investigate the difficulties that the national leadership had in organizing party work.[396] On his advice, new comrades had been brought into the leadership. But a reasonable division of labor failed to materialize. A part of the picture was captured in the frustrations of Sara Mehr, the vice president of the Bund in Sweden, who, even when Olberg was ill or on vacation, was not asked to carry out any significant tasks. During the summer of the same year, as noted, Rafal Ryba from the European Secretariat also visited the Swedish organization to help. Still, activity seemed to be fading.

Olberg bristled at the criticism by the young members of Trelleborg, which they expressed in long and somewhat arrogant instructions on how to systematically reorganize the central operations in Stockholm. "It sounds like you think that Perel [Shmul Perel, with title 'party secretary'] is a full-time employee of the party, but he works in a factory all day and spends almost all his free time engaged in party activity."[397] In fact, party operations, Olberg

[395] Letter from Vajskopf, Trelleborg to the National Land Committee, October 8, 1949. Vol. 208, ME18, 1400BA, YIVO.

[396] Letter from Novogrodski to Olberg, September 30, 1949, about travel to Europe with arrival information to Stockholm, October 21. Invitation from Olberg to Bund Uppsala, October 21, 1949: "Due to Novogrodski's visit, we have a meeting on the 23rd in *Folkets hus* in Stockholm." Vol. 208, ME18, 1400BA, YIVO.

[397] Letter from Olberg to Trelleborg, January 30, 1950. It is about a number of letters of criticism and a kind of reproach from the Trelleborg group towards the lack of a well-functioning organizational apparatus. Olberg's letter about Perel's factory work was, for example, a reply to an angry letter from Trelleborg's chairman Vajskopf to Perel on January 22, 1950, because the latter did not reply to a letter

assured, were being run successfully, even if there was a little personal friction. "You can be sure that we do everything we can. Instead of writing threatening letters to us, do your job, get in touch with Malmö and bring your own activities to life."[398] Whereupon the answer from Trelleborg, of course, was that they will not "stick their nose in, but just do our work!" with the addition: "We will send no more suggestions."[399]

In a circular in September 1950 to local groups from the board of the Stockholm group, it was claimed that the National Committee no longer functioned and that its operations had almost ceased. The board appointed during Novogrodski's visit had collapsed, and Olberg had not accepted Rafal Ryba's solutions from the summer.[400] The Bundists in Stockholm, led by Sara Mehr, said they were concerned about this development and, like the group in Trelleborg, called for the convening of a new National Assembly with representatives from all local associations and the election of a new national leadership. "We are confident that you will support it."[401]

But at the National Committee meeting in September, the criticisms were met with outrage.[402] Olberg said that activities were in fact extremely high, conflating his own efforts with the organization's operations. During the summer, he had visited local groups to discuss the situation and the consequences of the new American DP law, when, due to the Korean War, "most of our members were panicked." Olberg had been to Uppsala, Eskilstuna, the Vetlanda region – including Huskvarna, Borås and the Malmö region including Trelleborg and Landskrona. In Gothenburg, he had spoken with the American consul, all letters to the national leadership had been answered, *Unzer Tsayt* took a lot of time, as did the arrangement of Rafal Ryba's visit. What were the comrades really demanding? Sara Mehr presented the criticisms from the Stockholm group, but, according to the minutes, still considered Olberg's report positive and thought that some of the problems could now be fixed. However, party secretary Shmul Perel, who had received much of

quickly enough: "As secretary, you are solely responsible for it. We do not tolerate it and turn to a higher level." Vol. 208, ME18, 1400BA, YIVO.

398 Letter from Olberg and Perel to Bund Trelleborg. Vol. 208, ME18, 1400BA, YIVO.

399 Letter from Vajskopf, Trelleborg to the National Committee, March 13, 1950. Vol. 208, ME18, 1400BA, YIVO.

400 Letter to Bund's local associations from the Stockholm Board, September 10, 1950, signed by Sara Mehr, Raukh and Szechatow, among others. Also, letters from Sara Mehr to Novogrodski, June 18, 1950, Vol. 93, ME18, 1400BA, YIVO, and in the documents of local associations, such as Vetlandas, September 10, 1950. Vol. 213, ME18, 1400BA, YIVO.

401 Ibid.

402 Minutes of the meeting of the National Committee, September 23, 1950. Present Olberg, Perel, Mehr and Sobol. Vol. 206, ME18, 1400BA, YIVO.

criticism, objected: Why had the Stockholm group sent out its circular at all, without first asking the leadership. "If the national leadership has collapsed, then why is Sara Mehr here?" But Avrom Sobol from Stockholm turned the issue around and criticized the national secretariat, namely Olberg and Perel, for neglecting Mehr. He was also worried about the general sense of negativity among members, in Uppsala, Eskilstuna and Malmö. "Since Comrade Rafal's visit, the conflicts have increased," Sobol said, and he hoped that a new National Assembly would resolve the conflicts. Mehr stated that the Stockholm circular did not intend to offend either the chairman or the secretary, but at the same time she demanded that her responsibility in the party leadership be respected. If the minutes of the discussion seemed to express only a certain escalation of the disagreements, the resolution sent out after the meeting signaled something completely different.[403]

Outraged, the National Committee condemned the Stockholm branch's actions as irresponsible. The criticisms from Stockholm had been completely unfounded, it was untrue that the leadership had collapsed; on the contrary, it did all it could "in the interest of our party." Sending letters to the groups around the country without the Chairman Olberg's permission risked "breaking up our organization." Using lies and slander were "communist methods" that could ignite a fire that risked destroying the Bund in Sweden.

Thus, the final collapse of the small organization had begun. Sara Mehr wrote "with a heavy heart" about the "Bund's difficult situation in Sweden" in a personal letter to members around the country.[404] She had, she explained, always strived for unity, but it was no secret that there had been a conflict for a long time and that the leadership had not functioned properly for months. But "none of my questions were discussed, and Olberg made no concessions with respect to his own responsibilities." In fact, Mehr continued, Olberg cut off every discussion. Therefore, no proposals and no decisions could be made, meaning that not a single word of the national leadership's resolution, sent out to all groups, was correct. Nor was it true, she continued, that Olberg had visited the local branches, at least not on behalf of the National Committee. His presentation of the American DP law had not clarified anything; it had only upset people. In a dramatic tone, she maintained that the National Committee had collapsed, and that Olberg refused to share the work with her. He was using the leadership as his personal property and never gave financial accounts. Even if he had the best of intentions, he was working against the Bund's interests: "In

[403] Resolution adopted by the National Committee for the Bund in Sweden, September 23, 1950, signed by Olberg, Sobol and Perel. Vol. 206, ME18, 1400BA, YIVO.
[404] Letter from Sara Mehr to Bund Vetlanda, October 3, 1950. Vol. 213, ME18, 1400BA, YIVO.

a socialist organization, such autocratic methods are unacceptable, but they are characteristic of Olberg, who ignores all our decisions." She was convinced that the appeal from the Stockholm group for a new National Assembly – in her view, supported by New York – was decisive for the Bund's existence in Sweden, and she hoped for the help of all Bundists to bring about "normal, not dictatorial, relations between us."[405] For members across the country, the disagreement in the leadership naturally raised both concerns and questions. While several members, mainly in the Stockholm area, were linked to both sides in the conflict, others, such as the group in Vetlanda, declared themselves neutral, or, as in the case with Trelleborg, they left Sweden entirely.[406]

[405] In a letter to the Bund in Vetlanda, dated September 22, 1950, the day before the National Committee meeting, Mehr and Szechatow wrote: "Dear comrades, we have received full support from the Coordinating Committee for our initiative" and refer to a letter from Novogrodski. Vol. 213, ME18, 1400BA, YIVO.

[406] Letter from the Bund Vetlanda to the International Coordinating Committee, October 22, 1950. The group proposed that a national conference be held December 24–26 of the same year to resolve the disagreements "in a friendly manner." Vol. 213, ME18, 1400BA, YIVO.

The end

The crisis of the Bund in Sweden was brought to the attention of the Coordinating Committee in New York, who contacted the disputants and tried to mediate. For a time, the intervention of the New York leadership seemed to have borne fruit. Even if conflicts within the Swedish group had not been completely resolved, they had at least been reduced, and those involved promised to work together for the common cause. In January 1951, instead of a new national gathering with elected delegates, as proposed by the Stockholm group, a chairman's conference was announced by Olberg. The report from party secretary Perel to New York was almost fantastical in its levels of optimism.[407] The conference, held in Stockholm's People's House, had been a great success, and the reported activities extensive. The report went as follows: Olberg began by speaking about the international political situation, which was now so serious that time was almost up until a third world war broke out. On the basis of the communist attack on South Korea the year before, Moscow had turned the Cold War into a hot one. The decision of the United States to defend Korea had been enthusiastically welcomed by all the democratic states of the United Nations. The UN's "mighty army" had spurred the democratic world to resist "the appetite of Soviet imperialism." Sweden had equipped itself and was ready to defend its neutrality and independence from Russia militarily if war broke out in Europe. This also concerned a defense of the right to asylum for political refugees; no one would be deported. The Bund in Sweden was prepared to help comrades emigrate if Sweden found itself, geopolitically, in the danger zone. At the same time, the speaker had paradoxically emphasized, "we are categorically against creating panic among our comrades."

In the report, Perel dwelled on the Bund's successes in Sweden. Thanks to the initiatives of the national leadership and the devotion of the Bund groups around the country, the organization had succeeded in "increasing the Bund's influence on Jewish life in our small community" and contributed to the "flourishing of its cultural and social life." The eight local groups had held numerous cultural and social events, such as memorials for the ghetto fighters and celebrations of the founding of the Bund, the First of May demonstrations together with Social Democratic local organizations, and literary and musical cultural evenings. The members had been active in the "Jewish city councils,"

[407] Report from the Bund Secretary, Perel, to the International Coordinating Committee regarding the national meeting with the chairmen of the Bund Groups in Sweden, January 7, 1951. Vol. 207, ME18, 1400BA, YIVO.

i.e., the associations in different cities formed by the Mosaic congregations. With the help of JLC, they had distributed Yiddish literature and magazines. The Mendelsohn Library in Stockholm had a broad range of books to be borrowed, with about a hundred borrowers dotted around the country. Simultaneously with this flourishing activity, there had also been extensive internal discussions about the relationship to Zionism, the formation of the state of Israel and the rebirth of Yiddish as a language and culture. "Bundist socialist consciousness" among the members had deepened. A joint secretariat of former antagonists Olberg and Sara Mehr had been appointed to lead the organization together.

The conference ended with unanimous support for Olberg's introductory speech and Perel's organizational report. The comrades gathered sent greetings to the Bund's International Coordinating Committee and JLC in New York. Even though many of the comrades were preparing to leave Sweden, those who remained would do everything to successfully continue the extensive Bundist activity in Sweden.

Novogrodski very much welcomed their success and wrote that New York was confident this would put an end to the conflict in Sweden.[408]

Olberg's farce?

A few weeks after Perel's upbeat report, however, Emanuel Novogrodski received a completely different version. He had thanked Sara Mehr by letter for the fact that there was now peace in the Swedish organization and, now after the successful conference, was looking ahead to brighter days. Sara Mehr also assured him that the quarrel was now over; though the reason she gave made for very sobering reading: "Our people have left!"[409] As for the conference, "here in Stockholm as well as out in the country, we had not been told anything." If she hadn't read *Unzer Shtime*, she would not have known that she was "such an important person, who was elected to the Bureau and the Secretariat." She had in fact been ill during the conference and, she wrote bitterly, that she had not even been asked if she wanted to sit in the secretariat with Olberg. The conference itself was poorly organized. The invitation had reached the groups only a few days before it took place; only two of the six chairmen had been called; Uppsala's chairman, Perelmutter, had found it difficult to be recognized

[408] Letter from Novogrodski to Perel, January 23, 1951 and from Novogrodski to Olberg, January 23, 1951. Vol. 210, ME18, 1400BA, YIVO.

[409] Letter from Sara Mehr to Emanuel Novogrodski, February 1951. Vol. 93, ME18, 1400BA, YIVO.

as a representative.[410] Because she had fallen ill, Stockholm had been forgotten. Sziah Szechatow had finally been recognized as a replacement, but when he arrived at five in the afternoon, the conference was almost over. No one else from the Stockholm group had been invited. Neither the chairman nor the secretary had come from Eskilstuna, but only a comrade who was not even a member of the board. The only member from Borås attended, also. It was all a tragicomic spectacle, and Mehr would not have participated even if she had been healthy.[411] Why the farce? she wondered. Was it because he felt the need to send reports that no one could check to the Coordinating Committee, JLC and *Unzer Shtime*? Perel himself had now left Sweden for the United States, as had Sobol, "who both never lifted a finger" before they left.[412] Several months before, they had opposed the convening of a National Assembly, arguing that the Bundists were about to leave Sweden. Now, when this was a fact and they themselves were leaving, a conference was held. Was it just to show that there was a national leadership that does not consist only of Olberg?

Money

Once more, Mehr had become suspicious of Olberg. She wrote that she would not have commented on Novogrodski's letter had it not been for his call for the contributions for 1950. "Olberg will never send you the money he has or give me any back." Mehr said that he had paid large sums in support for ill comrades. According to her calculations, there should be between 3,000 and 3,500 kronor in the accounts, ($7000–8000 today) and there were no longer any major outgoings to be laid out in Sweden. Still, Olberg knows, she said, that there were old debts to settle, though he would avoid the subject: "You should demand the money from him!" Olberg had his good sides, she continued, at least at his desk, but his attitude toward party work and members was improper. Anyone who did not appreciate him was considered an enemy, and when the time came, there was "often bloody" payback. She had experienced

[410] The notice of the conference, signed by Olberg, chairman, and Perel, secretary, was dated January 3, 1951, and was addressed to the chairmen of the Bund's local organizations, stating that on Sunday, January 7, a special meeting with the chairmen of the Bund groups will take place in *Folkets hus*, hall N, in Stockholm. On the agenda: 1. The political situation 2. Reports 3. Discussion 4. The National Secretariat 5. Our tasks 6. Other. Vol. 206, ME18, 1400BA, YIVO.
[411] Letter from Sara Mehr to Emanuel Novogrodski dated only February, 1951. Vol. 93, ME18, 1400BA, YIVO.
[412] Sobol reportedly emigrated to Canada.

this firsthand. And she concluded: "I'm sorry to have disappointed you, but I'm so disappointed myself."[413]

Novogrodski responded with a series of personal reflections.[414] She could never disappoint him, only make him happy that she wrote to him. "I have begun to like you so much that there is nothing you ask for that I would not do for you." He was referring to Mehr's desire for literature and periodicals from the movement, and how tactlessly and uncompromisingly she had been treated. But, he explained, "I depend on you, comrade Sara, to turn this ill-treatment into something good for our movement." And he appealed to her directly: "Please rise above how badly you have been treated and say to yourself, for the Bund's sake, I am prepared to 'spit' on the insults and continue to cooperate with Olberg!" If she showed such generosity, the conference, despite its shortcomings, could have a positive impact.

Novogrodski also asked her for suggestions on how Olberg should be persuaded to send the financial contributions to New York. Mehr did not respond until three months later. The winter had been terrible, and her illness had not shown any signs of receding. She was over sixty, and she used to be so proud of her health, but "now I've received my punishment."[415] On the "Bund front", everything in Sweden had just become quieter. Only a few comrades were left. Novogrodski could now make the same joke about the Bund in Sweden as he once had made about the Menshevik exile organization and their leader, Rafael Abramovich: "The whole delegation could fit on Abramovich's sofa."[416] She continued bitterly: The Bundists met only occasionally, if Olberg so wished, and listed all of Olberg's different roles – sometimes the Bund, sometimes the JLC, sometimes the Congress for Yiddish Culture – but "he never contacts anyone, he does everything himself." Even though Mehr and Olberg formally constituted the secretariat, he never contacted her either in writing or by telephone, only through Wolf Goldberg, his new *shammes* (synagogue caretaker, derogatory in this context), – who had replaced Perel. "We have no contact regarding Bund issues. He does not need it." As an example, she gave the last memorial meeting for the ghetto uprising in Stockholm in April 1951. She had been contacted by Goldberg and made the preparations, "but without the help of the so-called secretariat, which consists of the two of us." During the event itself, without letting her or anyone else

[413] Letter from Sara Mehr to Emanuel Novogrodski dated only February 1951. Vol. 93, ME18, 1400BA, YIVO.

[414] Letter from Emanuel Novogrodski to Sara Mehr unclear date, 1951. Vol. 93, ME18, 1400BA, YIVO.

[415] Letter from Sara Mehr to Emanuel Novogrodski, May 17, 1951. Vol. 93, ME18, 1400BA, YIVO.

[416] Rafael Abramovitch was the leader of the Russian Menshevik exile organization in New York and the editor of its newspaper *Sotsialistitjeskij Vestnik* [The Socialist Messenger].

know in advance, Olberg had suddenly stepped up on stage himself; he officially opened the ceremony, gave the speech himself and ordered the pianist when exactly to perform. Finally, he muttered to Mehr, who was sitting far behind him: "Well, do you have anything to say?" She did not. So, Olberg declared the event to be over, by himself. Yet he could sometimes be the paragon of kindness, such as at meetings of the Congress for Yiddish Culture, but only as long as the issue was not about the Bund.[417]

Then there was the money. Olberg was simply afraid of the subject, Mehr thought, but he was so sophisticated that no one could believe that he had kept it for himself. She recalled the saying: "It is only when you start eating that you get an appetite." And she added, apologizing for her choice of words: "That is how he is. If he was ever honest, as I once thought, I doubt it now." Perhaps Sara Mehr did not know about the financial report from the Swedish organization's press committee that approved the accounts, but also noted that some of the money paid to *Unzer Tsayt* had been intended for the Coordinating Committee.[418] Perhaps it no longer mattered. Novogrodski replied, saying he understood her mood, but he urged her: "Please do not let these little things get to you. After all, your health is more important to us." He was convinced that she would succeed in convincing Olberg to send the money. "I know he knows we need it." And he congratulated her on the Swedish Social Democrats' success in passing the new law mandating three weeks paid vacation.[419]

Now, in May 1951, the history of the Bund in Sweden came to an end. With the breakdown in relations between Sara Mehr and Olberg – along with the leadership's dissolution, the suspicions, the bitterness and the departure of most comrades – not much needs to be added. In the autumn, Obranshka left for Australia, and the Vetlanda group was dissolved not long after.[420] At the same time, the group in Landskrona, which had escaped the collapse in Malmö, ceased to exist. "The Bund group in Landskrona was dear to me, but I could not prevent its collapse," the group's leader wrote to Olberg.[421]

But strangely enough, the Bund in Sweden lived on for a while, if only through Paul Olberg's name as a representative of the Bund in Sweden, a name that for many of the Jewish refugees and transmigrants represented salvation

[417] Letter from Sara Mehr to Emanuel Novogrodski, May 17, 1951. Vol. 93, ME18, 1400BA, YIVO.

[418] See letter on the financial report from Leysler Raukh to Olberg, December 20, 1950 and from Olberg to Stolar on the same date and earlier from Olberg to Stolar, November 20, 1950. Vol. 206, ME18, 1400BA, YIVO.

[419] Letter from Emanuel Novogrodski to Sara Mehr, May 21, 1951. Vol. 93, ME18, 1400BA, YIVO.

[420] Note, November 4, 1951, "Obranshka left for Australia". Vol. 207, ME18, 1400BA, YIVO.

[421] Letter from Sukienik, Landskrona to Olberg, November 4, 1951. Vol. 207, ME18, 1400BA, YIVO.

and the chance for a new life. From grateful comrades and others, Olberg's letter box continued to be filled year after year with postcards and letters from newlyweds, babies, and relatives hugging each other from different parts of the world.[422] To others, however, mainly those from the disintegrating inner kernel of the organization, the name Olberg had become associated with worry and even fear.

Olberg's name

Perelmutter had the same view of the Chairmen's conference as Sara Mehr.[423] Once such a devoted friend of Olberg's, Perelmutter had lost all confidence in him. Olberg just "pretended to do something." Had his commitment ever been genuine? "Olberg once said that Jews are swindlers – and since Bundists are Jews, we do not like him, as he does not like us," Perelmutter wrote. This contrasted, he thought, with Sara Mehr, who may not always have been the Bundist he had wanted, but was always committed in Jewish matters and "always treats us with motherly warmth."[424] Olberg's acts of self-harm should perhaps no longer play a role for Perelmutter, or for others, now that the Bund in Sweden was about to wind up its operations. "Those who leave no longer care about anything and have long since stopped being friends," sighed Perelmutter.[425] But, he said, those who traveled had to apply for travel documents through JLC and therefore had to meet Olberg, whether they wanted to or not. And all it took for Olberg to make things difficult, he continued, was someone simply holding a different opinion about the Bund's activities.

Szechatow had the same worries. A letter to Avram Stolar at *Unzer Tsayt* was spiced with words about Olberg being an "unparalleled fraud" and a "professional fraudster."[426] Szechatow himself no longer intended to deal with the organization in Sweden. The conflicts of the past year had finally been resolved not by the Bundists themselves, but by – Stalin! Under the threat of a new war, Szechatow continued, everyone was now trying to leave Sweden and Europe. Canada had opened its doors to them. Comrades also applied for visas to the United States, and a group from the countryside was already on its way to Australia. A few months later, almost no Bundists would remain in Sweden. However, the emigrating Bundists still needed the help of Olberg and JLC –

[422] See, among others, Vol. 29, PO 435, ARAB.
[423] Letter from Perelmutter to Novogrodski, April 24, 1951 (incorrectly dated 1950). Vol. 93, ME18, 1400BA, YIVO.
[424] Ibid.
[425] Ibid.
[426] Letter from Sziah Szechatow to Avram Stolar, February 12, 1951. Vol. 93, ME18, 1400BA, YIVO.

even if some tried to travel in secret. Many were, Szechatow claimed, simply afraid of Olberg. As the representative of the respected JLC, Olberg's words could have a decisive impact on their future. A comrade from Eskilstuna and his family who were about to leave for Canada suddenly had their visas revoked on the grounds that they were "undesirable elements," that is, communists. It was almost impossible to get Olberg to act and certify that the comrade was not a communist: "He never uses his contacts to help anyone."[427]

Szechatow and his wife were to leave for Canada in the spring, where their daughter and her family, along with their son, were soon to join them.[428] Even if he would like to speak out about the evil that had been committed in the Bund's name in Sweden, it was time to forget his experiences there and start thinking about his new life in Canada; he wanted to get away as soon as possible, even if it starting anew brings with it its own difficulties: "We so desperately want to have our own place to live." But he was worried that something would get in the way at the last minute, such as the visa suddenly being revoked or the cost of tickets becoming too high. "Olberg is an expert on such tricks."[429] Stolar had replied that JLC would contact Olberg, and he was sure that the painful experiences in Sweden would not be repeated.[430] But Szechatow was also worried about Olberg's letter.

Letters of introduction were part of the international Bund's routine when members traveled or moved. Local Bundist organizations needed to know if the new comrade was the in fact the person he or she was presenting themselves to be, preferably they would want to hear something about his or her previous participation in Bund. Olberg sent many such introductory letters, usually very friendly and with hopes that the comrade would be well taken care of.[431]

[427] Ibid.

[428] However, these could not leave Sweden until 1954 and went to Detroit, according to information received from Sara Ferdman Tauben, in a personal conversation with Håkan Blomqvist, Stockholm (20190530).

[429] Letter from Sziah Szechatow to Avram Stolar, February 12, 1951. Vol. 93, ME18, 1400BA, YIVO.

[430] Letter from Avram Stolar to Sziah Szechatow, February 20, 1951. Vol. 93, ME18, 1400BA, YIVO.

[431] For example: from Olberg Stockholm, May 10, 1949, unknown addressee: "We are pleased to confirm that Jankel Naimann, born in 1915 in Poland, has been a member of the Bund for many years and has always been active. Since 1948 he has lived in Sweden and been a member of Stockholm. We know him with confidence as a good friend and comrade. Take good care of him and give him all the support." Vol. 206, ME18, 1400BA, YIVO. October 13, 1950, to the Bund in New York: "The Bund in Sweden confirms that Rafael Vajskopf was an active member of Trelleborg. Help Vajskopf in any way you can." Vol. 210, ME18, 1400BA, YIVO. January 21, 1951 to the Bund in New York: "We certify that Comrade Spiro has been an active member of the Bund and recommend him to the Bund organization in New York. Vol. 210, ME18, 1400BA, YIVO. October 22, 1952, to the Bund in New York: "We confirm that Comrade Tromka came to Sweden in 1948. He was always devoted and trustworthy. Trust him and help him

However, there were exceptions. This could apply to new arrivals to Sweden when Olberg warned local groups to deal with some of them, as well as to members who left Sweden.[432] One of them concerned Avrom Goldberg in Södertälje, an industrial city close to Stockholm. Goldberg had been secretary of the Stockholm group, but was expelled in April 1950 after having been involved in a conflict between families who shared an apartment. According to Sara Mehr, he regained his membership three months later.[433] Goldberg had been one of Olberg's early critics and aired his doubts to Avram Stolar in New York. Even though Sweden was a small field to work in, Goldberg wrote, there were opportunities for the Bund, and every event attracted interest. Olberg, however, hindered these activities.[434] Unfortunately, Goldberg continued, Olberg kept the money and the technical resources. He regarded JLC as an extension of himself and did not let anyone else in. Even when he was on vacation, and Sara Mehr was meant to replace him, Olberg still did all the work. And Goldberg goaded the leadership in New York with a character assessment of Olberg: "He always follows orders, so it would be good if the Coordinating Committee gave him an order to involve others."[435] When Goldberg and his family arrived in Melbourne in early 1951, Olberg, on behalf of the National Committee in Sweden, had already sent a letter to the Australian Bund warning them of Goldberg. "I see it as my duty," Olberg wrote, to inform comrades that Goldberg had been expelled from the Bund in Sweden for "immoral and unethical conduct."[436] He "deserves to be ignored, and not get any attention or help from any Bundist." Olberg had "also heard" from a comrade now in New York that Goldberg had behaved badly in German camps. The board of the

recover in his new home in America." Equivalent letter of recommendation on the same date for "Comrade Figemann". Vol. 210, ME18, 1400BA, YIVO

[432] From Olberg to a comrade in Trelleborg, May 5, 1945: "F and P will no longer be in the party. They will be as unwelcome here as in Germany." Vol. 206, ME18, 1400BA, YIVO.

[433] In a letter from Sara Mehr and Wasserstrom to Avrom Goldberg on January 7, 1950, he is summoned to a comrade court regarding "your way against Sobol". Until the court ruled, he was deprived of his party rights. See also letter from Sara Mehr, January 10, 1950 that the Stockholm branch on January 3, appointed a court for the Sobol-Goldberg case. The first hearing was scheduled for January 12 at 7 pm. Letter to the Bund Committee in Melbourne, February 25, 1951, concerning the case of A. Goldberg, from the Stockholm Bund Committee, chaired by Sara Mehr, secretary S. Szechatow, members L. Raukh, Y. Nivinski. Vol. 210, ME18, 1400BA, YIVO.

[434] Letter from A Goldberg to A Stolar, July 21, 1949, Vol. 207, ME18, 1400BA, YIVO. In a letter from Olberg to Goldberg the month before, May 10, 1949, it is rather Olberg who criticizes Goldberg for inactivity, since he, as secretary of the Stockholm group, should have taken the initiative for a meeting after the First of May. Vol. 206, ME18, 1400BA, YIVO.

[435] Letter from A Goldberg to A Stolar, July 21, 1949. Vol. 207, ME18, 1400BA, YIVO.

[436] Letter from Olberg and Perel to the Bund Committee in Melbourne, Stockholm, December 3, 1950. Vol. 206, ME18, 1400BA, YIVO.

Bund's Stockholm branch had in turn contacted the Bund in Melbourne and explained that Goldberg, at the suggestion of Rafal Ryba from the European Secretariat, had regained his membership after a decision at a general membership meeting, and that he was never accused of anything political.[437]

Prior to his voyage to Canada, Szechatow wrote to the New York Coordinating Committee that he feared being subjected to the same treatment, and that letters from Olberg would catch up with him. "He's going to get dirty and lie, and something can go wrong."[438] Szechatow seemed really afraid of Olberg: "I admit that I am going to Canada with a sense of dread. I know what Olberg is capable of." The Bund's leadership in Sweden, he continued, consisted only of Paul Olberg, who "owned the stamp. Perhaps it was possible to rid themselves of this problem, though Olberg expected to live long, and so the Bund would have plenty of trouble with him in the future as well. For Szechatow's own part, he did not know if he even dared to rejoin the Bund in Canada. Novogrodski only replied prosaically that Szechatow should stop fighting with Olberg and others; in Canada he would not be judged by letters, but by his actions and Stolar assured him that no one "for a second" would believe the gossip.[439] However, as Szechatow had feared, a letter was soon on its way to Montreal in which Olberg again saw it as "his duty" to inform them about the new arrival's lack of character and misdeeds.[440] Szechatow had only caused problems while he lived in Sweden, Olberg said, but he could not hide his hurt feelings that the former comrade had not sided with him: "I helped him obtain asylum in Sweden, gave him support and made it easier for his son to bring his family here."

[437] Letter to the Bund Committee in Melbourne, February 25, 1951 regarding the case of A. Goldberg, from the Stockholm Bund Committee, chair Sara Mehr, secretary S. Szechatow, members L. Raukh, Y. Nivinski. According to Olberg's and Perel's letter, December 3, 1950, the Stockholm meeting in June 1950, in the presence of Rafal Ryba from the European Secretariat, had, on the contrary, decided to confirm the expulsion.

[438] Letter from Sziah Szechatow to the International Coordinating Committee in New York, undated (probably around February 25, 1951 when the Bund's Stockholm Committee sent a letter to the Bund in Melbourne). Vol. 93, ME18, 1400BA, YIVO.

[439] Letter from Emanuel Novogrodski to S. Szechatow, February 1951, letter from A Stolar to Szechatow, January 8, 1951. Vol. 93, ME18, 1400BA, YIVO.

[440] Letter from Olberg to the President of the Bund in Montreal, April 11, 1951. Vol. 210, ME18, 1400BA, YIVO.

Afterwards

In recent times, I have greatly missed the Jewish community, the contact with Jewish life. Linn, the former Bund group, which I knew best, no longer exists... Everyone has already set off in different directions, one after the other has left Sweden for good. With this group, our actors, poets, and writers have also made their journey, and after their departure, after their short but intense flowering period, cultural life has died out.

Zenia Larsson[441]

Some activities were conducted in the Bund's name in Sweden for a few more years. For example, memorial ceremonies for the ghetto uprising in Warsaw, the Bund's anniversary and the martyred Elrich and Alter were held, mainly in Stockholm and Eskilstuna. Several readers subscribed to *Unzer Tsayt* and *Unzer Shtime*, where First of May greetings were published from a shrinking number of Bundists in Sweden. In 1952, there were about forty, which then decreased through the 1950s to about ten in 1960, the year of Paul Olberg's death. There remained Sara Mehr, Ber Perelmutter and Olberg's "caretaker" Wolf Goldberg, plus a few others who had not left Sweden. Tobias Amster also remained, but left the Bund, merged *Kultur-Vinkl* with Hugo Valentin's Jewish Association, moved with his family to Stockholm and became a translator attached to Stockholm University. For his son, the journalist Harry Amster, it came as a surprise that his father had been a Bundist even for a period after the war: "Most of the time, he scolded Bundists."[442] Tobias Amster's grandson, Mattias, is presently the Orthodox rabbi of the Stockholm synagogue.

In 1966, Sziah Szechatow in Los Angeles published a greeting in *Unzer Tsayt* on the occasion of his seventieth birthday. The following year, the last greeting was sent from Sweden to the Bund's seventieth anniversary in November 1967. It was from Leyzer Raukh, who twenty years earlier had been part of the Stockholm group that organized the Bund in Sweden. Until his death, Paul Olberg represented the "Bund in Sweden" in the International Coordinating Committee and used alternately the Bund's and JLC's letterheading. But not only formally. As late as 1956, he had represented the Bund in the preparations for the Congress of the Socialist International but refrained from supporting a proposal to criticize Israel's war against Egypt the year before; instead he chose

[441] Larsson 1972, p. 107, "December 1948".
[442] E-mail to Håkan Blomqvist from Harry Amster (20141110) and call (20141212).

to abstain. "When the Coordinating Committee found out that I had refrained from condemning Israel, I was bombarded with letters," he wrote to Dr Emanuel Pat, son of Bundist leader Yankev Pat.[443] Emanuel Pat seems to have supported Olberg's decision not to criticize Israel. Olberg explained that he had come to the socialist congress to condemn Israel, "but having read the documents, I changed my mind." As a representative of the Bund's International Coordinating Committee, he was expected to represent the world organization's line, but "a delegate is not a postman, a delegate is not a soldier," he wrote indignantly. His report to *Unzer Tsayt* had also been censored, and his statement that Israel must defend itself had been deleted, and the International Coordinating Committee had called for the Bund's vote on the issue to be corrected.[444]

Paul Olberg died in May 1960, six months before his 82nd birthday; Sara Mehr died thirteen years later, at the age of 86, in the autumn of 1973. The International Bund maintained its distance from Zionism, but in the 1950s came to regard Israel as an established and significant fact of Jewish life that could not be ignored or simply condemned. According to David Slucki, the year 1956 and the Suez crisis marked a turning point for the Bund.[445] Already the year before, the Bund's Third World Congress in Montreal had adopted a somewhat less accusatory stance toward Israel, recognizing the Israeli state's right to security, but at the same time criticizing the treatment of the Palestinians, and advocating a two-state solution. That the state of Israel would be the center of Jewish life in the world was never accepted.[446]

As a socialist movement, the Bund mainly followed the development of international social democracy from its rebellious and almost revolutionary origins to its role as a representative of social reforms in the West. And like the rest of the Social Democrats, an overly simplified anti-communist position was challenged by the radical youth generation of the 1960s and the anti-Vietnam War movement. Whereas the Bund had plunged into condemnation of Soviet-

[443] Letter from Olberg to Emanuel Pat, February 24, 1957. Box 231, Doss. 22, Paul Olberg, corr. 1919–1950s, ME17, 1400BA, YIVO.

[444] Ibid. See also the Socialist International's Rundschreiben No. 99/56, December 21, 1956, p. 10 on the Bund distancing itself from Olberg's vote at the General Council meeting, November 30–December 2, 1956, in Copenhagen. Vol. 7, PO 435, ARAB. While the international Bund condemned the Israeli military action, the French Bund and *Unzer Shtime* were gentle with their criticism and took a positive view of the Franco-Israeli alliance against Nasser. The French Bund was also wary of criticizing the French Algerian War. David Slucki believes that the Bund's classic anti-colonialism in the French case was toned down by the intimate cooperation with the French Socialist Party, which held government power during the war years 1956–1957. Slucki 2012, pp. 84–91

[445] Slucki 2012, p. 84.

[446] Philip Mendes *Jews and the left. The rise and fall of a political alliance*, Palgrave Macmillan, Houndmills Basingstoke, New York 2014, p. 272.

backed aggression against South Korea, Vietnam was more complicated owing to the Bund's own basic anti-racist and original anti-colonial positions, not forgetting also the wave of youth radicalism in the 1960s. Aging Bundists and once young *Tsukunft* members participated together with the radical 60s generation in the American civil rights and anti-war movements, as well as in the Israeli peace movement.

The "if" that never happened

Today, when the owl of Minerva has long since flown over "Yiddishland" in Europe and the Bund, there is a renewed interest in the world that had perished in the east. This does not only apply to left-wing political contexts, where, after the end of Soviet communism, alternatives such as the Bund have gained renewed relevance in the search for more democratic socialist perspectives. The Bund's view on the "national question", often referred to in Marxist contexts, seems to coalesce around finding non-Zionist solutions to the Israeli-Palestinian conflict. Even in the context of academic research, interest in the Bund has increased since the end of the Cold War. Scattered monographs published at the beginning the 1990s have been followed by a growing and broadening of efforts to preserve archives, memories, and stories from a significant, but long-forgotten piece of European history.[447]

Within the research network Bundism.net, which was established in 2008 and has gathered about forty active researchers from various parts of the world, along with some sixty loosely connected academics and interested parties, a variety of aspects of the Bund are being studied: from Jewish identity formation within the Bundist-inspired school system *Tsysho* to the Bunds activities in different countries, its relations with other parts of the labor movement and ideological development. Central here, of course, is the Bund's view of the Jewish nation.

An imagined community?

In the age of globalization and (what many long imagined to be) post-nationalism, not only have national myths and stories been challenged and reconsidered. The work of Benedict Anderson, Ernest Gellner, Eric Hobsbawm, Michael Billig and others have fundamentally questioned accepted

[447] Gitelman formulates oblivion: "While Zionism achieved its primary goal, the founding of a Jewish state, the Jewish Labor Bund has practically disappeared. (…) Yet, perhaps more than Zionism, it was the Bund that profoundly changed the structure of Jewish society, politics and culture in Eastern Europe (…)", Zvi Gitelman (ed.), *The Emergence of Modern Jewish Politics: Bundism and Zionism in Eastern Europe* Univ. Of Pittsburgh Press, Pittsburgh 2003 p. 3.

notions about the origin of nations and the naturalness of nation-states, which were so prominent in the nineteenth and twentieth centuries. Instead, the nation appears as an "imagined community" constructed in and through historical processes where material and ideological factors intertwine – from the printing of books in popular idioms, the inventions of cartography, the telegraph and railway construction to schooling, museum activities and sporting events, not to mention the mass production of national ideology by intellectual elites.[448] When some years ago, the Israeli historian Shlomo Sand used these more up-to-date theories of nationalism as a way of problematizing the standard history of Zionism and Israeli historiography, this gave rise not only to heated debate erupt on matters of substance, but it generated much discussion on political questions, such as the contradiction between so-called civic versus ethnic nation-building (Israel as "Jewish state").[449] At the same time, other ideas about the relation between Jews and Jewish nationhood were brought to the fore. This included the Bund's world of concepts and ideas.

With today's theoretical conceptions of the nation, one could say that the Bund affirmed "the construction of Jewish ethnicity," but rejected projects of nation-state building predicated on ethnic belonging. In this way, the Bund belonged to the internationalist and quasi-cosmopolitan tendencies of the labor movement; they believed and hoped that the world would not have to undergo any phase of nation-state formation on the road to the universal ideals of socialism.[450] At the same time, the ethnic identification that the Bund affirmed did not differ in principle from, for example, Irish radical socialism under the leadership of James Connolly, which fought for an independent Irish nation-state. In fact, it did not even differ in these matters from Labor Zionism, whose Jewish identity building –linguistically, culturally, and geographically – took radically different expressions and aimed at nation-state building.[451]

Like other political and ideological perspectives, such as anarchism, syndicalism, and various branches of left-wing socialism that opposed the

[448] Key references may be represented here by Benedict Anderson, *Imagined Communities: reflections on the origin and spread of nationalism*, London, Verso, 2016. Michael Billig, *Banal Nationalism* London, Sage, 1995. Ernest Gellner, *Nations and nationalism* Malden, MA, Blackwell Publishing, 2006. E. J. Hobsbawm, Terence Ranger (eds), *The Invention of Tradition* Cambridge, Cambridge University Press, 1983. E. J. Hobsbawm, *Nations and Nationalism since 1780: programme, myth, reality*, Cambridge; Cambridge University Press, 1992.

[449] Shlomo Sand, *The Invention of the Jewish People* Verso, London, New York 2009.

[450] Håkan Blomqvist, *Nation, ras och civilization i svensk arbetarrörelse före nazismen* [Nation, race and civilization in the Swedish labour movement before Nazism], Carlsson bokförlag, Stockholm, 2006.

[451] For a discussion of the various answers within the Marxist labor movement to the so-called "national question", see Ephraim Nimni, *Marxism and nationalism: theoretical origins of the political crisis*, London 1991. Patrick Pasture & Johan Verberckmoes (eds), *Working-Class Internationalism and the Appeal of National Identity: Historical Debates and Current Perspectives*, Oxford, New York, 1998.

emergence of European (and overseas) nation-state projects, the Bund was under growing pressure from radicalized forms of nationalism during the tumultuous 1930s, culminating in World War II. This nationalist radicalization led to a growing and increasingly murderous anti-Semitism in Poland, Germany, Austria, Hungary, Romania and the Baltic countries. There was also pressure from the generally stronger nationalist tendencies within socialism, whether this concerned international social democracy or communism. It was the Bund's Jewish mass base that sustained the movement's position, mainly in Poland and the United States, and doing so for a long time. With World War II and the Holocaust, circumstances changed. While the multinational empires had long since dissolved, and nation-states had become the prevalent form of political representation in both the West and the East, the politico-discursive space within which the Bund operated was almost wiped out along with millions of Jews. From the east, the Stalinist version of socialism was hegemonic, while in the west, the so-called "Free World" was organized along capitalist lines. The Bundists, whose future was tied to the realization of socialism, in opposition to both Stalinist communism and bourgeois capitalism, were now faced with the choice of trying to rebuild their movement in the East against impossible odds or hoping to carve out some space for their socialism in the West. At the very beginning of the Cold War, the future was not yet decided, and the choice not yet made – a few years later, the doors of history had closed to alternative paths. Faithful to their non-Zionism and the principle of *doikayt*, the breakthrough years of the Zionist project and the founding of the State of Israel, forced the Bundists either to adapt or vanish. For Bundists who had to leave Poland and other annihilated East European Jewish communities to seek livelihoods elsewhere, the "place" was unmoored from its earlier point of anchorage in the experiences of being both proletarian and Jewish to a more prosaic geographical notion.

"The Bund was the answer," thought Eran Torbiner, who is not only a filmmaker, but also an activist in the Israeli peace movement. Among those newly interested in the Bund, there are many who lack the alternatives that seem to have perished or faded away – and who hope for the resurrection of ideas from the remnants of the Bund. For Zenia Larsson and others, that hope was lost. Israel's stabilization under the rule of workers' Zionism, as not only a haven for Jewish refugees, but also a Jewish welfare state, also made some former Bundists reevaluate or, at least, to come to terms with these developments. Paul Olberg had no difficulty appearing in pro-Israeli contexts during his last years, and in his wife Frida's estate, there are several gift receipts for various donations to Israel. Later in life, Sara Mehr and even Ber Perelmutter participated in Jewish events where Israel was seen as a natural and positive reference. Zenia Larsson came to actively advocate Jewish unity in connection with the Six-Day War in 1967, when she spoke in Stockholm at a demonstration in support of Israel; she would later publish a personal reflection on the Six-Day War.[452] In a press debate in 1979 with sympathizers of the Palestinian cause, she said she "deeply regrets" her own youth struggle for the Bund and the Bund's success in the Polish–Jewish world before the war. If the Bund had not been so successful, "perhaps more people would have listened to the warning voices of Zionist organizations, left Europe and survived the coming extermination."[453] A similar view was expressed as early as 1954 by the Jewish Marxist historian Isaac Deutscher: "If, instead of arguing against Zionism in the 1920s and 1930s, I had called on the Jews of Europe to go to Palestine, I might have helped save some lives which were to be wiped out in Hitler's gas chambers."[454] But history often wades in the "ifs" that never became reality. The victory of the Bund and Jewish socialism was one of them.

Afterword

"The three years in Sweden were the happiest times of my childhood. My mother was liberated, here it was rural and healthy, I bathed in the summer and skied in the winter. I was the only Jew in the class, but my teacher was so kind and so were my classmates," recalls Irena Klepfisz, a well-known American – and bilingual Yiddish-English – poet, as well as a lesbian, feminist activist for several decades, who was visiting Stockholm in 2019. She was 78 years old. It had been a long time since her father, Michal Klepfisz, smuggled her and her mother Roza out of the Warsaw Ghetto, where on April 19, 1943, people took to the streets against Nazism in an act of defiance. The year before, the "liquidation" of the ghetto had begun, and freight wagons had transported a quarter of a million of the population living in confinement to Treblinka. Under the leadership of the Bund, the *Tsukunft*, Labor Zionists and other Jewish groups, the Germans met a furious resistance that, with simple handguns and petrol bombs, held the world's strongest war machine at bay for a month. Irena's father, the 30-year-old engineer and leading Bundist, fell on the second day of the uprising. By then, two-year-old

[452] "Demonstration för Israel" [Demonstration for Israel], *Dagens Nyheter*, June 9, 1967. Zenia Larsson, *Morfars kopparslantar. Efter sexdagarskriget – en personlig reaktion* [Grandfather's copper coins. After the Six Day War – a personal reaction], Rabén & Sjögren, Stockholm 1970.

[453] "Zenia Larsson i debatten om sionismen: Judar är ett folk inte en ras" [Zenia Larsson in the debate on Zionism: Jews are a people not a race], *Dagens Nyheter*, March 19, 1979.

[454] Isaac Duetscher "Israel's Spiritual Climate", *The Reporter*, April 27, and May 11, 1954. https://www.marxists.org/archive/deutscher/1954/israel.htm (20190616).

Irena was already hidden in a Catholic convent, while her mother served as a maid in a Polish home under false papers. In the spring of 1946, the two came to Sweden as migrants and were housed among *khaveyrim* in Neglinge. In archival documents from YIVO and the Robert F. Wagner Labor Archives, they are noted in arrival lists and residential addresses. Roza Klepfisz was one of the "ghetto widows," who Eda Rak had mentioned in a conversation we had together, and who participated in the presidium when, in 1947, the Stockholm Bund commemorated the memory of the uprising. She and her daughter Irena were on their way to Australia, where a relative had managed to settle. In Melbourne, surviving Bundists gathered as far away from Europe as possible and tried to rebuild their movement around socialism and Yiddishkeit. The city became, and still is, a center of Jewish socialism where the children and grandchildren of the once viable Jewish labor movement maintain their traditions. Along the way, however, mother and daughter stayed with an aunt in New York. In the large Jewish immigrant community of hundreds of families gathered in the Amalgamated Housing Cooperative in the Bronx, surviving Bundists came to create a community around Yiddish culture and socialism with politics, school, theater, music, literature, sports, and everything that once belonged to the secular Jewish labor movement in Poland. Eda Rak guided me around the neighborhood. "Emanuel Pat lived there," and "Up here, Shloime Krystal has just turned 100; he was also in Stockholm." As one of the few remaining elderly Bundists in the area, Krystal still remembered his time spent in Sweden; now he is gone too. Together with Eda, I met Bundist "children," now no longer so young, who together spent their summers from the late 1950s onwards participating in Yiddish socialism and culture at Camp *Hemshekh* – "Continuation" – there Bund and SKIF's summer camp in the Catskills Mountains, New York. Many *Hemshekhistn* remain in contact with one another.

In Tel Aviv, we met Bella Bryks Klein, then director of the *Brith Haavoda Arbeter-Ring,* born in Stockholm of parents who survived the extermination camps and were rooted in the Bund's socialist Yiddishkeit. Now the Bund house in Tel Aviv is no more. At the Centre *Medem* in Paris and the *Bibliothèque Medem – Maison de la culture yiddish*, old Bundists guided us around both its literature and history. Not to mention at YIVO in New York, where aged Bundists volunteer to sort and preserve the archives. Those still alive attended the annual ghetto uprising ceremony at *Der Shteyn*, the memorial stone in New York's Riverside Park, where there were plans after the war to erect a large monument. At the seventy-fifth anniversary in 2018, Irena Klepfisz and Marcel Kshensky spoke, among others. Marcel's father Markus, or Motl, was the leader of the young Bundists at Mälarbaden's manor and got especially cold during his stay in the Eskilstuna barracks.

In 2019, Sara Ferdman Tauben and her husband Irwin came to Stockholm to revisit her childhood home in Neglinge and Kumla manor in Tyresö. As the granddaughter of Sziah Szechatow, one of Olberg's antagonist – and vice versa – she spent a few childhood years in Stockholm's Bundist milieu before her family moved on, first to Detroit and then Los Angeles. Finally, Sziah and his wife Eta, who later tragically died in a car accident, also made the voyage to the US. Sziah Szechatow worked in the textile industry, where he sewed baseball caps until his retirement at the age of 75. "Sziah continued throughout his life to be known for his passion for argument," says Sara Ferdman Tauben, and "remained devoted to Bund's ideals to the last," and she added, "to the detriment of his family relations." In the mid-1970s, she says, Szechatow published an autobiographical memoir (*Yorn fun kamf un gerangl*) under the English title *Years of Fighting and Struggle.* In a chapter she translated with the title "Sweden: Land of Humanism. Memories and Impressions," he presented a sympathetic account of "the country with social democracy," where his own gloomy memories of the conflicts within the Bund had faded away. The refugees from war-torn Europe who were mentally and physically exhausted after their experiences had, he thought, been able to bring Sweden a new influx of Jewish life with the richness and traditions of Jewish Poland. Even though great opportunities were open in Swedish society, he writes with melancholy, most, including him and his family, chose to move on to relatives and friends in North America, away from the threat of Soviet communism. Those who passed through Sweden and lived there for a time on their way west, will always, Szechatow concluded, "have in their hearts the warmest feelings for the country and its people."

Leib Gnacik from the Bund group in Eskilstuna had a similar experience. His granddaughter contacted me after some photos from the Swedish edition of this book had been published on the Internet. She recognized her grandfather on a picture from the Eskilstuna Bund group and put me in contact with her mother, Hanna Cohen, who immediately corrected a caption to one of the photos. "No, the woman beside my father on the picture is not my mother but my aunt Perla".[455] Her mother's name was Sara Gitla and met Leib Gnacik in Sweden where Hanna herself was born in 1948, joined three years later by her little sister Esther; they ended up growing up in Eskilstuna. The family left

[455] E-mail from Hanna Cohen to Håkan Blomqvist (20201014), telephone Håkan Blomqvist with Hanna Cohen (20210117), e-mail from Hanna Cohen to Håkan Blomqvist (20210131, 20210227, 20210311).

Sweden after eleven years, as late as 1956, for the US where they settled in Albany, New York. Hanna Cohen writes: "My mother didn't like it here. She said it was dirty, and the apartment had mice. She cried and wanted to go back to Sweden. But it was she who wanted to leave Sweden, because she was afraid of a new war. We even moved from a nice new apartment to a smaller and cheaper one in Eskilstuna to save money for the travel. My father wanted to stay in Sweden, as he had a good job and we lived well."

In Lodz, Leib Gnacik had been a shoemaker, a trade he practiced also at the Cooperative movement's shoe repair workshop in Eskilstuna. Before the war he had a wife and child in Poland and Hanna remembers: "Once when I was about fifteen years old, I was looking at a photo of my father with a small child (4–6 years old). I thought it was me, but I couldn't recognize it, and I didn't remember the coat and hat she was wearing. So, I asked my mother, and she told me it was a picture of his daughter in Poland. His wife and daughter died in the holocaust." He never talked about it.

Sara Gitla was sixteen years younger than her husband and the only survivor of her family. "They didn't know each other before Sweden, but met and married there in 1947; they were married first by a peace officer, but then they took the train to Stockholm where a rabbi married them." She was born in 1921 and grew up on a farm with her parents, grandparents, and younger sister and brother. Later she moved to Radom with her family and lived in the Radom's ghetto during the occupation where she was forced into slave labor producing ammunition. She was separated from her family, who were all killed, and was taken to Auschwitz and then to an ammunition factory in Berlin; Hannah contends that it might have been " because she was skilled with her hands and very handy". When she arrived in Sweden via Denmark, Malmö and Norrköping, she was ill with typhus and weighed only 70–75 pounds. In Sweden, Hanna continues, Sara Gitla learned to be a seamstress and her husband bought a sewing machine, which she then brought with her to the US. "Pretty soon she learned to love the sewing machine and became very talented. She landed a job as a seamstress, and sewed lots of clothes for her children." She was, Hanna writes, a good cook and made everything from scratch with fresh vegetables, meats and herbs. "Once when I came home from school, a fish was swimming in the bathtub, so fresher it couldn't be!" In Sweden she learned how to make Swedish food, like pancakes and a four-layer birthday cake with strawberries, nuts, and homemade whipped cream.

After a few years, the parents could buy a house in Albany because of restitutions from Germany. Leib Gnacik worked as an employee repairing shoes and jackets until he was about 75 years old. He died in 1987 of kidney and heart problems at the age of 82. While he didn't return to his Bund activities in the US, he joined the *Arbeter-Ring* (Workmen's Circle, branch 320), and attended meetings and, according to newspaper clips, sometimes talked about his war time experiences.

Sara Gitla had different jobs in Albany. In the beginning, she worked full time in a meat factory – "that's why she never had a hot dog in her life." Later, Hanna remembers, she worked part time, four hours a day, as a cleaning woman at a state office. At the age of 65 she learned to swim at the Jewish Community Center, and then went swimming three days a week. But, later, she was diagnosed with Alzheimer's and lived with it for about twenty years, living with her daughter Hanna and her husband. She died in March 2019, "at the age of 97 years and 11 months." She was buried next to Leib Gnacik at the Workmen's Circle Cemetery in Albany.

Hanna's memories from the years in Eskilstuna are vivid. The family spent the summer weeks in Mälarbaden, perhaps not far from the Bund home at the mansion guest house in the 1940s. "There were fruit, pears, apples, fresh blueberries and bushes with red berries we would pick. My sister sat on a blanket while my mother, father and I picked blueberries. Esther's face, hands and clothes were all blue. There were strawberries and wildflowers. I remember we picked the wildflowers and decorated a big pole, the maypole. There was music, and people danced around the maypole. The lake had rowing boats, but my father, mother and I could not swim. My father gave me the tube of a tire to swim with."

Hanna was close to her father and can still recall her fishing excursions and cycle rides with him. She still remembers how, during wintertime, she would take a kick sled to school. All the neighbors in Eskilstuna were Swedes as were her best friends, Inga and Margareta.

Hanna thinks her parents had lost their belief. "My father had a very religious upbringing, and went to the Yeshiva, but the war ended all that. If there was a God, where was he? I think my parents believed in the culture and enjoyed celebrating the holidays with all the food. They certainly considered themselves Jewish, but just couldn't follow it the way they were brought up to do. They would go to the synagogue during the holidays, but I don't think they were believers, and they did not keep kosher." She remembers that her father played soccer with the Swedes and that her parents participated in a traditional outdoor cray feast in Mälarbaden during the summer. At Christmas however there was a compromise. "I was the only Jewish child and wanted a Christmas tree like in my friend's homes. I didn't get it, but my father took a fir tree branch indoors on which I could place my toys".

Hanna thinks that the family had a good life in Sweden. "The Swedish government was great at the time, and the Swedes were friendly. When my parents arrived in Sweden, they were sick and weighed only about 70–75 pounds. With Swedish food and cakes they put on weight." In Poland, even before the war, Hanna writes, it was hard to live as a Jew. "Many Poles were anti-Semites, sometimes even more than the Germans. The Swedish people were different. My father would never have played soccer with Poles."

On a beautiful early summer day with Irena Klepfisz, more than seventy years after she and her mother arrived in Sweden, we were on our way to Saltsjöbaden's primary school in sunny Neglinge where hawthorn and lilac float over the garden fences and fill the air with early summer scents. "But where did my bike path go, I took it for two years and remember it so clearly?" In seven decades, much had changed; many buildings had either been constructed or demolished during the intervening period.

Still, two former playmates met with an air of familiarity. Ewa Heller, one year older, was also born in the ghetto and was smuggled out. With her surviving parents, she lived for a time in the Bundist home in Neglinge, but remained in Sweden when her parents decided to stay. Now, after seventy years, the two embraced each other, and reminisced over black and white photographs where they, as little girls with bows in their hair, smiled at the camera. In the classrooms we got to meet the fourth grade in class. Irena had her class photo from the 1940s with her; curious pupils tried to recognize the surroundings; some worn out benches with lids and space for inkwells remained in the hall. "We learned to write with ink," Irena remembered, while talkative ten- and eleven-year-olds spoke with her in English as if they had never done anything else. "But how can you speak English so fluently?" Irena asked. She herself had difficulties with the English language when coming to America. "Computer games," they laughed. The school has been rebuilt and the old chairs are gone, but in a classroom, Irena recognizes the surroundings, and the stairs and railings are the same. "This was the best thing that happened this week," said one of the kids in the class; he probably got the words from Irena Klepfisz.

Irena's mother Roza, referred to as Rose in the USA, maintained her commitment to the Bund until her death in 2016, at the age of 102. She had not only lost her husband at the age of 29, she managed to save herself and her daughter – yes, even kidnapped her from the convent, which wanted to keep the child – from Nazism. As a seamstress, she sewed clothes for the children in the Bund home and threw herself into the work of saving the memories of life in Jewish Poland and the Bund. She worked on the first multilingual bibliography of the Holocaust for YIVO and then at the Jewish aid organization JOINT. Irena became a poet, lesbian activist as well as proponent of Yiddish and Yiddish culture. "I thought they were 'fake Jews', who went to the Sabbath and so on," she explained of her first encounter with the Jewish diaspora in New York when mother and daughter first arrived from Sweden. The Neglinge house, Irena recollects, had been completely bilingual Polish – Yiddish, "I was the only one who knew Swedish." She heard Yiddish, understood it, but never spoke it. "I really didn't start speaking Yiddish, and that very hesitatingly, until I came to New York". English was difficult since she had to learn and start using it everywhere.

Maybe it was "my language frustration" that opened the way to poetry. There she could express herself more freely and put the words together as she knew them. In her commitment and poetry, life experience was combined with the desire to highlight the lives of the repressed, overlooked or forgotten. During the wave of feminist activism in the United States in the 1970s, which "highlighted voices that had not been heard," Irena Klepfisz became synonymous with the struggle to make Jewish women visible in the history of Eastern European Jewish life and in Yiddish culture.

As a lesbian feminist and Yiddish activist, she worked for Jewish women to rediscover Yiddish and the world that while having been lost, still has left its traces in their lives today. She wanted to maintain and defend a secular Judaism in the face of the imagined choice between religion and assimilation. She gathered opinion against the Israeli occupation of the West Bank. And she decided to "come out" as a lesbian, something that at that time was met with reluctance not only in conservative homophobic environments but at first also in secular and socialist Jewish contexts.

During the work on this book, which began in 2013, history and the present have flowed together, notes and information in the archive documents have been followed by human encounters, travels, and correspondence, where past and present interweave.

As a political movement, the Bund belongs to history. But as an idea and a way for thinking political strategy, it remains an abiding experience when seeking to negotiate democratically the tension between universalism and particularism, between pragmatic *doikayt* and national utopianism – or fanaticism – in a time of dead ends and divisiveness. "You could very well say that our attitude is inconsistent," Novogrodski once wrote in response to criticism that the Bund both tried to help Jewish refugees escape from Poland, but at the same time supported the reconstruction of Jewish communities there. "You're right. However, at the same time, we do not have the right to be consistent. Our lives are broken, therefore our actions cannot follow an unbroken line."

Words that refuse to sink without trace.

Sources and literature

Arbetarrörelsens arkiv och bibliotek, Stockholm, ARAB, [Workers' Movement's Archive]
Sara Mehr personal archive, No. 400
Paul Olberg personal archive No. 435

Arbetarrörelsens arkiv, Trelleborg [Worker's movement's archive]
Trelleborgs arbetarekommun [Trelleborg labour constituency]
Trelleborgs soc.dem. ungdomsklubb FRIHET [Trelleborg Social Democratic Youth Club Freedom]

YIVO 1400 Bund Archives
ME 17 Dossier 22 Paul Olberg
ME18 Bund in Sweden
Vol. 93
World Coordinating Committee
Correspondence with Denmark and Sweden 1950–51
Vol. 206
Kulturfarband Arbeter-Ring
Jewish Labor Committee
Malmö: Jidiszer Kultur Farband Arbeter-Ring
photos
Vol. 207
Jewish Social Democratic Labor Party 1946–1952
About deportees, letters, applications, alphabetically arranged letter register, correspondence (Yiddish), entry lists, Social Democratic member books in Yiddish. Telegram to the 50th anniversary celebrations in 1947.
Vol. 208
Land Committee 1949–50.
Letters, circulars.
Vol. 209
1948
Material from the Polish Bund. Extensive correspondence, including with the Coordinating Committee in New York.
Vol. 210
Bund in Stockholm Central Office
Editor of Unzer shtime (correspondence with Paris). Support for Jewish repatriates, lists, prizes, gift packages, fundraisers.
Vol. 211
Stockholm 1950
Correspondence, membership cards, accounts, notebooks.
Vol. 212
Uppsala
Correspondence 1950
Vol. 213
Vetlanda 1948–50

Minutes books 1948–50, correspondence.
Vol. 214
Correspondence 1948–50.
Vol. 215
Trelleborg
Minutes, accounts, letter folder.
Vol. 216
Malmö
Minutes, documents, correspondence, accounts, handwritten minutes books 1941–49. Jewish Cultural Association Arbetar-Ring Malmö. Correspondence with the association 1945 saved Jews in Malmö.

The Tamiment Library & Robert F. Wagner Labor Archives (TAMWAG)
Jewish Labor Committee of America, JLC

Microfilm on a reel where a "Reel" comprises several boxes which in turn consist of several folders with documents arranged chronologically. The transition from one folder to another does not appear on anything other than the date of the document. A box can also be microfilmed over several reels.

Series III: Foreign Countries;
Sweden
Box 36, folder 13–19 (undated, 1939–Nov 1945) Reel 102
Box 36, folder 20 (dec 1945) Reel 103
Box 36, folder 21–25 (Jan 1946–Apr 1946), Box 37 folder 1 (May 1946) Reel 105
Box 37, folder 2–4 (Jun 1946–Aug 1946) Reel 106
Box 37, folder 5–7 (Sep 1946–Now 1946) Reel 107
Box 37, folder 8–11 (Dec 1946–Feb 1947) Reel 108
Box 37, folder 12–15 (Mar 1947–Jun 1947) Reel 109
Box 38, folder 1–3 (Jul 1947–Sep 1947) Reel 110
Box 38, folder 4–6 (Oct 1947–Dec 1947) Reel 111
Box 93, folder 29–33 (Jan 1948–May 1948) Reel 275
Box 94, folder 1–5 (Jun 1948–Oct 1948) Reel 276
Box 94, folder 6–8 (Nov 1948–Dec 1948) Reel 277
Box 94, folder 1–4 (Jan 1949–Apr 1949) Reel 278
Box 94, folder 5–9 (May 1949–Sep 1949) Reel 279
Box 94, folder 10–16 (Oct 1949–Jun 1950) Reel 280
Box 94, folder 17–20 (Jul 1950–Jun 1951) Reel 281
Box 94, folder 12–18 (Jul 1951–1956) Reel 282
Box 94, folder 20–23 (1949–1956) Reel 283
Series IV: Rescue and Relief (med subseries)
Subseries IV: A: Rescue: A:1: General
Box 39 folder 46 (Olberg, Paul and Frieda 1940) Reel 115
Subseries IV:B:2: Immigration: Individual files
Box 51 folder 40–43 (Jan 1945–1946), Box 52 folder 1–2 (Jan 1947–Dec 1947) Reel 152
Series V: Supplement
Subseries V:C: Addendum
Box 53B folder 25 (1947), Reel 167

Newspapers and magazines
Arbetet
Dagens Nyheter
Expressen
Folket
Forverts
Frihet
Jewish Labor Bund Bulletin
Lebns-fragn
Morgon-Tidningen
Rundschreiben (Socialist International)
Sotsialistitjeskij Vestnik
Unzer shtime
Unzer tsait
Värmlands Folkblad

Interviews, conversations, correspondence, Among others:
Harry Amster
Bella Bryks Klein
Hanna Cohen
Stacey Cohen
Leo Greenbaum
Irena Klepfisz
Liliane Kshensky Baxter
Marcel Kshensky
Eda Rak
Sara Ferdman Tauben
Eran Torbiner
Marek Web
Christel Winberg

Literature

A Great Collection: The Archives of the Jewish Labor Movement, New York 1965.

Annual Gathering Commemorating the Warzaw Ghetto Uprising. 75th Anniversary April 19, 2018, Congress for Jewish Culture, New York 2019.

Benedict Anderson, *Imagined communities: reflections on the origin and spread of nationalism,* Verso, London, 2016.

Abraham Ascher, *Pavel Axelrod and the Development of Menshevism,* Harvard University Press, Cambridge, Massachusetts, 1972.

Michael Billig, *Banal Nationalism,* Sage, London, 1995.

Hans Björkegren, *Ryska posten: de ryska revolutionärerna i Norden 1906–1917,* Bonniers, Stockholm 1985.

Daniel Blatman, *For our freedom and yours: The Jewish Labour Bund in Poland 1939–1949,* Vallentine Mitchell, London, Portland, 2003.

Håkan Blomqvist, *Nation, ras och civilisation i svensk arbetarrörelse före nazismen* Carlsson Bokförlag, Stockholm, 2006.

Håkan Blomqvist, "Lost Worlds of Labour: Paul Olberg, the Jewish Labour Bund, and Menshevik Socialism" in Norbert Götz, ed, *The Sea of Identities: A Century of Baltic and East European Experiences with Nationality, Class and Gender*, Södertörn Academic Studies, Huddinge, 2014.

Mikael Byström, *Utmaningen: Den svenska välfärdsstatens möte med flyktingar i andra världskrigets tid* Nordic Academic Press, Lund 2012.

Constance Pâris de Bollardière, "The Jewish Labor Committee's Bundist Relief Network in France 1945–1948", i *Jewish History Quarterly*, no 2 (246), June 2013.

Alain Brossat, Sylvia Klingberg *Revolutionary Yiddishland: A History of Jewish Radicalism* Verso, London, New York, 2016 (Balland 1983).

Vladimir N. Brovkin, *The Mensheviks after October: Socialist Opposition and the Rise of the Bolshevik Dictatorship* Cornell University Press, Ithaca and London, 1987.

Oleg Budnitskii, Russian Jews between the Reds and the Whites 1917–1920, University of Pennsylvania Press, Philadelphia, 2012 (Rosspen 2005).

Anthony Carew, *American Labour's Cold War Abroad: From Deep Freeze to Détente, 1945–1970*, AU Press, Edmonton, 2018.

Catherine Collomp, "'Relief is a political gesture:' The Jewish Labor Committee's interventions in war-torn Poland, 1939–1945", *Transatlantica*, no 1/2014

Isaac Duetscher, "Israel's Spiritual Climate", *The Reporter*, April 27 and May 11 1954. https://www.marxists.org/archive/deutscher/1954/israel.htm (20190616).

Björn Elmbrant, *Stockholmskärlek. En bok om Hjalmar Mehr*, Atlas, Stockholm 2010.

Per Enerud *Den farligaste av flyktingar. Paul Olberg – antinazist, anticommunist och dissident I folkhemmet*, Carlsson Bokförlag, Stockholm 2017.

Ernest Gellner, *Nations and nationalism* Malden, MA, Blackwell Publishing, 2006.

Bernard Goldstein, The stars bear witness, The Viking Press, New York 1949.

Zvi Y. Gitelman, *Jewish Nationality and Soviet Politics. The Jewish sections of the CPSU, 1917–1930* Princeton New Yersey 1972.

Zvi Gitelman (ed.), *The Emergence of Modern Jewish Politics: Bundism and Zionism in Eastern Europe* Univ. of Pittsburgh Press, Pittsburgh 2003.

Martin Grass, "Ryska emigranternas läsesal i Stockholm 1907–1910" ARAB 2006, http://www.arbark.se/2006/07/ryska-emigranternas-lasesal-i-stockholm-1907-1910

Jan T. Gross, *Fear: Anti-Semitism in Poland after Auschwitz*, Random House, New York, 2006.

Leopold H. Haimson (ed.), *The Mensheviks: from the revolution of 1917 to the second world war* The University of Chicago Press, Chicago and London, 1974.

Svante Hansson, *Flykt och överlevnad – flyktingverksamhet i Mosaiska församlingen i Stockholm 1933–1950*, Hillelförlaget Stockholm 2004.

Henrik Erlikh un Viktor Alter, a lebn fun kemfer, a toyt fun martirer [Henryk Erlich and Viktor Alter, a life of struggle, a death of martyrdom], New York, 1943.

E. J. Hobsbawm & Terence Ranger (eds), *The Invention of Tradition*, Cambridge University Press, Cambridge, 1983.

E. J. Hobsbawm, *Nations and nationalism since 1780: programme, myth, reality*, Cambridge University Press, Cambridge, 1992.

Peter Hudis & Kevin B Anderson (eds), *The Rosa Luxemburg Reader*, Monthly Review Press, New York, London 2004.

Jack Jacobs (ed.), *Jewish Politics in Eastern Europe: The Bund at 100*, Palgrave, Houndmills 2001.

Aleksander Kan, *Hemmabolsjevikerna: Den svenska socialdemokratin, ryska bolsjeviker och mensjeviker under världskriget och revolutionsåren 1914–1920*, Carlsson bokförlag, Stockholm 2005.
Samuel D. Kassow, *Vem ska skriva vår historia? Det dolda arkivet i Warszawagettot*, Bonniers, Stockholm 2010.
Harry Kelber, "AFL-CIO's Dark Past (3)", 2004, http://www.laboreducator.org/darkpast3.htm (20190604)
Irena Klepfisz & Daniel Soyer, *The Stars Bear Witness - The Jewish Labor Bund, 1897–2017*, YIVO, New York, 2017.
Zenia Larsson, *Morfars kopparslantar. Efter sexdagarskriget - en personlig reaktion*, Rabén & Sjögren, Stockholm, 1970.
Zenia Larsson, *Brev från en ny verklighet*, Rabén & Sjögren, Stockholm, 1972.
André Liebich, *From the Other Shore: Russian Social Democracy after 1921*, Harvard University Press, Cambridge, Massachusetts, and London, England, 1997.
Beatriz Lindqvist, *Drömmar och vardag i exil. Om chilenska flyktingars kulturella strategier*, Carlsson bokförlag, Stockholm, 1991.
Christin Mays, "For the Sake of Democracy - Samarbetskommittén för demokratiskt uppbyggnadsarbete and the the Cultural Reconstruction of Post-World War II Europe", master thesis, Uppsala university, 2011.
Philip Mendes, *Jews and the left. The rise and fall of a political alliance*, Palgrave Macmillan, Houndmills Basingstoke, New York, 2014.
Henri Minczeles, *Histoire générale du BUND: un mouvement révolutionnaire juif*, Denoël, Paris, 1999.
Goldie Morgentaler, "Chava and Zenia", *Tablet*, https://www.tabletmag.com/jewish-arts-and-culture/253817/chava-and-zenia
Ephraim Nimni *Marxism and nationalism: theoretical origins of the political crisis*, Pluto Press, London, 1991.
Lennart Olausson, *Demokrati och socialism. Austromarxismen under mellankrigstiden*, Arkiv förlag, Lund, 1987.
Paul Olberg, *Antisemitismen i Sovjet*, Natur och Kultur, Stockholm 1953.
Patrick Pasture & Johan Verberckmoes (eds), *Working-Class Internationalism and the Appeal of National Identity: Historical Debates and Current Perspectives*, Oxford, New York 1998.
Pontus Rudberg, *The Swedish Jews and the victims om Nazi terror, 1933–1945*, Uppsala Universitet, Uppsala, 2015.
Martyna Rusiniak-Karwat, *Nowe zycie na zgliszczach: Bund w Polsce w latach 1944–1949*, Instytut Studiów Politycznych Polskiej Akademii Nauk, Warszawa 2016.
Shlomo Sand, *The Invention of the Jewish People* Verso, London, New York, 2009.
Edward W. Said, "Tankar om exil" i *Från exilen*, Ordfront, Stockholm, 2006.
David Slucki, "A Party of Naysayers: The Jewish Labor Bund after the Holocaust", *AJS Perspectives*. The Magazine of the Association for Jewish Studies, No. 42–43, 2013.
David Slucki, *The International Jewish Labor Bund after 1945: Toward a Global History*, Rutger University Press, New Brunswick, New Jersey, and London, 2012.
Solomon Schwarz, *The Jews in the Soviet Union*, Syracuse Univ. Press, Syracuse, 1951.
Shaye Shikhatov (Szaje Szechatow), Yorn fun kamf un gerangl (Years of fighting and struggling), Tel Aviv: Lior, 1973.
Morten Thing, *De russiske jöder i Köbenhavn 1882–1943*, Gyldendal, Köpenhamn, 2008

Malin Thor Tureby, *Hechaluz – en rörelse i tid och rum. Tysk-judiska ungdomars exil i Sverige 1933–1943*, Växjö, 2005.
Salomon Shulman, *Jiddischland. Bland rabbiner och revolutionärer*, Nya Doxa, Nora 1996
Enzo Traverso *Les marxistes et la question juive*, Paris, 1997.
Marek Web, "Between New York and Moscow: the Fate of the Bund Archives" in Jacobs, 2001.
Nathan Weinstock, *Le pain de misère: Histoire du mouvement ouvrier juif en Europe Tome 1: L'Empire russe jusqu'en 1914* och *Tome II: L'Europe centrale et occidental jusqu'en 1945*, La Découverte, Paris, 2002.
Noach Zelazo, *Who were exterminated in the depths of loneliness by the German caused Jewish Holocaust*, Stockholm 2001.
Klas Åmark, *Att bo granne med ondskan: Sveriges förhållande till nazismen, Nazityskland och Förintelsen*, Albert Bonniers förlag, Stockholm, 2011.

Internet

Research, archives
Arbetarrörelsens arkiv och bibliotek, Huddinge
https://www.arbark.se/sv/ (20190623)
Arbetarrörelsens arkiv Trelleborg
https://www.abf.se/distrikt-avdelningar/abf-skane/abf-sydvastra-skane/arbetarrorelsens-arkiv/ (20190623)
www.bundism.net (20190623)
JLC archive
http://dlib.nyu.edu/findingaids/html/tamwag/wag_025_002/dscaspace_ref1918.html (20190623)
YIVO
https://yivo.org (20190623)
Transcription, names
http://www.yivoencyclopedia.org/article.aspx/Names_and_Naming (20190623)
Persons
Frank Atran
https://www.jta.org/1952/06/12/archive/frank-atran-noted-jewish-philanthropist-dies-in-new-york (20190623)
Chaim Nahman Bialik
http://www.yivoencyclopedia.org/article.aspx/Bialik_Hayim_Nahman (20190617)
Sara Mehr
Ansökan om uppehållsbok 1918–1924, *Stadsarkivet*,
http://digitalastadsarkivet.stockholm.se/Databas/ansokan-om-uppehallsbok-1918–1924/Visa/sara-mehr-fodd-matles/731?sidindex=73 (20181123)
Shlomo Mendelson
https://www.jta.org/1948/02/11/archive/shlomo-mendelson-jewish-writer-and-socialist-leader-dies-in-los-angeles
Beinish Michalewicz (1876–1928), se The Jewish Labor Bund Bulletin no 14, 1949
https://www.marxists.org/subject/jewish/bund-bulletin/two-14.pdf (20181126)
Emanuel Novogrodski (1891–1967)
http://www.yivoarchives.org/index.php?p=collections/controlcard&id=34168 (20181227)

Yankev [Jacob] Pat (1890–1966)
http://yleksikon.blogspot.com/2018/06/yankev-jacob-pat.html (20190623)
Shmuel Zygielbojm,
http://www.yivoencyclopedia.org/article.aspx/Zygielbojm_Shmuel_Mordkhe

Film
Eran Torbiner Bundaím
https://www.youtube.com/watch?v=3bE6uhKxmYU (20190623)

Organizations
Centre Medem Arbeter Ring
https://www.centre-medem.org/ (20190623)
Gotteiner "Bund" institute
https://data.bnf.fr/15891556/gotteiner_institute_for_the_history_of_the_bund_and_the_jewish_labor_movement_haifa__israel/ (20190616)
Jewish Labour Bund Melbourne
https://www.bundist.org (20190623)
Jewish Socialists' Group
https://www.jewishsocialist.org.uk (20190623)
Maison de la culture yiddish
https://www.yiddishweb.com/histoire/ (20190623)
ORT
https://www.ort.org/ (20190623)
TOZ
http://www.yivoencyclopedia.org/article.aspx/TOZ (20181227)
World Congress for Jewish Culture
http://congressforjewishculture.org/ (20190623)

Various
History of the Jewish Community of Grodno
https://www.jewishgen.org/Yizkor/grodno/gro137.html (20190623)
Holocaust Survivors and Victims Database
https://www.ushmm.org/online/hsv/person_view.php?PersonId=4182297 (20190623)
Lärbro
https://www.hembygd.se/larbro/krigssjukhusmuseet (20180721)
http://www.lakartidningen.se/Aktuellt/Kultur/Kultur/2014/10/Krigssjukhuset-pa-Gotland-en-tillflykt-for-krigets-offer-/ (20181227)
http://www.tjelvar.se/sjalavard/7-1.htm (20190623)
Sveriges Officiella Statistik, Lönestatistisk Årsbok för Sverige 1948.
https://www.scb.se/Grupp/Hitta_statistik/Historisk_statistik/_Dokument/SOS/Loner/Lonestatistisk-arsbok-for-Sverige-1948.pdf (20180721)
Sveriges Riksbank
www.riksbank.se, Statistisk Årsbok/Sveriges Riksbank, Årsbok/Sveriges Riksbank, Sveriges Riksbank, 1931: *Sveriges Riksbank 1668-1918-1924*, band V, samt www.eh.net. Länkat till Riksbankens mittkurser. Sammanställt av Rodney Edvinsson. (20190623)

Personal register

www.ingramcontent.com/pod-product-compliance
Ingram Content Group UK Ltd.
Pitfield, Milton Keynes, MK11 3LW, UK
UKHW021838270726
14058UKWH00002B/227